First Certificate

Language Practice

with key

Michael Vince

with Paul Emmerson

English Grammar and Vocabulary

MACMILLAN

Macmillan Education
Between Towns Road, Oxford OX4 3PP
A division of Macmillan Publishers Limited
Companies and representatives throughout the world

ISBN-13 : 978 1 4050 0765 8 without key
ISBN-13 : 978 1 4050 0766 5 with key

Text © Michael Vince 2003
Design and illustration © Macmillan Publishers Limited 2003

First published 1993
This edition published 2003

Designed by Mike Brain Graphic Design Limited
Layout and composition by Mike Brain Graphic Design Limited

Illustrated by:
Rowan Barnes-Murphy pp 9, 42; Ben Hasler pp 3, 218;
Ian Kellas pp 96, 97; Gillian Martin pp 141; Janek Matysiak pp 227, 232, 260;
Julian Mosedale pp 53, 78, 103, 120, 121, 129, 143, 155, 183, 202, 264, 289;
David Parkins pp 18, 145; Martin Shovel pp 36, 61, 84, 107, 127, 135, 153, 160,
192, 214, 248, 282, 295; Bill Stott pp 94, 100, 111.

Photographs by:
Eyewire, Photodisc and Andrew Oliver.

The author would like to thank the many schools and teachers who
have commented on these materials. Also special thanks to
Paul Emmerson and Sarah Curtis.

Printed and bound in Malaysia

2011 2010 2009 2008
13 12 11 10 9

Contents

Vocabulary

Introduction

This book is designed to revise and consolidate grammar points at the level of First Certificate. It also provides practice in key lexical areas.

There are regular consolidation units which include forms of testing commonly used in the First Certificate examination.

It can be used as a self-study reference grammar and practice book, or as supplementary material in classes preparing for examinations.
If used for classwork, activities can be done individually or co-operatively in pairs or small groups. The grammatical information provided can be used for reference when needed, or worked through systematically.

The grammar section includes recognition and concept-checking activities, as well as production activities.
Each vocabulary section includes focus on phrasal verbs, prepositions and particles, and collocations.

Past time

Explanations

Describing events in the past

- Main events
  The past simple is used to describe finished actions and events in the past.
  *Susan **went** into the station and **bought** a ticket.*

- Background description
  The past continuous is used to describe actions in progress in the past. It gives information about the background situation.
  *There were a lot of people waiting in the station. Some **were sleeping** on the benches, and others **were walking** up and down. Susan **was looking for** Graham, so she didn't sit down.*

- Past before past
  The past perfect is used to make it clear that one past event happens before another past event. We use the past perfect for the earlier event.
  *By the time the train arrived, Susan **had managed** to push her way to the front of the crowd.*
  It is not always necessary to use the past perfect if a time expression makes the order of events clear.
  *Before the train arrived, Susan **managed** to push her way to the front of the crowd.*

- Past continuous used with past simple
  We often use the past continuous first to set the scene, and then the past simple for the separate, completed actions that happen.
  *Susan **was looking** for Graham, so she **didn't sit down**. Instead, she **tried** calling him on her mobile phone.*
  We often contrast an action in progress with a sudden event which interrupts it.
  *While Susan **was trying** to get onto the platform, a man **grabbed** her handbag.*

- Participle clauses
  Participle clauses are introduced by the time expressions *before, after* and *while*. They have the same subject as the following clause.
  *After **struggling** with him, Susan **pulled** the bag from his hands.*

Habits in the past

- Past simple
  The past simple is used to describe past habits or states. A time expression is usually necessary.
  *I always **got up** at six in those days.*   (habit)
  *I **lived** in Austria for several years.*   (state)

■ *Used to*
Used to is used to describe past habits or states. A time expression is not necessary.

> I **used to get up** at six, but now I get up at eight.
> I **used to own** a horse. (I owned a horse once.)

With negatives and questions *used to* becomes *use to*.

> I **didn't use to** like beer.
> **Did** you **use to** swim every day?

When we use *used to* we suggest that the action is no longer true and so make a strong contrast with the present.

■ *Would*
Would is used to describe a person's typical activities in the past.
It can only be used to describe repeated actions, not states. It is mainly used in writing, and in personal reminiscences.

> *Every evening was the same. Jack **would turn on** the radio, light his pipe and fall asleep.*

■ Past continuous
The past continuous can be used to describe a repeated action in the past, often an annoying habit. A frequency adverb is necessary.

> *When Peter was younger, he **was always getting** into trouble.*

Politeness and uncertainty

We can use the past continuous with *think, hope* and *wonder* to give a polite or uncertain meaning.

> I was **thinking** of having a party next week.
> I was **hoping** you would join us at the café tonight.
> I was **wondering** if you could help me.

Practice

1 **Choose a suitable description for each picture.**

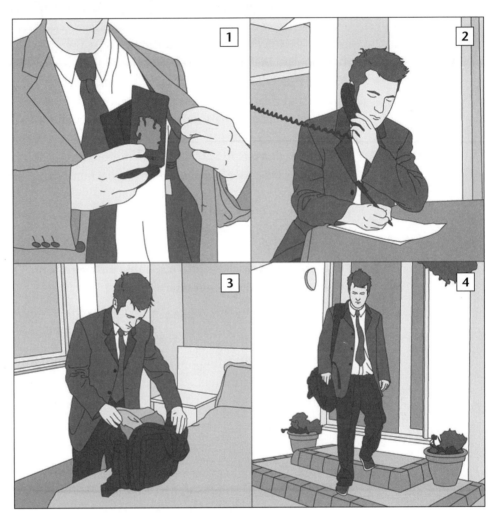

a) When he left the house, Peter forgot that he had put his passport and wallet in his other jacket.

b) After phoning the airport, Peter packed his suitcase.

c) When he returned from Portugal in March, Peter put his passport and wallet in his jacket pocket.

d) A few days before leaving for his summer holiday, Peter phoned the airport to check his flight.

e) While Peter was packing his suitcase, he realised that he hadn't checked his flight.

f) While Peter was packing his suitcase, the phone rang.

2   Underline the most suitable verb form in each sentence. The first one is done for you.

a) I suddenly remembered that I *forgot/had forgotten* my keys.

b) While Diana *watched/was watching* her favourite television programme, there was a power-cut.

c) Tom *used to live/would live* in the house at the end of the street.

d) Who *was driving/drove* the car at the time of the accident?

e) By the time Sheila got back, Chris *went/had gone*.

f) David *ate/had eaten* Japanese food before, so he knew what to order.

g) I *did/was doing* some shopping yesterday, when I saw that Dutch friend of yours.

h) I *used to like/was liking* sweets much more than I do now.

i) What exactly *were you doing/did you do* when I came into your office yesterday?

j) Laura missed the party because no-one *was telling/had told* her about it.

k) Tanya *would/used to* be a doctor.

3   Put each verb in brackets into a suitable past verb form. Only use the past perfect where this is absolutely necessary.

a) While I (try) ...*was trying*... to get my car started, a passing car (stop) .... and the driver (offer) .... to help me.

b) The police (pay) .... no attention to Clare's complaint because she (phone) .... them so many times before.

c) Mary (not wear) .... her glasses at the time, so she (not notice) .... what kind of car the man (drive) ....

d) Nick (lie) .... down on the grass for a while, next to some tourists who (feed) .... the ducks.

e) Tony (admit) .... that he (hit) .... the other car, but said that he (not damage) .... it.

f) Sorry, I (not listen) .... to you. I (think) .... about something else.

g) Helen (feel) .... very tired, and when she (finish) .... her work, she (fall) .... asleep.

h) The police (get) .... to Clare's house as fast as they could, but the burglars (disappear) ....

i) I (phone) .... you last night but you (not answer) .... What (you do) .... ?

j) We (not go) .... out yesterday because it (rain) ....

4   Decide whether the verb form in *italics* is suitable or unsuitable.

a) While I *had* a bath, someone knocked on the door. ..... *unsuitable* ...

b) Sally *didn't go* to a boxing match before. ....

c) Harry tried to repair the car, but he didn't really know what he *was doing*.
   ....

d) What *did you wear* to the Ponsonby's party? ....

e) *Were you eating* spaghetti every day when you lived in Italy? ....

f) I didn't know you *had bought* a new car. ....

g) They all wanted to believe her, but suspected she *was lying*. ....

h) As Peggy walked home, she tried to remember what *happened*. ....

i) 'What a terrible day!' thought Lucy. Everything *had gone* wrong!
   ....

j) Although it rained a lot, I *was enjoying* my holiday last year. ....

5   Put each verb in brackets into a suitable past verb form.

When Professor Mallory, the famous archaeologist, (1) ..... *invited* ....
(invite) me to take part in his expedition to find the Lost City of the Himalayas,
I (2) .... (not hesitate) to accept his invitation. Mallory
(3) .... (discover) an ancient map showing the position of the
city, although no European (4) .... (ever go) to the area before.
In fact, most of Mallory's colleagues either (5) .... (believe)
that the city (6) .... (never exist) or (7) .... (feel)
that it (8) .... (vanish) long ago and (9) ....
(become) simply a legend. According to the Professor, the builders of the city
(10) .... (hide) it among the mountains in order to protect its
immense riches. He (11) .... (believe) that the descendants of
these ancient people (12) .... (still keep) themselves apart from
the rest of mankind for the very same reasons. So when we
(13) .... (set off) on a cool May morning towards the distant
mountains, each of us (14) .... (look forward) to exciting
discoveries. For a week or more we (15) .... (climb) higher and
higher, following the map, which Mallory (16) .... (study) from
time to time. Then one afternoon, while we (17) .... (rest) at the
top of a valley, we (18) .... (notice) that a rider on a horse
(19) .... (wave) at us from the other side of the valley. A rider
whose clothes (20) .... (shine) like gold!

6 Rewrite each sentence beginning as shown. Use a participle clause.

a) Norman collected the parcel, but then he realised it was the wrong one.
   After *collecting the parcel, Norman realised it was the wrong one.*

b) Sue left the house but first she checked that she had her keys.
   Before ....

c) Mark was parking his car when he noticed the wing-mirror was broken.
   While ....

d) Julia cleaned the house, but then she fell asleep on the sofa.
   After ....

e) Brian bought a new television, but first he checked all the prices.
   Before ....

f) Alan was skiing in Switzerland and met his old friend, Ken.
   While ....

g) Kate took two aspirins, and then she felt a lot better.
   After ....

h) Sheila went out for the evening, but first she washed her hair.
   Before ....

Key points

1   The past simple describes completed events in the past, such as the main events in a narrative. It can also describe habits and routines in the past.

2   The past continuous is used for:
    a) background description.
    b) actions in progress, often contrasted with a sudden event.
    The past continuous cannot be used to describe past routines and habits.

3   Participle clauses can introduce a clause giving the main event.
    The subjects of both clauses must be the same.

4   The past perfect describes a past event which took place before another past event. If *before* or *after* is used, the past perfect is optional.
    The past perfect is not used for an event that happened a long time ago in the past.

5   *Used to* only refers to past time, and has no present form.

6   *Would* can be used to describe habitual actions in the past, usually in writing. It does not make such a strong contrast with the present as *used to*. Compare:
    Jim **would always make** his mother a cup of tea after lunch.
    Jim **used to drink** tea, but now he prefers coffee.
    Would cannot be used to describe states.
    Sally used to be a dancer.

 SEE ALSO

Grammar 2: Present perfect
Grammar 5: Consolidation 1
Grammar 7 and 8: Conditionals, Wishes and related forms
Grammar 14: Time expressions

Present perfect

Explanations

Recent events

Present perfect simple
The present perfect simple is used to describe recent events.
> *I've **left** my shopping bag behind.*

The event happened in the past, but there is a result in the present.
> *I've **broken** my arm, as you can see.*

No definite time is given for the event, but to emphasise the idea of recentness we can use *just*.
> *I've **just broken** my watch.*

We can also describe events that have not happened.
> *I **haven't found** her phone number **yet**.*

Indefinite events

- Present perfect simple
No definite time is given for the events. They are a series of actions in our life up to now.
> *I've **been** to France three times.*

After *It's/This is the first/second time* we use the present perfect. It also refers to our life up to now.
> ***This is the first time I have eaten** Japanese food.*

- Compared with past simple
Events described using the past simple have definite times.
> *I **went** to France **last year**.*
> *I **ate** at a Japanese restaurant **on Saturday**.*

If we think of a definite place for an event, this may suggest a definite time.
> *I **left** my shopping bag **on the train**.*

Extended or repeated events

- Present perfect simple
The present perfect simple describes a state which lasts up to the present.
> *I've **lived** in this house for five years.*

The present perfect simple can describe a habitual action in a period of time up to the present.
> *I've **never worn** a tie to work, and I refuse to start now!*

- Present perfect continuous
The present perfect continuous can also describe a state which lasts up to the present moment.
> *I've **been living** in this house for five years.*

There is little difference in meaning between simple and continuous in this case, or with *How long* questions.
> *How long have you **lived/been living** in this house?*

The verbs *wait, sit, lie, stay* prefer the present perfect continuous.
> *I've **been waiting** for ages.*

For, since, ago	See Grammar 14 for contrast between these time expressions.

Present perfect simple or continuous?

■ Completed action

The present perfect simple can show that an action is complete.

*I've **finished** my homework!*

If we say *how many* or *how much* we use the simple form. A certain amount has been completed.

*I've **written ten pages** of my homework!*

■ Not completed

The present perfect continuous can show that an action is not completed, or that it has finished recently.

*We**'ve been walking** for hours! Let's have a rest.*

*I've **been digging** the garden. That's why I'm so dirty!*

■ Present result or action in progress

We use the present perfect simple if our attention is on the present result.

*I've **written** my homework. Now I can watch the television.*

We use the present perfect continuous if our attention is on the action in progress.

*I've **been writing** my homework all evening! I didn't know it would take so long.*

Practice

1 Choose a suitable description for each picture.

a)

1) Did you enjoy the match?
2) Have you enjoyed the match?

b)

1) What have you been doing?
2) What have you done?

c)

1) He was married six times.
2) He has been married six times.

d)

1) How long have you been here?
2) How long are you here for?

e)

1) I've been waiting for two hours.
2) I waited for two hours.

f)

1) Where did Wendy go?
2) Where has Wendy been?

2   <u>Underline</u> the most suitable verb form in each sentence.

a) *Did you see/<u>Have you seen</u>* my bag anywhere? I can't find it.

b) Larry *is writing/has been writing/has written* his novel for the last two years.

c) From the minute he got up this morning Gary *asked/has asked/has been asking* silly questions!

d) *Have you given/Did you give* Helen my message when you *have seen/saw* her?

e) Sorry, could you say that again? I *didn't listen/haven't listened/haven't been listening* to you.

f) The police think that they *found/have found* your wallet, so call this number.

g) *Did you two meet/Have you two met* before? Eric, this is Amanda.

h) *Did you meet/Have you met* anyone interesting at the reception?

3   Put each verb in brackets into a suitable verb form.

a) I'm sorry about not coming last week. I (have) ....*had*............ a cold and so I (stay) .... at home.

b) Wait a minute! I (have) .... an idea. Let's go and see Roger. We last (see) .... him a long time ago.

c) It's nice to be back here in London. This is the second time I (come) .... here.

d) I'm phoning about your bicycle for sale, which I (see) .... in the local paper. (you sell) .... it? Or is it still available?

e) This place is in a terrible mess! What on earth (you do) .... ?

f) And now for an item of local news. Hampshire police (find) .... the dangerous snake which (go) .... missing earlier in the week.

g) This tooth (kill) .... me lately! So I (make) .... an appointment with the dentist for next Tuesday.

h) I can't give you the report I (promise) .... for today because I (not finish) .... it.

4   <u>Underline</u> the most suitable time expression.

a) I haven't seen Gerry <u>*for*</u>/*since* a long time. How is he?

b) It's ages *ago/since* I last went to a football match.

c) I've written to Deborah *last week/recently*.

d) What have you been doing *today/yesterday*?

e) Have you eaten Italian food *before/already*?

f) I've been living here *in/since* the end of last year.

g) Actually I had dinner with Sue *last night/lately*.

h) I've been trying to get in touch with David *for ages/for the last time*.

i) Terry hasn't been to Edinburgh *since/when* we went there together.

j) I can't remember *how long/when* I've had this watch.

5 Complete the second sentence so that it has a similar meaning to the first sentence, using the word given. Do not change the word given. You must use between two and five words, including the word given.

a) Steve started learning the violin a month ago.

   learning

   Steve ....*has been learning*.................... the violin for a month.

b) I haven't been to an Indian restaurant for ages.

   since

   It's ages .... an Indian restaurant.

c) When she heard the results, Mary began to feel more confident.

   become

   Since hearing the results .... more confident.

d) The last time Nancy came here was in 1986.

   since

   Nancy hasn't .... 1986.

e) This is my first visit to Japan.

   time

   This is the first .... to Japan.

f) How long have Helen and Robert been married?

   get

   When .... married?

g) Jack bought those trousers last month, and has been wearing them ever since.

   for

   Jack has .... a month.

h) It's a long time since our last conversation.

   spoken

   We .... long time.

i) Thanks, but I had something to eat earlier.

   already

   Thanks, but I've .... eat.

j) This is my first game of water-polo.

   played

   I .... before.

6   Put each verb in brackets into either the present perfect simple or the present perfect continuous.

a) Someone (eat) ......*has eaten*...... all the cakes. I'll have to buy some more.

b) What (you buy) .... your sister for her birthday?

c) My throat is really sore. I (sing) .... all evening.

d) Brenda (learn) .... Russian, but she finds it difficult.

e) How many people (you invite) .... to your party?

f) Those two cats (sit) .... on that branch for the last hour.

g) It (rain) .... all day! Why can't it stop?

h) Diana (wear) .... twelve different dresses in the past week!

i) I (do) .... everything you asked. What should I do now?

j) Graham and Pauline (try) .... to find a house for ages, but they can't find one they can afford.

7   Put each verb in brackets into either the past simple, the present perfect simple, or the present perfect continuous.

It was announced in London this morning that the British Oil Corporation (1) ......*has discovered*......... (discover) oil under the sea near the Welsh coast. The company, which (2) .... (drill) for oil in the area since 2001, (3) .... (find) small amounts of oil near Swansea last month, and since then (4) .... (discover) larger amounts under the seabed nearby. Last year the government (5) .... (lend) over £50,000,000 to BOC, and (6) .... (give) permission for the company to build an oil refinery and other facilities in South Wales.

   The reaction of local people to today's news (7) .... (be) mixed so far. Local MPs (8) .... (already welcome) the news, pointing out that the oil industry will bring badly needed jobs to the area. But local residents are worried about the danger of pollution. 'Nobody (9) .... (ask) us yet what we want,' said Ann Griffiths, leader of the Keep Out The Oil Campaign. 'Look what (10) .... (happen) when they (11) .... (find) oil in Scotland in the 1960s. The oil companies (12) .... (get) rich, not the local people. BOC (13) .... (not tell) us the truth about what this is going to mean for our people.' A BOC spokesman later (14) .... (refuse) to comment. Meanwhile local campaigners (15) .... (ask) the government to hold an inquiry.

8 Look carefully at each line. Some of the lines are correct, and some have a word which should not be there. Tick each correct line. If a line has a word which should not be there, write the word in the space.

A letter from the builders

Dear Mrs Sangster,

Just a quick note to explain what we have been done	......*been*......
so far this month. The work on the kitchen has gone	........✓........
well so far, although we haven't already finished	1) ....
knocking down the outside wall yet. So I wrote	2) ....
to you last week and have explained that two of	3) ....
my workmen were ill. They have quite recovered	4) ....
now, I am glad to say, and they have came back	5) ....
to work yesterday. As the weather has been bad	6) ....
we have been work inside most of the time, and	7) ....
all the painting is now been finished. We have	8) ....
also put in a new window in the kitchen, as you	9) ....
have instructed in your last letter. As you	10) ....
have not been visiting here for two weeks	11) ....
we have not had the chance to discuss the walls.	12) ....
When we checked them we have discovered	13) ....
that they are in a dangerous condition. I'll	14) ....
let you know what we have do to them.	15) ....

Best wishes,

Andrew Turner, Builder

Key points

1   The present perfect simple describes events without a definite time. Either these events take place in a period of time leading up to the present moment, or the result of the event is still evident.

The choice between the present perfect simple and the past simple can depend on how the speaker thinks. Compare:

A: *What's the matter?*   A: *What's the matter?*
B: *I've had an accident.*   B: *I had an accident.*

In the second example, the speaker thinks of the event as finished rather than still connected with the present.

2   Events described with the present perfect simple may be recent, or not.

3   The present perfect continuous is used for an action in progress. It suggests that the action is unfinished, or recently finished. Compare:

I've read this book.   (completion of the action is emphasised)
I've been reading this book. (the action itself is emphasised – it may not be complete)

The present perfect continuous can also emphasise the length of time of the action.

4   *For* refers to a finished or unfinished period of time.

*I waited **for three hours**.*
*He's been sitting there **for ages**.*

Since refers to the point at which an unfinished period of time began.

*He's been sitting there **since two o'clock**.*

Ago refers to the time of a finished event.

*Jill arrived **a week ago**.*

 SEE ALSO

Grammar 1: Past time
Grammar 5: Consolidation 1
Grammar 14: Time expressions

Explanations

Prediction

■ *Will*
Will is used to make predictions. It is often preceded by *I think* or by opinion words like *perhaps*. A time expression is also necessary.
> *I think it'll rain tomorrow.   Perhaps she'll be late.*

In speech, *will* is contracted to *'ll*.
See also Grammar 18 and 19 for functional uses of *will*.

■ *Going to*
Going to is also used for predictions. It is especially common when we can see the cause of the event.
> *Look out! There's a bus coming! It's going to hit us!*
> *I can see you're going to have a baby. When is it due?*
> *You're going to fall!*

Going to is also common in impersonal statements.
> *Liverpool are going to win the Cup.*

But *will* can also be used for most examples like this, with no change of meaning.

■ Future continuous
The future continuous is used to describe a situation in progress at a particular time in the future.
> *This time next week I expect I'll be living in London. And I'll probably be cycling to work.*

■ Future perfect
The future perfect looks back from a point in the future.
> *By the time we get there, the film will have started.*

It refers to indefinite time up to that point. This means that when we get to the future point we can say:
> *The film has started.*

Intention

■ *Going to*
Going to is used to describe a present intention or plan. This is something we have already decided to do.
> *I'm going to fix the television tomorrow.*

■ *Will*
Will is used for instant decisions made at the time of speaking.
> *I know, I'll get him a wallet for his birthday.*

Fixed
arrangements and
timetables

■ Present continuous
The present continuous is used to describe definite, fixed arrangements.
*Sorry, I can't help you, **I'm leaving** in the morning.*
The arrangements are often social arrangements or appointments and may be written in a diary.

■ Present simple
The present simple is used to describe future events which are based on a timetable, programme or calendar.
*My train **leaves** at 11.30 tomorrow morning.*

When, until, as
soon as

After the time expressions *when, until* and *as soon as* a present tense form is used, although this refers to future time.
*I'll wait for you here **until** you **get** back.*
The present perfect is often used in cases like this to emphasize the completion of an event.
*I'll wait here **until** you **have finished**.*

Practice

1 Underline the most suitable future form in each sentence.

a) Why *are you going to buy*/*will you buy* a new mountain bike?

b) Don't phone between 8.00 and 9.00. *I'll study*/*I'll be studying* then.

c) Look out! That tree *will*/*is going to* fall!

d) Let me know as soon as Louise *will get*/*gets* there.

e) Great news! Jean and Chris *will come*/*are coming* to stay with us.

f) According to this timetable, the bus *is going to arrive*/*arrives* at 6.00.

g) Can you call me at 7.00, because *I'll leave*/*I'm leaving* tomorrow.

h) If you arrive late at the sale, the best things *will go*/*will have gone*.

2 Put each verb in brackets into a suitable future form. More than one answer may be possible.

a) I can't see you on Thursday afternoon. I (visit) ....*am visiting*........... our Birmingham branch.

b) George (not be) .... back until six. Can I take a message?

c) What (you buy) .... with the money you won in the lottery?

d) I don't think you (have) .... any problems at the airport.

e) (you take) .... your dog with you to Scotland?

f) All the hotels are full. Where (we spend) .... the night?

g) You'd better not come in July. My mother (stay) .... with me then.

h) What time (your plane leave) .... ?

3 Put each verb in brackets into a suitable future form. More than one answer may be possible.

a) By the time we reach home, the rain (stop) ....*will have stopped*...........

b) This time next week I (lie) .... on the beach in Spain.

c) In ten years' time I (work) .... for a different company.

d) If we don't get there by 6.00, Jack (leave) ....

e) In July they (be married) .... for twenty years.

f) In the year 2500 a lot of people (live) .... on the Moon.

g) When you get to the station, I (wait) .... for you outside.

h) Don't worry! The plane (land) .... in a moment.

i) By the time you come home, I (finish) .... the decorating.

j) Come round between eight and nine. We (watch) .... the match on television then.

4 Put each verb in brackets into a suitable future form.

Have you ever wondered what exactly (1) ...*you will be doing*... (you do) in ten years time? Well, according to computer expert Tom Vincent, computers (2) .... (soon be able) to make accurate predictions about the future. Professor Vincent, from Cambridge, (3) .... (hold) a press conference next week to describe the computer which he calls 'Computafuture'. 'This computer can tell us what life (4) .... (be) like, based on data describing past events,' explains Professor Vincent. For example, Computafuture can predict how many people (5) .... (live) in a particular area, or whether there (6) .... (be) a lot of rain during a particular period. Professor Vincent also believes that by the year 2050, computers (7) .... (replace) teachers, and (8) .... (also do) most of the jobs now being done by the police. 'Computers are becoming more intelligent all the time,' says Professor Vincent. 'Soon they (9) .... (direct) traffic and (10) .... (teach) our children. And telling us about the future.'

5 Put each verb in brackets into a suitable verb form. All sentences refer to future time.

a) When I (see) ....*see*........ you tomorrow, I (tell) .... you my news.

b) As soon as we (get) .... there, we (phone) .... for a taxi.

c) I (go) .... to the library before I (do) .... the shopping.

d) We (wait) .... here until the rain (stop) ....

e) I (get) .... £50 from the bank when it (open) ....

f) After you (take) .... the medicine, you (feel) .... better.

g) You have to stay until you (finish) .... your work.

h) I (let) .... you know the minute I (hear) .... the results.

i) Before we (paint) .... the wall, we (have) .... a cup of tea.

j) We (climb) .... over the wall as soon as it (get) .... dark.

6 Look carefully at each line. Some of the lines are correct, and some have a word which should not be there. Tick each correct line. If a line has a word which should not be there, write the word in the space.

Keeping a diary

Are you one of those people who will know	........*will*........
exactly what they will be doing every day next	........✓........
week? When the different days will arrive,	1) ....
will you have get out your diary, or are	2) ....
you the kind of person who will just guess?	3) ....
Some people will write their appointments	4) ....
in a diary, but others just hope that they will	5) ....
remember. For example, tonight I'm be going	6) ....
to the cinema, but perhaps I'll not forget all	7) ....
about it. You see, I will never keep a diary.	8) ....
I try not to forget my appointments, but I know	9) ....
that I will usually do. I just don't like planning	10) ....
my future. I know that one day I'm going to	11) ....
make a serious mistake. I'll be miss an important	12) ....
examination, or by the time I remember it and	13) ....
get there, it will have been finished. Perhaps	14) ....
that will be when I have finally buy a diary.	15) ....

Key points
1 For functional uses of *will*, see Grammar 18 and 19.

2 The present continuous is used to describe fixed arrangements, and to ask about social arrangements.

Are you doing anything this evening?

3 The present simple and present perfect can be used to refer to future time after the words *when, until* and *as soon as*.

*I'll tell you the news **when I see you**.*

*Call me **when** you **have finished**.*

 SEE ALSO

Grammar 5: Consolidation 1
Grammar 14: Time expressions
Grammar 18 and 19:
Functional uses of *will*

Present time

Explanations

Present simple

■ Facts which are always true
The present simple is used to describe permanent facts, for example in science and geographical descriptions.

*The light from the Sun **takes** 8 mins 20 secs to reach the Earth.*
*The River Po **flows** into the Adriatic Sea.*

The present simple is also used for situations that are generally true.

*I **work** in an office and **live** in a flat in the suburbs.*

■ Habitual actions
The present simple is used to describe habits and routines. A frequency adverb is often used.

*I usually **take** the bus to work.*

■ Summary of events
The present simple can be used to make a summary of the events in a narrative, for example in a film or book. It can also be used for a table of historical events.

*In Chapter 1, Susan **meets** David, and **agrees** to go to the school dance with him.*
*In 1789 the French Revolution **begins**.*

Present continuous

■ Actions which are in progress now
The present continuous is used to describe actions which are temporary and not yet finished.

*I**'m doing** the washing-up.*

The action may be happening right now, or around now.

*I**'m reading** one of the Harry Potter books at the moment.*

■ Habits during a temporary situation
The present continuous can describe a habit that happens over a short period of time. A time expression is necessary.

*At the moment we**'re sending** all the mail by courier, because the Post Office is on strike.*

■ A repeated temporary action
The present continuous can describe a single action that is repeated. A time expression is necessary.

*Whenever I see Tom he**'s smoking**.*
*You**'re making** the same mistake again!*

In examples like this we are often exaggerating or complaining. This is particularly true when we use *always*.

*You**'re always borrowing** money from me!*

Problems with
simple and
continuous

■ Some verbs are not normally used in the continuous form, because they
   describe activities which already extend in time. These are called 'state'
   verbs.
   be, believe, cost, depend, have, hear, know, matter, smell, suppose, taste, think,
   understand

■ Some of these verbs can be used in continuous forms with a change of
   meaning.
*Tim **is being** rather difficult at the moment.*	(behave)
*I'm **having** breakfast.*	(eat)
*I'm **tasting** the soup, to check if it needs more salt.*	(sample)
*I'm **thinking** of buying a new car.*	(consider)

■ In many situations we can use either a simple or continuous form. The
   simple form is for a permanent situation or general habit, the continuous
   form is for a temporary situation.
*I **live** in London.*	(it's my permanent home)
*I'm **living** in London.*	(just for a year – my home is in Athens)
*Do you **sleep** a lot?*	(Is it your habit?)
*Are you **sleeping** enough?*	(What is happening at the moment?)

Practice

1   <u>Underline</u> the most suitable verb form in each sentence.

a) What sort of work *do you do/are you doing*?

b) I can't talk now. *I cook/I'm cooking* the dinner.

c) What shall we have? *Do you like/Are you liking* fish?

d) Can I borrow this typewriter? Or *do you use/are you using* it?

e) What *do the people here do/are the people here doing* in the evenings?

f) Follow that bus. Then you *turn/are turning* left.

g) A lot of people think that the Sun *goes/is going* around the Earth.

h) Excuse me, *do you read/are you reading* your newspaper? Could I borrow it?

i) *Do you wait/Are you waiting* for the bus to Newcastle?

j) Andy *builds/is building* his own house in the country.

2   Put each verb in brackets into either the present simple or the present continuous.

a) There's nobody here, and the door's locked. What (we do) *do we do* now?

b) What (you look) .... at? (I wear) .... the wrong clothes?

c) I (look after) .... Jack's dog this weekend. (you want) ....
to take it for a walk?

d) Who (drive) .... the Mercedes that's parked outside?

e) I (still have) .... a pain in my leg but it (get) .... better.

f) Who (Sue dance) .... with? That's not her brother, is it?

g) Harry always (look) .... untidy! He (wear) .... dirty jeans.

h) I (write) .... in reply to your advertisement in the *Daily News*.

i) That plant I bought (not grow) .... very much. And I (water)
.... it every day.

j) Which hotel (you stay) .... in when you (come) .... here?

3   Decide whether the verb form in *italics* refers to present or future time.

a) Where *are you staying* on Saturday night? *future*

b) George *retires* at the end of next year. ....

c) What are we doing when the guests *arrive*? ....

d) *I'm trying* really hard to understand this book. ....

e) Wait for me here until I *get* back. ....

f) Sue *is leaving* in the morning. ....

g) *I'm waiting* for the bus. ....

h) I'm off now and *I'm taking* the car. ....

i) They*'re showing* a Woody Allen film on Channel 4 tonight. ....

j) *I'm going* for a walk this evening. ....

4   Write each verb in the *-ing* form, then complete the spelling rules below.

> write ...*writing*...   swim ....   get ....
>
> admit ....   annoy ....   begin ....
>
> study ....   like ....   try ....
>
> decide ....

a) If a word ends in vowel + consonant + *-e* (write) ....

....

b) If a word ends in vowel + consonant (swim) ....

....

c) Words which end in *-y* (try, annoy) ....

....

5   Rewrite each sentence. Use a verb from the box to replace the words in *italics*.

> be   cost   feel   have   see   ~~smell~~   taste   have   think of   have

a) This flower *has* a wonderful *perfume*.
    ......*This flower smells wonderful.*..

b) I think you *are behaving in a* very silly way.

....

c) She *is expecting* a baby in the summer.

....

d) Nancy *is considering* moving to Scotland.

....

e) Don't go in. They *are holding* a meeting.

....

f) I *am meeting* Janet this evening actually.

....

g) Good clothes *are becoming* more and more *expensive*.

....

h) I *am trying* the soup to see if it needs more salt.

....

i) Helen *is taking* a bath at the moment.

....

j) I *think* that you would be happier in another job.

....

6 Put each verb in brackets into either the present simple or the present continuous.

Dear Aunt Jean,

I (1) ..*am just writing*.. (just write) to tell you how much I

(2) .... (appreciate) the money you sent me, and to tell you

how I (3) .... (get on) in my first term at university. Actually, I

(4) .... (really enjoy) myself! I (5) .... (study)

quite hard as well, but at the moment I (6) .... (spend) a lot of

time just making friends. I (7) .... (still stay) with my friend

Sue, and I (8) .... (look for) somewhere of my own to live. Only

a few of the first-year students (9) .... (live) in college here,

and I (10) .... (seem) to be spending a lot of time travelling

backwards and forwards. I (11) .... (go) to lectures every

morning, and most afternoons I (12) .... (study) in the library.

In fact I (13) .... (write) this letter instead of an essay on

Hamlet! I (14) .... (think) I'll buy some new clothes with the

money you sent. Everything (15) .... (cost) a lot here, and I

(16) .... (save) to buy a winter coat. It

(17) .... (get) really cold here in the evenings. I now

(18) .... (know) some other students and generally speaking

we (19) .... (have) quite a good time socially! I

(20) .... (also learn) to drive. See you soon.

Katherine

Key points   1   The present simple describes facts and habitual actions. The present continuous describes actions which are still in progress at the time of speaking.

2   Many verbs which describe states rather than momentary events can only be used in the simple form. Many verbs describing mental activities (*understand, know*) are of this kind.

3   Some verbs have both state and event meanings, but the meanings are not the same.

4   When describing a photograph, we usually describe the scene as if it is happening now, and use the present continuous.

5   Present tense forms are also used to refer to future time. See Grammar 3.

6   Where some languages use present tenses, English uses the present perfect. See Grammar 2.

   I've lived in Milan all my life.

→ **SEE ALSO**

Grammar 3: Future time
Grammar 5: Consolidation 1

Consolidation 1

1 **Complete the second sentence so that it has a similar meaning to the first sentence, using the word given. Do not change the word given. You must use between two and five words, including the word given.**

a) There's a party at Mary's house next week.

having

Next week .... *Mary's having a* .... party at her house.

b) When you phoned me, it was my lunch time.

I

When you phoned me .... lunch.

c) I started working here three years ago.

for

I've .... three years.

d) Our meeting is tomorrow.

a

We .... tomorrow.

e) I haven't had a Chinese meal for ages.

since

It's .... a Chinese meal.

f) David went home before we arrived.

had

When we .... home.

g) The arrival time of Helen's flight is 8.00.

at

Helen's flight .... 8.00.

h) Hurry up! We'll get to the theatre after the beginning of the play.

will

By the time we get to the theatre, the play ....
begun.

i) Oh no! My wallet is missing.

lost

Oh no! I .... wallet.

j) I've only recently started wearing glasses.

wear

I .... recently.

2   **Put each word in brackets into a suitable verb form.**

Moving house

I come from a very large family, and recently my parents (1) ....*decided*....... (decide) that they (2) .... (spend) long enough living in an overcrowded house in Birmingham. 'We (3) .... (move) to the country', my father (4) .... (announce) one evening. 'I (5) .... (sell) this house, and we (6) .... (live) on a farm.' So last week we (7) .... (load) all our possessions into two hired vans, and for the last few days we (8) .... (try) to organize ourselves in our new home. Yesterday, for example, my three brothers and I (9) .... (start) painting the downstairs rooms. Unfortunately while I (10) .... (mix) the paint, one of my sisters (11) .... (open) the door. Nobody (12) .... (tell) her that we (13) .... (be) in the room, you see. So instead of painting the walls, we (14) .... (spend) all morning cleaning the paint off the floor. But worse things (15) .... (happen) since then. This morning when I (16) .... (wake up), water (17) .... (drip) through the ceiling next to my bed. We (18) .... (spend) today so far repairing the roof. It's not all bad news, though. The school in the village nearby (19) .... (close down) two years ago, and my parents (20) .... (not find) another school for us yet.

3   **Complete the second sentence so that it has a similar meaning to the first sentence, using the word given. Do not change the word given. You must use between two and five words, including the word given.**

a) Jack left the office before I arrived there.

already

When I arrived at the office ......*Jack had already*........................... left.

b) Do you know how to drive this kind of car?

ever

Have .... this kind of car before?

c) This is my first visit to Scotland.

I

This is the first time .... Scotland.

d) During dinner, the phone rang.

I

While .... phone rang.

e) Do you have any plans for Saturday evening?

    doing

    What .... Saturday evening?

f) I started this job five years ago.

    been

    I have .... five years.

g) Is this car yours?

    you

    Do .... car?

h) Look at those black clouds! There's rain on the way!

    to

    Look at those black clouds! It's .... rain.

i) Our twenty-fifth wedding anniversary is in June next year.

    for

    By June next year we .... twenty-five years.

j) I haven't been to the cinema for two months.

    time

    The .... the cinema was two months ago.

4   **Put each verb in brackets into a suitable verb form.**

At the dentist's

I was on time for my dentist's appointment, but the dentist was still busy with

another patient, so I (1) ....*sat*............ (sit) in the waiting room and

(2) .... (read) some of the old magazines lying there. While I

(3) .... (wonder) whether to leave and come back another day, I

(4) .... (notice) a magazine article about teeth. It

(5) .... (begin): 'How long is it since you last

(6) .... (go) to the dentist? (7) .... (you go)

regularly every six months? Or (8) .... (you put off) your visit for

the last six years?' Next to the article was a cartoon of a man in a dentist's chair.

The dentist (9) .... (say): 'I'm afraid this (10) ....

(hurt).' I (11) .... (suddenly realise) that my tooth

(12) .... (stop) aching. But just as I (13) .... (open)

the door to leave, the dentist's door (14) .... (open). 'Next please,'

he (15) .... (call), as the previous patient (16) ....

(push) past me. 'Actually I'm not here to see you, I (17) .... (wait)

for my friend,' I (18) .... (shout), leaving as rapidly as I could.

(19) .... (you ever do) this kind of thing? Surely I can't be the

only person who (20) .... (hate) the dentist!

5 Look carefully at each line. Some of the lines are correct, and some have a word which should not be there. Tick each correct line. If a line has a word which should not be there, write the word in the space.

Meeting again

Dear Harry,

Do you remember me? ....✓..........

We have met last year when you were on holiday ......*have*......

in Brighton. I'm sorry I haven't been written to you 1) ....

since by then. I have been working abroad and 2) ....

I have only just come back home to England. 3) ....

Next week I am planning is to be in Bristol, and 4) ....

I was thinking about that we could meet. 5) ....

Do you remember Shirley, the girl we have met 6) ....

in Brighton? We are getting married next month, 7) ....

and we are want you to come to the wedding. 8) ....

I have lost your phone number, but when 9) ....

I have get to Bristol I'll try to contact you. 10) ....

It will be great to see you again. Are you still 11) ....

studying, or I have you found a job? 12) ....

You won't recognise me when you will see me! 13) ....

I had my hair cut last week, and now I look at 14) ....

completely different. Shirley doesn't like men 15) ....

with long hair, you see!

Best wishes,

Graham Norris

6 Decide which answer (A, B, C or D) best fits each space.

The latest news

Dear Linda,

I'm sorry I (1) .... *B* .... to you for so long, but I (2) .... very busy lately. All last month I (3) .... exams, and I

(4) .... anything else but study for ages. Anyway, I

(5) .... studying now, and I (6) .... for my exam

results.

As you can see from this letter, I (7) .... my address and

(8) .... in Croydon now. I (9) .... that I wanted a

change from central London because it (10) .... so expensive. A

friend of mine (11) .... me about this flat, and I

(12) .... here about two months ago. When you

(13) .... to London this summer, please visit me. I

(14) .... here until the middle of August. Then I

(15) .... on holiday to Scotland.

Please write soon,

Margaret

	A	B	C	D
1)	A don't write	B haven't written	C am not writing	D wasn't writing
2)	A was being	B had been	C am	D have been
3)	A had	B was having	C had had	D have had
4)	A haven't done	B don't do	C wasn't doing	D am not doing
5)	A stop	B will have stopped	C have stopped	D was stopping
6)	A wait	B am waiting	C have waited	D was waiting
7)	A am changing	B had changed	C will change	D have changed
8)	A will live	B have been living	C live	D have lived
9)	A decided	B have decided	C was deciding	D decide
10)	A will become	B becomes	C has become	D will have become
11)	A tells	B told	C was telling	D will tell
12)	A have moved	B had moved	C was moving	D moved
13)	A will come	B came	C come	D were coming
14)	A am staying	B stayed	C stay	D have stayed
15)	A have gone	B went	C am going	D will have gone

Indirect speech

Explanations

With tense changes

- Summary of tense changes
  Tenses move back in time after a past tense reporting verb.
    'I agree.'   *Peter said **he agreed**.*
    'I'm leaving.'   *Jane said **she was leaving**.*
  But the past perfect remains the same.
    'No, I hadn't forgotten.'   *Greg said that **he hadn't** forgotten.*
  For Modals (*can, may, must, should*) see Grammar 16.

- Main verb changes
  In complex sentences, only the first verb is changed.
    'I was walking home when I saw the accident.'
    *James said he **had been walking** home when he saw the accident.*

- Reference words
  Some words referring to people, places and time change in indirect speech, because the point of reference changes.
    *'I'll see **you here tomorrow**, Jack,' said Mary.*
    *Mary told Jack she would see **him there the next day**.*

    *'I gave **you this yesterday**.'*
    *John said he had given **it** to **her the day before**.*
  Other words of this kind appear in the Practice section.

Without tense changes

- Present tense reports
  If the reporting verb is in the present tense, there is no change.
    *Brenda **says** she's arriving at about 6.00.*

- Past tense reports
  If the reported words are 'always true', there is no change.
    *Harry told me that **he still likes you**.*
  If a message is being repeated immediately, there is no change.
    *Mary said **she's too busy** to come.*

Questions

- Reporting questions
  Yes/No questions are reported using *if*. The verb does not have a question form, but has the form of a normal statement. There is no question mark.
    ***'Do you like** hamburgers?*
    *Charles asked me **if I liked** hamburgers.*
  Wh- questions are reported with the question word. The verb has the form of a normal statement. There is no question mark.
    *'Where **are we going**?'*   *I asked Sue where **we were** going.*

■ Reporting polite questions

We can use a phrase like *Could you tell me* or *Do you know* to ask for information in a polite way. Note the word order.

 'Where is the station?' *'Could you tell me **where the station is?**'*

When we report this kind of question we use *ask* and the usual tense change rules.

 *I **asked** him where the station **was**.*

Commands and requests

■ Commands are reported with *tell* and the infinitive.

 'Go away!' *He **told** me **to go** away.*

■ Requests are reported with *ask* and the infinitive.

 'Please help me.' *He **asked** her **to help** him.*

Reporting verbs

■ *Say* or *tell*?

We *say* something and we *tell* somebody.

 *I **said** I could meet you this evening, but I'm really busy.*

 *I **told you** I could meet you this evening, but I'm really busy.*

We can use *to* after *say*, but we never use *to* between *tell* and the object.

 *I **said to him** that I'd meet him this evening.*

■ Other reporting verbs

Exercises 8 and 9 in the Practice section use some other common reporting verbs. The meaning and grammar of each verb can be found in a good dictionary and should be learned. For example:

 *She suggested go**ing** to the beach.* (*suggest* + *-ing* form)

 *She offered **to give** me a lift.* (*offer* + infinitive)

 *She reminded **me to call** my mother.* (*remind* + object + infinitive)

Paraphrase

It is often impossible or unnecessary to report every word spoken.

 'Excuse me, do you think you could tell me the time?'

 *He asked me **what the time was**.*

Practice

1 Underline the most suitable verb form in each sentence.

a) Helen asked me if I liked visiting old buildings.
    '*Do you like*/*Did you like* visiting old buildings?' asked Helen.

b) Bill asked Mary if she had done anything the previous weekend.
    '*Have you done* /*Did you do* anything last weekend?'

c) The policeman asked me if the car belonged to me.
    '*Does*/*Did* this car belong to you?' asked the policeman.

d) Fiona asked me if I had seen her umbrella anywhere.
    '*Did you see*/*Have you seen* my umbrella anywhere?' asked Fiona.

e) Joe asked Tina when she would get back.
    'When *will you get*/*have you got* back?' asked Joe.

f) Eddie asked Steve who he had been to the cinema with.
    'Who *did you go*/*had you been* to the cinema with?' asked Eddie.

g) My parents asked me what time I had got home the night before.
    'What time *did you get*/*have you got* home last night?' my parents asked.

h) David asked a passer-by if it was the right road for Hastings.
    '*Is*/*Was* this the right road for Hastings?' asked David.

2 Rewrite each sentence as direct speech.

a) Graham told Ian he would see him the following day.
    'I'll see you tomorrow, Ian,' said Graham.

b) Pauline told the children their swimming things were not there.

    ....

c) David told me my letter had arrived the day before.

    ....

d) Shirley told Larry she would see him that evening.

    ....

e) Bill told Stephen he hadn't been at home that morning.

    ....

f) Margaret told John to phone her on the following day.

    ....

g) Tim told Ron he was leaving that afternoon.

    ....

h) Christine told Michael she had lost her lighter the night before.

    ....

3 Rewrite each sentence as indirect speech, beginning as shown.

a) 'You can't park here.'

The police officer told Jack ...*that he couldn't park there.*..................

b) 'I'll see you in the morning, Helen.'

Peter told Helen ....

c) 'I'm taking the 5.30 train tomorrow evening.'

Janet said ....

d) 'The trousers have to be ready this afternoon.'

Paul told the dry-cleaners ....

e) 'I left my umbrella here two days ago.'

Susan told them ....

f) 'The parcel ought to be here by the end of next week.'

Brian said ....

g) 'I like this hotel very much.'

Diana told me ....

h) 'I think it's going to rain tonight.'

William said ....

4 Rewrite each question in indirect speech, beginning as shown.

a) 'What time does the film start, Peter?'

I asked *Peter what time the film started.*..............................

b) 'Do you watch television every evening, Chris?'

The interviewer asked ....

c) 'Why did you apply for this job?' asked the sales manager.

The sales manager asked me ....

d) 'Are you taking much money with you to France?'

My bank manager wanted to know ....

e) 'When will I know the results of the examination?'

Maria asked the examiner ....

f) 'Are you enjoying your flight?'

The flight attendant asked me ....

g) 'How does the photocopier work?'

I asked the salesman ....

h) 'Have you ever been to Japan, Paul?'

Sue asked Paul ....

FIRST CERTIFICATE **LANGUAGE PRACTICE**

5 **Complete the sentences. Use the number of words given in brackets.**

a) 'Do you think you could possibly tell me what the time is?'
David asked me ...*to tell him the time.*............................... (five words)

b) 'Excuse me, but I wonder if you'd mind opening the window.'
The man sitting next to me asked me ....
(four words)

c) 'You go down this street, turn left, then take the second turning on the right.
The cinema is just down the street on the left.'
A passer-by told me how .... (five words)

d) 'I want to know how much this bike costs. Can you tell me?'
John asked how .... (four words)

e) 'Look, don't worry, I'll help you if you like.'
Sue said she .... (three words)

f) 'All right, I tell you what, the car's yours for £500.'
The salesman said I could .... (five words)

g) 'I hope you don't mind my saying this, but you're being a bit silly, aren't
you?'
Peter told me I .... (five words)

h) 'It doesn't look as if I'll be arriving until after eight, I'm afraid.'
Jane said she probably .... (five words)

6 **Rewrite each sentence, beginning as shown. Do not change the meaning.**

a) What time does the next boat leave?
Do you think you could tell me ....*what time the next boat leaves*.... ?

b) Where can I change some money?
Can you tell me .... ?

c) Where is the toilet?
Could you possibly tell me .... ?

d) How much does this pullover cost?
I'd like to know .... ?

e) How do I get to Victoria Station?
Can you explain .... ?

f) Does this train go to Gatwick Airport?
Could you tell me .... ?

g) Where do you come from?
Would you mind telling me .... ?

h) What do you think of London?
Do you think you could tell me .... ?

7 **Put the correct form of either *say*, *tell* or *ask* in each space.**

a) I ....*told*.......... you that you had to be on time. Why are you late?

b) When you .... her if she'd work late, what did she
   .... ?

c) I think that Alan .... us a lie abut his qualifications.

d) When I .... him what he was doing there, he
   .... me it was none of my business.

e) I .... I would help you, so here I am.

f) Did you hear what Sheila .... about her new job?

g) What did Carol .... you about her holiday?

h) There, you see! I .... you the bus would be on time.

8 **Put the correct form of one of the verbs in the box into each space.**

accuse	decide	admit	apologise	~~deny~~	offer
remind	advise	confess	doubt	suggest	

a) 'No, it's not true, I didn't steal the money!'
   Jean ....*denied*.......... stealing the money/that she had stolen the money.

b) 'Why don't we go to the cinema this evening?'
   Peter .... going to the cinema/that they went to the cinema.

c) 'I've broken your pen. I'm awfully sorry, Jack.'
   David .... for breaking Jack's pen.

d) 'Don't forget to post my letter, will you, Sue?'
   Diana .... Sue to post her letter.

e) 'Let me carry your suitcase, John.'
   Harry .... to carry John's suitcase.

f) 'All right, it's true, I was nervous.'
   The leading actor .... to being nervous/that he had been nervous.

g) 'I don't think Liverpool will win.'
   Vanessa .... whether Liverpool would win.

h) 'If I were you, Bill, I'd buy a mountain bike.'
   Stephen .... Bill to buy a mountain bike.

i) 'You murdered Lord Digby, didn't you, Colin!'
   The inspector .... Colin of murdering Lord Digby.

j) 'It was me who stole the money,' said Jim.
   Jim .... to stealing the money.

k) 'Right. I'll take the brown pair.'
   Andrew .... to take the brown pair.

9   Rewrite each sentence, beginning as shown. Do not change the meaning.

a) 'Sue, can you remember to buy some bread?'

Paul reminded ...*Sue to buy some bread.*...

b) 'I don't really think it'll snow tomorrow.'

I doubt ....

c) 'I'm sorry I didn't phone you earlier.'

Jill apologised ....

d) 'Yes, all right, I'll share the bill with you, Dave.'

Brenda agreed ....

e) 'No, I'm sorry, I won't work on Saturday. Definitely not!'

Catherine refused ....

f) 'Let's go out to the café for lunch, shall we?'

Wendy suggested ....

g) 'It's not true! I have never been arrested.'

Larry denied ....

h) 'If you like, I'll help you do the decorating, Bob.'

Ann offered ....

i) 'I'll definitely take you to the park on Sunday, children.'

Tom promised the ....

j) 'I really think you should see a doctor, Chris.'

William advised ....

10 Look carefully at each line. Some of the lines are correct, and some have a word which should not be there. Tick each correct line. If a line has a word which should not be there, write the word in the space.

Satellite television

When my parents decided that to get a new	........*that*........
satellite television, I asked them why they	........✓........
thought this was a good idea. I doubted it	1) ....
whether it was really necessary, and told to them	2) ....
that I had thought they spent too much time	3) ....
watching television. They agreed they didn't	4) ....
go out very much, but were insisted that they	5) ....
had had thought about the matter very carefully.	6) ....
'We enjoy television,' they said me, 'and when we	7) ....
asked you, you said that you agreed with us.'	8) ....
I replied them that I didn't remember being asked,	9) ....
and that I would have tried to stop them. Then	10) ....
they were admitted that they had asked me while I was	11) ....
watching my favourite programme. I asked them	12) ....
what was I had been watching, and they said	13) ....
it was a football match. 'You told us that	14) ....
to keep quiet, so we thought that you agreed!'	15) ....

Key points

1 Tense changes are usually necessary after a past tense reporting verb.

2 Words referring to time and place also change in indirect speech.

3 Indirect questions are of two types. *Yes/No* questions are reported with *if* and *Wh-* questions are reported with the question word. The verb is not put into a question form in an indirect question.

4 Indirect speech is often introduced by a reporting verb. These verbs are followed by a variety of grammatical constructions. A good dictionary will include this information.

5 Indirect speech may also involve paraphrasing the main points of what was said.

SEE ALSO

Grammar 10: Consolidation 2
Grammar 16: Modal verbs: present and future
Grammar 17: Modal verbs: past

Conditionals

Explanations

Real/likely situations: first conditional

- With *if*

  A first conditional describes a real or likely situation. A present tense is used after *if*, but the time referred to is the future. *Will/Won't* are common in the result clause.

  > If you **fall**, I **won't be able to** catch you!

  This means that there is a real possibility this will happen.

  Going to can be used instead of *will*.

  > If it rains, we**'re going to** get wet.

  The modal verb *can* is also common in first conditional sentences.

  > If the cases **are** too heavy, I **can** help you carry them.

- *Unless, provided, as long as*

  Unless means *If ... not*.

  > **Unless** you **leave** at once, I**'ll call** the police.
  > **If** you **don't leave** at once, I**'ll call** the police.

  Provided and *as long as* can also introduce a condition.

  > **Provided** you leave now, you'll catch the train.

- With the imperative

  It is common to use the imperative instead of *if*.

  > **Get** me some cigarettes, and I**'ll pay** you later.

- With *should*

  We can use *should* instead of *if* in a conditional sentence. It means *if by any chance* ... and makes the action less likely.

  > **Should** you see John, can you give him a message?

Unreal/imaginary situations: second conditional

- With *if*

  A second conditional describes an unreal or imaginary situation. A past simple tense is used after *if*, but the time referred to is the future. *Would* is common in the result clause.

  > If you **fell**, you **would hurt** yourself.

  This means that there is a small possibility that this will happen. The situation and its result are imagined.

  The modal verbs *might* and *could* are common in second conditional sentences.

  > If you **became** a millionaire, you **might be** unhappy.

- *Were*

  Were is often used instead of *was* in formal language. Note that *were* is not stressed in speech.

> If I **were** taller, I**'d join** the basketball team.
>
> If I **were** you, I**'d leave** now. (*I* and *you* are stressed in speech)

■ *Were to*

Were to is another way of expressing a second conditional sentence.

> If they **were to offer** me the job, I**'d turn** it down.

Unreal/imaginary past situations: third conditional

■ With *if*

A third conditional describes an unreal or imaginary situation in the past. A past perfect tense is used after *if*. *Would* + *have* + past participle is used in the result clause.

> If John **had studied** more, he **would have got** better marks.

This means that John didn't study more. A past situation, different to the one that really happened, is imagined.

The modal verbs *might* and *could* are common in this kind of sentence.

> If you **had tried** harder, you **might have succeeded**.

■ Mixed conditions

For past events which have a result continuing in the present, it is possible to use the form of a third conditional in the *if*-clause, and the form of a second conditional in the result clause.

> If you **had saved** some money, you **wouldn't be** so hard up.

Other *if* sentences

If can mean *when* in the sense of *whenever*.

> If/When/Whenever it **rains**, we **play** football indoors instead.

In this type of sentence we use the present simple in both the *if*-clause and the result clause.

If can also mean *if it is true that*.

> If (it is true that) you **have** a job like that, you **are** very lucky.
>
> If (it is true that) nothing **happened**, you **were** lucky.

If + past simple can be used for past events with a real possibility, or that we know are true. This type of sentence does not have any special grammar rules.

> If you **missed** the TV programme last night, you can borrow my recording.
>
> If the police **arrested** him, they must suspect him.

Practice

1 <u>Underline</u> the most suitable verb forms in each sentence.

a) If the machine <u>stops</u>/will stop, you <u>press</u>/will press this button.

b) I can't understand what he sees in her! If anyone *treats/will treat/treated* me like that, I *am/will be/would be* extremely angry!

c) If you *help/helped* me with this exercise, I *will/would* do the same for you one day.

d) According to the timetable, if the train *leaves/left* on time, we *will/would* arrive at 5.30.

e) If it *is/will be* fine tomorrow, we *go/will go* to the coast.

f) If we *find/found* a taxi, we *will get/would get* there before the play starts.

g) It's quite simple really. If you *take/will take/took* these tablets every day, then you *lose/will lose/lost/would lose* weight.

h) I don't like this flat. I think *I am/I will be/I'd be* happier if I *live/will live/would live/lived* in a house in the country.

i) I don't know how to play baseball, but I'm sure that if I *will do/did*, I *play/will play/would play* a lot better than anyone in this awful team!

j) If I *phone/will phone/phoned* you tonight, *are you/will you be/would you be* in?

2 <u>Underline</u> the most suitable verb forms in each sentence.

a) Why didn't you tell me? If you *told*/<u>had told</u> me, I *had helped*/<u>would have helped</u> you.

b) If Bill *didn't steal/hadn't stolen* the car, he *wasn't/wouldn't be/hadn't been* in prison now.

c) If Ann *wasn't driving/didn't drive/hadn't driven* so fast, her car *didn't crash/wouldn't crash/wouldn't have crashed* into a tree.

d) Let me give you some advice. If you *smoked/would smoke/had smoked* less, you *didn't feel/wouldn't feel/wouldn't have felt* so tired.

e) What bad luck! If Alan *didn't fall/hadn't fallen/wouldn't fall* over, he *won/would win/would have won* the race.

f) If you *invited/had invited* me last week, I *was able/had been able/would have been able* to come.

g) I'm sure your letter hasn't arrived yet. If it *came/had come* I'm sure I *noticed/had noticed/would have noticed* it.

h) We have a suggestion to make. How *do you feel/would you feel* if we *offered/would offer/had offered* you the job of assistant manager?

i) If you *lent/had lent* us the money, we *paid/would pay/had paid* you back next week.

j) Terry never catches anything when he goes fishing. And if he *catches/caught/had caught* a fish, he *throws/would throw* it back!

3   Put each verb in brackets into a suitable verb form.

a) Why didn't you phone? If I (know) ....*had known*................... you were

coming, I (meet) .... you at the airport.

b) It's a pity you missed the party. If you (come) .... ,

you (meet) .... my friends from Hungary.

c) If we (have) .... some tools, we (be able)

.... to repair the car, but we haven't got any with us.

d) If you (not help) .... me, I (not pass)

.... the exam.

e) It's a beautiful house, and I (buy) .... it if I (have)

.... the money, but I can't afford it.

f) I can't imagine what I (do) .... with the money if I

(win) .... the lottery.

g) If Mark (train) .... harder, he (be)

.... a good runner.

h) If Claire (listen) .... to her mother, she (not marry)

.... David in the first place.

4   Rewrite each sentence, beginning as shown. Do not change the meaning.

a) I didn't have an umbrella with me and so I got wet.

I wouldn't ......*have got wet if I'd had an umbrella with me.*.........

b) I'll call the police if you don't leave me alone!

Unless ....

c) In the snowy weather we don't go to school.

If ....

d) Without Jack's help, I wouldn't have been able to move the table.

If ....

e) Make me some coffee, and I'll give you one of my biscuits.

If ....

f) If you hadn't told me about Sue's hair, I wouldn't have noticed.

Unless ....

g) If you see Peter, tell him to be here at 8.00.

Should ....

h) I wouldn't accept if you asked me to marry you!

If you were ....

5 **Choose the most appropriate description for each picture.**

a)

1) If she falls, she'll land in the safety net.

2) If she fell, she'd land in the safety net.

3) If she had fallen, she would have landed in the safety net.

b)

1) It's worse if we order soup.

2) It would be worse if we ordered soup.

3) It would have been worse if we'd ordered soup.

c)

1) If I own a dog like that, I'll keep it on a lead.

2) If I owned a dog like that, I'd keep it on a lead.

3) If I had owned a dog like that, I'd have kept it on a lead.

d)

1) I like it more if it looks like someone I know.

2) I'd like it more if it looked like someone I knew.

3) I'd have liked it more if it had looked like someone I knew.

6   **Rewrite each sentence. Use contracted forms.**

a) If I had known, I would have told you.
......*If I'd known, I'd have told you.*..

b) Tony would not have crashed if he had been more careful.

....

c) If I had my credit card with me, I would have bought the coat.

....

d) You would not have got lost if you had taken the map.

....

e) If Graham had not lost his watch, he would not have missed the plane.

....

f) If you had not told me her name, I would have found out from someone else.

....

g) If I were you, I would try getting up earlier.

....

Key points

1   The present tense form in first conditional sentences does not refer to present time. It refers to future time.

2   The past tense form in second conditional sentences does not refer to past time. It refers to future time.

3   The difference between first and second conditional sentences can depend on the attitude of the speaker. The future situation might have a high possibility of happening (first conditional) or a low possibility (second conditional).
    If she falls, she'll land in the safety net.
(This means that there is a real possibility that she will fall.)
    If she fell she would land in the safety net.
(I am commenting on an imaginary situation, and I do not think she is likely to fall.)

4   *Might* and *could* are common in conditional sentences when we are uncertain about our predictions.
    *If you leave now, you **might catch** the train.*
    *If you asked him nicely, he **might agree**.*
    *If you'd continued driving in that way, you **could have hit** another car.*

5   Mixed conditional forms are possible, especially where a past event has a present result.
    *If Brenda **hadn't stolen** the money, she **wouldn't be** in prison.*

6   *Unless, provided*, and *as long as* can introduce conditions.

→ SEE ALSO

Grammar 10: Consolidation 2
Grammar 17: Modal verbs: past
Grammar 18: Functions 1

Wishes and related forms

Explanations

Wishes

- Wishes about the present
  For wishes about the present we use *I wish* + the past simple. The time referred to is an imaginary present.
  > *I wish I **knew** the answer to this question.*   (I do not know the answer.)
  > *I wish I **didn't have** so much work to do.*   (I do have a lot of work.)

- Wishes about the past
  For wishes about the past we use *I wish* + the past perfect. The time referred to is past time.
  > *I wish I **had gone** to your party last week.*   (I did not go.)

- Wishes about the future
  We can use *could* to refer to a future event.
  > *I wish June **could meet** me next week.*
  We also use *could* to refer to something that is generally difficult or impossible.
  > *I wish I **could drive**.*
  > *I wish I **could contact** him, but I don't have my mobile phone with me.*
  We can also use *have to* to refer to a future event.
  > *I wish I **didn't have to get up** early tomorrow.*

- Wishes using *would*
  When we want to complain about a bad habit we use *I wish* + *would*.
  > *I wish Peter **wouldn't chew** gum all the time.*
  We also use *I wish* + *would* to refer to something that we would like to happen.
  > *I wish the police **would do** something about these people!*

If only

We can replace *I wish* with *If only* for emphasis.
> ***If only** I knew the answer to this question!*
> ***If only** I had gone to your party last week!*
In speech, *only* is often heavily stressed.

It's time

- The construction *it's time I/you/we ...* is followed by a past tense.
  > *Sorry, but it's time we **went** home.*
  The meaning here is similar to a second conditional.
  > *If we went home, it would be better.*
  High can be added for extra emphasis.
  > *It's **high time** you **learned** to look after yourself!*

- *It's time* can also be used with the infinitive. The meaning changes slightly.
  > *It's time **you started** work!*   (you are being lazy and not working)
  > *It's time **to start** work.*   (a simple statement of fact)

I'd rather

The construction *I'd rather I/you/we ...* is followed by a past tense.

> *I'd rather you **didn't tell** John about this.*

The meaning here is similar to a second conditional.

> *If you didn't tell John about this, it would be better.*

Suppose and *imagine*

In informal speech we can use *suppose* or *imagine* in place of *if*. The construction is a normal second conditional.

> *Suppose you **lost** your keys. What **would** you do?*
>
> *Imagine you **were** rich. How **would** you feel?*

Practice

1 <u>Underline</u> the most suitable verb form in each sentence.

a) I wish Peter *doesn't live/<u>didn't live</u>/wouldn't live* so far away from the town centre. We'll have to take a taxi.

b) I feel rather cold. I wish I *brought/had brought* my pullover with me.

c) What a pity. I wish we *don't have to/didn't have to/wouldn't have to* leave.

d) I wish you *tell/told/had told* me about the test. I haven't done any revision.

e) I wish the people next door *hadn't made/wouldn't make/couldn't make* so much noise. I can't hear myself think!

f) Darling, I love you so much! I wish we *are/had been/would be/could be* together always!

g) I'm sorry I missed your birthday party. I really wish I *come/came/had come/would come*.

h) I like my new boss but I wish she *gave/would give/could give* me some more responsibility.

i) Having a lovely time in Brighton. I wish you *are/were/had been* here.

j) This car was a complete waste of money. I wish I *didn't buy/hadn't bought* it.

2 Put each verb in brackets into a suitable verb form.

a) This train journey seems endless! I wish we (go) ...*had gone*...... by car.

b) I wish I (have) .... the money to buy some new clothes, but I can't afford any at the moment.

c) I wish the government (do) .... something about the pollution in the city.

d) I'm getting really soaked! I wish I (not forget) .... my umbrella.

e) I wish you (not do) .... that! It's a really annoying habit.

f) That was a lovely meal, but I wish I (not eat) .... so much.

g) I wish I (study) .... harder for my exams. I'm not going to pass.

h) I wish you (not leave) .... your dirty shoes in your bedroom!

i) I'm afraid I have no idea where Diana has gone. I wish I (know) ....

j) I really enjoyed our trip to the theatre. I wish we (go) .... more often.

3 <u>Underline</u> the most suitable verb form in each sentence.

a) A cheque is all right, but I'd rather you *pay/<u>paid</u>* me cash.

b) Imagine you *live/lived* in New York. How would you feel?

c) If only I *have/had/would have* a screwdriver with me.

d) If you want to catch the last train, it's time you *leave/left*.

e) I'd rather you *don't/didn't* tell anyone about our conversation.

f) I've got a terrible headache. If only I *didn't drink/hadn't drunk* that wine.

g) If you don't mind, I'd sooner you *practised/had practised/would practise* your violin somewhere else.

h) It's high time you *learn/learned* to look after yourself.

i) Jean thinks that everyone likes her. If only she *knows/knew* what people say behind her back!

j) I'd rather we *stay/stayed* at home this Christmas for a change.

4 Look carefully at each line. Some of the lines are correct, and some have a word which should not be there. Tick each correct line. If a line has a word which should not be there, write the word in the space.

Losing your memory

Imagine it that one day you woke up and	*it*
discovered that you had completely lost your	✓
memory. How would you have feel exactly?	1) ....
I have thought about this recently after I was	2) ....
involved in a traffic accident. I woke up in	3) ....
hospital, and said to myself 'It's the time I	4) ....
got up and have went to school!' I soon realised	5) ....
my mistake. A nurse came in and asked to me	6) ....
what my name was. I thought about it for a	7) ....
moment and then said, 'I would wish I knew!'	8) ....
Then I tried to get up. 'I'd rather prefer	9) ....
you didn't do that,' said the nurse. 'Don't worry	10) ....
you'll have it your memory back soon.'	11) ....
'I wish you hadn't have said that,' I replied.	12) ....
'Now I am really worried! If I hadn't looked	13) ....
in my wallet, I wouldn't have been known my	14) ....
own name!' Unfortunately my memory soon came	15) ....
back, and I realised I had a maths test the next day!	

5 Put each verb in brackets into a suitable verb form.

a) What can we do to get in touch with Robert? If only we (know)
.........._knew_............ his phone number.

b) Come on children! It's time you (be) .... in bed.

c) Actually I'd rather you (not smoke) .... in here.

d) Suppose you (see) .... a ghost. What would you do?

e) I'm so annoyed about my car accident. If only I (be) ....
more careful!

f) It's high time you (start) .... working more seriously.

g) I'd rather you (not put) .... your coffee on top of my
book.

h) I've no idea where we are! If only we (have) .... a map.

i) Your hair is rather long. Don't you think it's time you (have)
.... a haircut?

j) Visiting museums is interesting, but I'd sooner we (go) ....
swimming.

6 Complete the second sentence so that it has a similar meaning to the first
sentence, using the word given. Do not change the word given. You must use
between two and five words, including the word given.

a) It would be nice to be able to fly a plane.
could
I wish I ...._could fly_... a plane.

b) Please don't eat in the classroom.
you
I'd rather .... classroom.

c) I think we should leave now.
we
I think it's .... left.

d) What a pity we ate all the food.
only
If .... all the food!

e) It's a shame we don't have a video.
wish
I .... a video.

f) Don't shout all the time, it's so annoying!
wouldn't
I .... shout all the time!

g) I don't want you to buy me a present.

sooner

I'd .... buy me a present.

h) I don't like being so tall.

wish

I .... so tall.

i) We ought to start work now.

started

It's .... work.

j) I regret not going to university.

had

I .... to university.

Key points

1 Wishes about the present use a past tense form, and wishes about the past use a past perfect form.

2 Wishes with *would* refer either to annoying habits or to something we would like to happen.

3 Past tense forms are used after *It's time* and *I'd rather* to show an imaginary situation.

> *It's time we left.*

4 *I hope* ... can be used in a similar way to *I wish* ... But *I hope* is used only for wishes that are actually possible, and it usually has a good meaning.

> *I hope you have a good time.*
>
> *There's a lot to see. I hope you won't be late.*

Wish cannot be used in this way.

I hope ... can be used with the infinitive.

> *I hope **to see** you next week.*

But *I wish* with the infinitive has a different meaning. It is a formal way of saying *I'd like to* (or *I want to*).

> *I wish **to interview you for the job** next week.*

Note also these expressions:

> *I wish you luck/success in your new job.*
>
> *We wish you a happy New Year.*

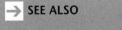

SEE ALSO

Grammar 10: Consolidation 2

Explanations

Uses

■ Transitive and intransitive verbs
  Only verbs with an object (transitive verbs) can be made passive.
  They sent the letter.   *The letter **was sent**.*
  They arrived late.   (cannot be made passive)
  Verbs with both direct and indirect objects can be made passive in two ways:
  They sent me the letter. *I **was sent** the letter.*
                      ***The letter was sent** to me.*
  Some transitive verbs cannot be made passive in some uses. For example *like*
  and *love*.
  I like this place.   (a passive form of this sentence is not possible)

■ Focus on important information
  By placing the object at the beginning of the sentence, the passive can
  change the focus of interest in a sentence.
  United were beaten by Arsenal.   (we are more interested in United)

  The passive is used in a variety of contexts. Notice how the agent (person
  who does the action) is unimportant, unknown or clear from the situation.
  Impersonal statements   *Students **are asked** not to smoke.*
  When the agent is unknown   *My bike **has been stolen!***
    (Here we could say *Someone/They have stolen my bike.*)
  When the agent is obvious   *Mr Jones **will be arrested**.*
  How something was done   *The box **was opened with a knife**.*

Reporting verbs

■ The passive is often used with *say, believe, understand, know* and similar verbs
  used in reporting speech to avoid an impersonal *they* or *people*.
  People say that John Wilson lives in New York.
  *John Wilson **is said** to live in New York.*

■ Other verb forms can also be reported in this way.
  They say John Wilson is travelling in Africa.
  *John Wilson **is said to be travelling** in Africa.*
  People say John Wilson has arrived in Australia.
  *John Wilson **is said to have arrived** in Australia.*

*Have/Get
something done*

■ When someone does some work for us, we can use *have something done.*
  *Last year I **had** new tiles **put** on the roof.*
  ***I'm having** my hair **cut** this afternoon.*

■ The same construction can describe bad luck caused by an unspecified person.

> *Peter **had** his car **stolen** last week.*
> *And then he **had** his leg **broken** playing football.*

■ Using *get* instead of *have* in the examples in paragraph 1 above would be more informal.

Using *get* can also suggest managing to do something difficult.

> *It was difficult but we **got** the painting **done** in the end.*

Needs doing

This is an idiomatic way of expressing a passive sentence where a thing or person needs some kind of action.

> *The floor is filthy. It needs to be cleaned.*
> *The floor is filthy. It **needs cleaning**.*

Verbs and prepositions

The preposition stays with the verb in a passive sentence.

> *People **shouted at** the Prime Minister during his speech.*
> *The Prime Minister **was shouted at** during his speech.*

Other problems

■ *Be born* is a passive form but does not have an obvious passive meaning.

> *I **was born** near Kyoto.*

■ *Make* (when meaning *force*) is followed by *to* in the passive.

> *They made David work hard.*
> *David **was made to** work hard.*

■ Because the agent is unimportant, unknown or obvious, it is often not included. If we want to say who does the action we use *by*.

> *This letter was delivered this morning.*
> *This letter was delivered this morning **by** courier.*

Practice

1   Underline the verb forms which are not possible.

a) My car <u>has being</u> stolen.

b) Jack was borned on a Thursday.

c) Then I realised that none of the guests had been sent an invitation.

d) Mary's car is being serviced today.

e) Your order will been sent as soon as possible.

f) The hole in the road was being repaired when I came home.

g) This swimming pool is used by over a thousand people each week.

h) When was this church built?

i) An address is writing on the back of the envelope.

j) Customers are request to ask for a receipt.

2   Underline the most suitable verb form in each sentence.

a) Their new house *hasn't been finished*/*wasn't finished* yet.

b) The robbers *were arrested*/*have been arrested* as soon as they left the bank.

c) Sue told us her baby *is born*/*had been born* two weeks earlier than expected.

d) If there is too much snow, the match *has been cancelled*/*will be cancelled*.

e) By the time we got there, the rain *had stopped*/*had been stopped*.

f) When *were you told*/*have you been told* about the new rules?

g) Most of the passengers *were swimming*/*were swum* easily to the shore.

h) The winning horse *was ridden*/*was riding* by Pat Murphy.

i) I looked again for the old man, but he *was vanished*/*had vanished*.

j) I don't think that you *will be asked*/*are being asked* to show your passport.

3   Put each verb in brackets into a suitable passive form.

a) I'm sorry, madam, but this carpet (already sell) *has already been sold.*

b) The old house on the corner (knock down) .... last year.

c) When exactly (John give) .... his prize?

d) Most people agree that America (not discover) .... by Christopher Columbus.

e) All complaints about products (deal with) .... by our customer services department.

f) Police confirmed that the murder weapon (since discover) .... in a nearby lake.

g) It (announce) .... yesterday that the government has decided not to raise income tax.

h) Good news! I (ask) .... to take over as the new manager.

i) I don't believe that this play (write) .... by Shakespeare.

j) Ann really likes (invite) .... to dinner parties.

4 **Rewrite each sentence, putting the verb in *italics* in the passive where possible. Do you need to mention the agent?**

a) I really *like* this hotel.

   ...*not possible*...

b) Jane *won* the poetry competition.

   ...*The poetry competition was won by Jane.*...

c) Peter's new car *cost* over £20,000.

   ....

d) Martin always *wears* casual clothes.

   ....

e) One of our visitors *lost* this cigarette lighter.

   ....

f) They *haven't decided* the exact time of the match yet.

   ....

g) Most of the guests *had left* the hotel by midday.

   ....

h) Some parents *read* to their children every night.

   ....

i) This bike *belongs* to my sisters.

   ....

j) People *ate* most of the food at the party.

   ....

5 Complete the second sentence so that it has a similar meaning to the first sentence, using the word given. Do not change the word given. You must use between two and five words, including the word given.

a) Last Thursday we appointed a new marketing manager.

   was

   A new ...*marketing manager was appointed*........... last Thursday.

b) Smith Ltd are supplying our company with furniture.

   supplied

   Our company .... by Smith Ltd.

c) William the Conqueror built the castle in the 11th century.

   by

   The castle .... William the Conqueror in the 11th century.

d) No decision has yet been made.

   decided

   Nothing .... yet.

e) People believe that someone murdered Jenkins.

   was

   It .... murdered.

f) Your hair needs cutting.

   get

   You ought .... cut.

g) The police were following the suspects.

   were

   The suspects .... police.

h) No-one has seen Peter since the day of the party.

   been

   Peter .... the day of the party.

i) We put up a notice about the trip on the notice board yesterday.

   was

   A notice .... up on the notice board yesterday.

j) People think that an apple a day is good for you.

   to

   An apple a day .... for you.

6 Rewrite each sentence so that it contains a form of *have something done.* Do not include the agent.

a) A painter painted our house last month.
...*We had our house painted last month.*...

b) The hairdresser is cutting my hair this afternoon.

....

c) Someone has stolen my motorbike.

....

d) The dentist has taken out all of Ricky's teeth.

....

e) I haven't been to the car-wash for a long time.

....

f) The men are coming to put in the new central heating on Saturday.

....

g) Someone broke Harry's nose in a fight.

....

h) Isn't it time someone fixed your television?

....

7 Rewrite each sentence so that it contains a passive form, and does not contain the words in *italics.*

a) *Apparently,* Freddie has a wife in Scotland.
Freddie is said to have a wife in Scotland....

b) *Nobody* knows *anything* about Brenda's family.

....

c) *People* think that *someone* started the fire deliberately.

....

d) You should *ask* a doctor to see to that cut.

....

e) *People* say that Chris was in the army.

....

f) My trousers *need* to be pressed before I leave.

....

g) *No-one* has signed this letter.

....

h) Mary's hair still *needs* cutting.

....

8 Look carefully at each line. Some of the lines are correct, and some have a word which should not be there. Tick each correct line. If a line has a word which should not be there, write the word in the space.

Opening of new Gulliver Sports Centre

The Gulliver Sports Centre, which has been	..........✓..........
completely rebuilt, was been reopened yesterday	.....*been*.....
by the Minister of Sport. The building it was	1) ....
originally used to as a market, but was sold	2) ....
to Fairdene Council in 1981, and it then converted	3) ....
into a sports hall. Local schools were played football	4) ....
and basketball indoors, and keep-fit classes were held	5) ....
there. In 1990 the hall was damaged when by a fire	6) ....
which was broke out in the heating system. The hall	7) ....
could not be used, and remained empty while discussions	8) ....
continued about its future. It was then and decided that	9) ....
the hall would to be rebuilt, and an appeal for money	10) ....
was launched. Two years ago a local businessman offered	11) ....
to pay for the building work, and plans were drawn up.	12) ....
The new hall is includes a swimming pool, running track	13) ....
and other sports facilities which can be used by anyone	14) ....
in the Fairdene area. The Minister was made a speech	15) ....
in which she congratulated everyone involved.	

Key points

1 Not all verbs can be made passive. You can check in a dictionary whether the verb is transitive or intransitive.

2 The agent is only included if this information is needed.

3 Passive forms are often used to give an impersonal view.

4 When we change from passive to active the meaning changes slightly. In particular, the focus of interest changes. A passive form may be more suitable in some contexts but unsuitable in others.

5 Passive forms tend to be used more often in writing, especially in scientific and technical language.

→ SEE ALSO

Grammar 10: Consolidation 2

Consolidation 2

1 Complete the second sentence so that it has a similar meaning to the first sentence, using the word given. Do not change the word given. You must use between two and five words, including the word given.

a) Please don't open the window.

you

I'd ......*rather you didn't*... open the window.

b) Fiona wanted to know the time.

what

Fiona wanted to know .... was.

c) We won't go out if the weather is bad.

won't

We .... the weather is good.

d) I would like you to be here!

wish

I .... here.

e) Catherine refused to let me go.

couldn't

Catherine .... go.

f) If I were you, I'd try to get some sleep.

advise

I .... to try to get some sleep.

g) What a pity we didn't see the match.

wish

I .... the match.

h) The old man introduced himself.

us

The old man .... name.

i) David told me the time of the next train.

what

David told .... train left.

j) The police inspector said I had killed Mrs Burns.

of

The police inspector .... killing Mrs Burns.

2   **Decide which answer (A, B, C or D) best fits each space.**

The stolen bike

One morning last week I realised that my bike (1) ....*B*......... stolen from my garden. I phoned the police and two officers called at my house the next day. They (2) .... me if I had seen or heard anything. I told (3) .... I had been out that evening, and hadn't noticed anything suspicious when I came home. 'If I had seen anything, I (4) .... you,' I replied. 'It was raining hard too. If the weather (5) .... so bad, I would have ridden my bike.' The officers told me that lots of people (6) .... their bikes stolen lately. 'The thieves (7) .... to have put the bikes in a van,' said one of the officers. 'I (8) .... I had known about that,' I said. 'I saw a black van that evening. In fact, it (9) .... opposite my house.' The officers asked me what the van's number (10) .... , but I couldn't remember. '(11) .... you saw the van again, (12) .... you recognise it?' one of them asked. 'It (13) .... painting. I remember that,' I replied. However, there was a happy ending to this story. After the officers had left, I (14) .... by a friend of mine. 'By the way', she said, '(15) .... you want your bike, I'll bring it back this afternoon. I borrowed it a couple of days ago.'

1)	A had	B had been	C had had itself	D had not
2)	A reminded	B questioned	C told	D asked
3)	A them	B that	C if	D later
4)	A called	B would	C had called	D would have called
5)	A wasn't	B wouldn't be	C hadn't been	D wouldn't have been
6)	A had	B had had	C had to have	D hadn't
7)	A think	B are thought	C have thought	D are thinking
8)	A would	B realise	C wish	D thought
9)	A was parked	B had parking	C is parked	D has parked
10)	A is	B was	C had	D wrote
11)	A If	B When	C Remember	D Suppose
12)	A do	B can	C would	D if
13)	A needed	B had been	C looked like	D seemed
14)	A called up	B was phoned	C had a phone call	D heard some news
15)	A unless	B if only	C if	D as long as

3 Complete the second sentence so that it has a similar meaning to the first sentence, using the word given. Do not change the word given. You must use between two and five words, including the word given.

a) Excuse me, is somebody serving you, sir?

being

Excuse me, ...*are you being served*..., sir?

b) I think we should go home.

went

It's .... home.

c) The painters painted our house last month.

had

We .... last month.

d) It's a pity that Charles always complains so much.

wouldn't

I .... so much.

e) Someone will meet you at the airport.

be

You .... at the airport.

f) People think that train-robber Dave Briggs has escaped.

have

Train-robber Dave Briggs .... escaped.

g) 'Don't forget to buy some bread, Mum,' said Pauline.

reminded

Pauline .... buy some bread.

h) Have you received your salary yet?

been

Have .... yet?

i) I think I'll manage to finish the letters by 4.00.

get

I think I'll .... by 4.00.

j) My parents made me study every night.

was

I .... every night by my parents.

59

4 Put each verb in brackets into a suitable verb form.

A friend in the rain

Last week I (1) ...*was walking*... (walk) home after playing tennis when it
(2) .... (start) raining very heavily. 'Oh no, I (3) ....
(get) soaked before I (4) .... (reach) home,' I thought. 'I wish I
(5) .... (remember) to bring my raincoat.' But unfortunately I
(6) .... (leave) it at home. How stupid of me! I (7) ....
(always forget) to bring it with me. Luckily just then a friend of mine passed in
her car and offered me a lift. '(8) .... (you go) home?' she asked,
'or (9) .... (you want) to go for a drink?' 'I think I'd rather you
(10) .... (take) me home,' I said. 'If I (11) .... (not
change) my clothes, I know I (12) .... (fall) ill, and then I
(13) .... (not be able) to play in the tennis tournament next week.
And I (14) .... (practise) hard for the last month.' 'I
(15) .... (wait) for you to change if you (16) ....
(like),' she told me. 'I think it's time you (17) .... (relax) for a
change. You (18) .... (worry) too much about things lately. And
people who (19) .... (worry) too much (20) .... (fall)
ill more easily. It's got nothing to do with the rain!'

5 Put each verb in brackets into a suitable verb form.

The facts about sugar

Packet sugar from the supermarket (1) ....*is extracted*.... (extract) from either
sugar cane or sugar beet. These products (2) .... (mix) with hot
water, which (3) .... (dissolve) their natural sugar. Sugar
(4) .... (also find) in fruit some of which, such as dates and grapes,
(5) .... (contain) very high amounts of sugar. To be a little more
specific, sugar should (6) .... (call) sucrose. Sucrose
(7) .... (make up) of two substances: glucose, which
(8) .... (use) for instant energy, and fructose, which
(9) .... (last) longer as a source of energy. The sugar in fruit is
mainly fructose. So when we (10) .... (eat) fruit, we
(11) .... (also eat) quite large amounts of natural sugar. Some
scientists (12) .... (believe) that too much sugar
(13) .... (eat) in sweets, cake and biscuits. It (14) ....
(say) to be generally bad for the health, although nothing (15) ....
(definitely prove) so far. However, it (16) .... (known) that sugar
(17) .... (cause) tooth decay. As one expert put it: 'If other foods
(18) .... (damage) our body as much as sugar (19) ....
(damage) our teeth, they (20) .... (ban) immediately.'

6 Look carefully at each line. Some of the lines are correct, and some have a word which should not be there. Tick each correct line. If a line has a word which should not be there, write the word in the space.

A holiday in Scotland

Some friends of mine decided to go on holiday	................✓................
to Scotland. They asked me if I was wanted to go	........*was*........
too, but I had already arranged to go to Italy.	1) ....
I told them so that I had been to Scotland before,	2) ....
so they asked me to give them some ideas.	3) ....
I advised them to take up warm clothes and	4) ....
raincoats. 'If I were like you, I'd always carry	5) ....
umbrellas!' I told them. 'I doubt that whether	6) ....
you'll have any sunny days.' I didn't see	7) ....
them again until was after their holiday. They	8) ....
were all very sun-tanned, and they told to me	9) ....
that they had had very hot weather.	10) ....
'If we had been taken your advice, we would	11) ....
have made a terrible mistake,' they said me.	12) ....
'Luckily we were told us before we	13) ....
left that it was very hot in Scotland.	14) ....
It is said to they have been the hottest summer ever!	15) ....

Explanations

Subject or object

■ Subject or object

Relative clauses give extra information about a noun in the main clause. Relative clauses begin with a relative pronoun (*who, which, that, whom, whose*). The relative pronoun can be the subject of the clause:

> *That's the woman **who bought my car**.*

The woman (subject) bought my car (object).

Or the object of the clause:

> *That's the car **that I used to own**.*

I (subject) used to own the car (object).

■ Combining sentences

Note how sentences are combined.

> Subject: *This is Jean. She bought my car.*
>
> *Jean is the person who bought my car.*

She is not repeated, as the person is the subject.

> Object: *That is Jean's car. I used to own it.*
>
> *That's the car that I used to own.*

It is not repeated, as *the car* is the object.

Defining or non-defining

■ Defining

Defining clauses give important information which tells us exactly what is being referred to.

> *That book **which you lent me** is really good.*

This indicates which book we are talking about. Without the relative clause, it might be difficult to understand the meaning.

■ Non-defining

Non-defining clauses add extra information. They are separated by commas in writing, and by a pause on either side (where the commas are) in speaking.

> *The book, **which I hadn't read**, was still on the shelf.*

This gives extra information about the book. We could miss out the relative clause and the meaning would still be clear.

Omitting the relative pronoun

■ Defining relative clauses

In a defining relative clause we can leave out the relative pronoun if it is the object of the clause.

> *That's **the car (that) I used to own**.*

We cannot miss out the relative pronoun if it is the subject of the clause.

> *That's the woman **who bought my car**.*

■ Non-defining relative clauses

In a non-defining relative clause we cannot leave out the relative pronoun.

Which, who and *that*

- *That* instead of *which*
  When we talk about things, *that* is often used instead of *which*. This is very common in speech.
  > *Is this the house **that** you bought?*

- *That* instead of *who*
  When we talk about people, *that* can be used instead of *who*. This is less common, but we still do it, especially in speech.
  > *Have you met the boy **that** Sue is going to marry?*

- *Which* in non-defining clauses
  That cannot be used to introduce a non-defining clause.
  > *The hotel, **which** was a hundred years old, was very comfortable.*

- Prepositions
  That cannot be used after a preposition.
  > *This is the car (**that/which**) I paid £2000 **for**.* (speech)
  > *This is the car **for which** I paid £2000.* (formal)

Whom and *whose*

- *Whom* is the object form of *who*. It has to be used after prepositions. Its use is formal and quite rare.
  > *This is the person (who) I sold my car to.* (speech)
  > *This is the person **to whom** I sold my car.* (formal)

- *Whose* means *of whom*, and usually refers to people.
  > *This is Jack. His sister is staying with us.*
  > *This is Jack, **whose** sister is staying with us.*

Practice

1 <u>Underline</u> any relative pronouns that can be left out in these sentences.

a) I think that my boss is the person <u>who</u> I admire most.
b) Harry, who was tired, went to bed very early.
c) We're taking the train that leaves at 6.00.
d) Have you seen the book that I left here on the desk?
e) The film which we liked most was the French one.
f) My radio, which isn't very old, has suddenly stopped working.
g) The clothes which you left behind are at the reception desk.
h) The couple who met me at the station took me out to dinner.
i) Last week I ran into an old friend who I hadn't seen for ages.
j) Don't cook the meat that I put in the freezer – it's for the dog.

2 Replace the relative pronouns in *italics* with *that*, where possible.

a) This is the magazine *which* I told you about.
   This is the magazine that I told you about.

b) John's flat, *which* is in the same block as mine, is much larger.

c) The girl *whose* bag I offered to carry turned out to be an old friend.

d) The policeman *who* arrested her had recognised her car.

e) I work with someone *who* knows you.

f) We don't sell goods *which* have been damaged.

g) Brighton, *which* is on the south coast, is a popular holiday resort.

h) I don't know anyone *whose* clothes would fit you.

i) There's a café near here *which* serves very good meals.

j) People *who* park outside get given parking tickets.

3   Underline the most suitable word in each sentence.

a) My friend Jack, *that/who/ who* parents live in Glasgow, invited me to spend Christmas in Scotland.

b) Here's the computer program *that/whom/whose* I told you about.

c) I don't believe the story *that/who/whom* she told us.

d) Peter comes from Witney, *that/who/which* is near Oxford.

e) This is the gun with *that/whom/which* the murder was committed.

f) Have you received the parcel *whom/whose/which* we sent you?

g) Is this the person *who/which/whose* you asked me about?

h) That's the girl *that/who/whose* brother sits next to me at school.

i) The meal, *that/which/whose* wasn't very tasty, was quite expensive.

j) We didn't enjoy the play *that/who/whose* we went to see.

4   Put a suitable relative pronoun in each space, or leave the space blank where possible.

a) My bike, ...*which*.... I had left at the gate, had disappeared.

b) The shoes .... I bought were the ones .... I tried on first.

c) The bag in .... the robbers put the money was found later.

d) The medicine .... the doctor gave me had no effect at all.

e) Peter, ... couldn't see the screen, decided to change his seat.

f) I really liked that tea .... you made me this morning.

g) What was the name of your friend .... tent we borrowed?

h) The flight .... Joe was leaving on was cancelled.

5   Make one new sentence from each pair of sentences. Begin as shown, and use the word given in capitals.

a) Brenda is a friend. I went on holiday with her.   WHO
   Brenda is ...*the friend who I went on holiday with.*.....................

b) This is Mr Smith. His son Bill plays in our team.   WHOSE
   This is Mr Smith ....

c) Her book was published last year. It became a best seller.   WHICH
   Her book ....

d) This is the bank. We borrowed the money from it.   WHICH
   This is the bank from ....

e) I told you about a person. She is at the door.   WHO
   The person ....

f) Jack's car had broken down. He had to take a bus.   WHOSE
   Jack, ...

6   **Make one sentence from each group of sentences, beginning as shown.**

a) The hotel was full of guests. The hotel was miles from anywhere. The guests had gone there to admire the scenery.

The hotel, which *was miles from anywhere, was full of guests who had gone there to admire the scenery.*

b) I lent you a book. It was written by a friend of mine. She lives in France.

The book I ....

....

c) A woman's jewels were stolen. A police officer was staying in the same hotel. The woman was interviewed by him.

The woman whose ....

....

d) A goal was scored by a teenager. He had come on as substitute. This goal won the match.

The goal which ....

....

e) I was sitting next to a boy in the exam. He told me the answers.

The boy I ....

....

f) My wallet contained over £100. It was found in the street by a schoolboy. He returned it.

My wallet, ...

....

g) My friend Albert has decided to buy a motorbike. His car was stolen last week.

My friend Albert, ...

....

h) Carol is a vegetarian. I cooked a meal for her last week. She enjoyed it.

Carol, ...

....

7   **Put one suitable word in each space, or leave the space blank where possible.**

Murder At The Station by Lorraine Small. Episode 5. *Trouble on the 6.15*. The story so far: Jane Platt, (1) ......*who*...... is travelling to London because of a mysterious letter, is the only person (2) .... witnesses a murder at Victoria Station. The detective to (3) .... she gives her statement then disappears. Jane goes to an office in Soho to answer the letter (4) .... she had received. There she discovers that her uncle Gordon, (5) ....

lives in South America, has sent her a small box (6) .... she is only to open if in trouble. Jane, (7) .... parents have never mentioned an Uncle Gordon, is suspicious of the box, (8) .... she gives to her friend Tony. They go to Scotland Yard and see Inspector Groves, (9) .... has not heard of the Victoria Station murder, (10) .... was not reported to the police. Jane gives Inspector Groves the murdered man's ticket (11) .... she found beside his body. Then Jane and Tony decide to go to Redhill, (12) .... was the town (13) .... the murdered man had come from. On the train they meet a man, (14) .... face is somehow familiar to Jane, (15) .... says he knows her Uncle Gordon...

8 **These sentences are all grammatically possible, but not appropriate in speech. Rewrite each sentence so that it ends with the preposition in *italics*.**

a) Margaret is the girl *with* whom I went on holiday.
   Margaret is the girl I went on holiday with.

b) The golf club is the only club *of* which I am a member.
   ....

c) That's the girl *about* whom we were talking.
   ....

d) It was a wonderful present, *for* which I was extremely grateful.
   ....

e) This is the school *to* which I used to go.
   ....

f) Is this the case *in* which we should put the wine glasses?
   ....

g) Can you move the chair *on* which you are sitting?
   ....

h) That's the shop *from* which I got my shoes.
   ....

i) Is that the person *next to* whom you usually sit?
   ....

j) This is Bill, *about* whom you have heard so much.
   ....

9 **Make one sentence from each group of sentences, beginning as shown.**

a) I got on a train. I wanted to go to a station. The train didn't stop there.

The train I *got on didn't stop at the station I wanted to go to.*

b) I read a book. You recommended a book to me. This was the book.

The book I ....

c) The ship hit an iceberg and sank. Warning messages had been sent to it. The ship ignored these.

The ship, ...

d) The postman realised I was on holiday. You had sent me a parcel. The postman left it next door.

The postman, ...

e) I used to own a dog. People came to the door. The dog never barked at them.

The dog I ....

f) I bought my car from a woman. She lives in a house. You can see the house over there.

The woman I ....

g) We went to a beach on the first day of our holiday. It was covered in seaweed. This smelled a lot.

The beach we ....

h) My neighbours have three small children. The children make a lot of noise. My neighbours never apologise.

My neighbours, ...

i) I bought a new computer. It cost me a lot of money.

The new ....

Key points

1 Long sentences with relative clauses are more common in writing. In speech it is more usual to join shorter clauses with conjunctions.

The hotel, which was miles from anywhere, was full of guests. (writing)
The hotel was miles from anywhere. It was full of guests. (speech)
The hotel was miles from anywhere, and it was full of guests. (speech)

2 In speech, relative pronouns are usually left out when they are the object of the clause.

This is the book I told you about.

3 In speech it is common to end relative clauses with a preposition.

That's the girl I live next door to.

→ SEE ALSO

Grammar 15: Consolidation 3

Explanations

Movement

Prepositions used with verbs of motion (*come, go, run*, etc) show the direction of the movement.

> *Jack ran **out of** the room.*   *Sue moved **towards** the door.*

Other examples: *to, into, across, around, along, up, down, past*

Position and place

Prepositions can show position.

> *Ted was sitting **next to** Janet.*   *The bank is **opposite** the cinema.*

Other examples: *before, below, beside, in front of, near, on top of, under*

Prepositions can show place.

> *I live **in** France.*   *Sue lives **on** an island.*   *John is **at** school.*

See below for problems of use.

Other uses

■ Prepositions are also used in time expressions.

■ Prepositions cover a wide range of other meanings.
> *This book is **about** Napoleon.*
> *I can't drink tea **with/without** sugar.*

Problems of use

■ *To* and *at*
With verbs of motion *to* means *in the direction of*. *At* is not used with verbs of motion. It is used to say where someone or something is.
> *We went **to** the cinema.*   *We arrived **at** the cinema.*

■ *Next to* and *near*
Next to means *very close, with nothing in between*. It is the same as *beside*. *Near* means *only a short distance from*, which can be a matter of opinion.
> *Peter always sits **next to** Mary.*
> *I live **near** the sea, it's only ten miles away.*

■ *Above* and *over*
Both words mean *in a higher position than*, but *over* suggests closeness or touching.
> *There was a plane high **above** them.*
> *Put this blanket **over** you.*

There may be little difference in some contexts.
> *There was something written **above/over** the door.*

■ *In* and *at*: places

In refers to towns, countries and the 'inside' of places.

> *She lives **in** Paris.*   *They arrived **in** Peru.*   *He's **in** the kitchen.*

At refers to points with a particular purpose rather than inside.

> *She lives **at** home.*   *I'll meet you **at** the bus stop.*

Compare:

> *They met **in the cinema**.*   (inside)
> *They met **at the cinema**.*   (place)

■ Prepositions at the end of a sentence

Study these common examples:

> *Who are you waiting **for**?*   (question)
> *You are very difficult to live **with**!*   (infinitive)
> *That's the company that I work **for**.*   (relative clause)

Prepositions without an object	Some prepositions can be used without an object. *Ted was walking **along**, whistling.* In this example we mean *along the street*, but it is clear from the context or unimportant. Other prepositions used like this are: *around, along, behind, opposite*
Prepositions with more than one word	Examples: *according to, on behalf of, by means of* Other examples are included in the Practice section.
Prepositional phrases	There are many fixed phrases containing prepositions. Examples: *by mistake, on purpose, out of order* Other examples are included in the Practice section.

Practice

1 <u>Underline</u> the most suitable prepositions.

a) I got *at/to* the station just in time to see Jack getting *from/off* the train.

b) The cafe is *among/between* the chemist's and the butcher's and *across/opposite* the library.

c) Sue lives *at/in* Wales, which is a country *at/in* the west of Britain.

d) I was brought up *in/on* an island *near/next to* the coast of Scotland.

e) Travelling *by/in* your own car is better than going *by/on* foot.

f) Jack was leaning *by/against* the wall with his hands *in/into* his pockets.

g) Ann had a hat *on/over* her head and a veil *above/over* her face.

h) We arrived *at/in* England *at/in* Gatwick Airport.

i) I left my bags *at/from* the station *at/in* a left luggage locker.

j) Peter came running *into/to* the room and threw his books *at/onto* the floor.

2 Complete each sentence with a suitable word or phrase from the box.

| according to | because of | ~~instead of~~ | apart from | by means of |
| in favour of | on behalf of | as for | in case of | regardless of |

a) I think I'd rather have coffee ......*instead of*...... tea.

b) .... the danger, Paul ran back into the burning house.

c) .... fire, smash the glass and push the button.

d) Personally, I am .... banning cigarette smoking completely!

e) I would like to thank you, ... everyone who was rescued.

f) .... you, no-one else knows that I have escaped.

g) .... Steve, he believes that we should stay where we are.

h) Jim managed to climb into the house .... a ladder he found.

i) .... the rain, the match was postponed.

j) .... the timetable, the next train isn't for two hours.

3 Decide whether it is possible to leave out the words in *italics*.

a) Most people are wandering around *the streets*, taking photos. ...*possible*...

b) I gave my bike to *my little sister*, when it became too small for me. ....

c) The people who live in the house opposite *our house* are Italian. ....

d) I left my coat *on the bed* in here but it seems to have disappeared. ....

e) I'll wait for you outside *the cinema*, on the pavement. ....

f) Peter took a deep breath, and then went under *the water* again. ....

g) Don't worry, the hotel's quite near *to where we are now*. ....

h) The children can sit behind *you in the back seats*. ....

4 Complete each sentence with a suitable word or phrase from the box.

at	by	for	in	on	~~off~~	out of	to	under	without

a) Police officers don't have to wear uniform when they are ....*off*........ duty.

b) I feel very tired. .... times I consider giving up work.

c) The children were all upset, and some were .... tears.

d) This factory needs modernising. Everything here is .... date.

e) Don't worry, everything is .... control.

f) Sorry, I seem to have taken the wrong umbrella .... mistake.

g) Please hurry. We need these documents .... delay.

h) That wasn't an accident! You did it .... purpose.

i) We thought the two films were very similar .... each other.

j) We decided to take a holiday in Wales .... a change.

5 <u>Underline</u> the most suitable phrase in each sentence.

a) I can't disturb John now. He's *at bed/<u>in bed</u>*.

b) Tony always arrives exactly *in time/on time* for his lesson.

c) Two pounds for each ticket, that makes £12 *in all/with all*.

d) I can't pick that last apple. It's *out of hand/out of reach*.

e) Joe and I met on the plane completely *by chance/by surprise*.

f) The children spend most of their time *out of doors/out of place*.

g) I'm sorry but Jane isn't here *at present/at a time*.

h) How can Sam love Lucy? They have nothing *in common/in general*.

i) They should be here soon. They are *in the way/on the way*.

j) Terry isn't here. He's away *in business/on business*.

6 Complete each sentence with a suitable word from the box.

breath	fail	impression	secret	strike	~~costs~~	return	stock

a) This is important. You must catch the two men at all ......*costs*...... .

b) I was under the .... that you enjoyed working here.

c) Please hand your work in on Tuesday, without ....

d) We can't go by train. The train-drivers are on ....

e) Martin is supposed to have given up smoking, but he smokes in ....

f) I'm afraid we don't have your size, we are out of ....

g) If I give you the information, what will you give me in .... ?

h) I ran for the bus, and now I'm out of ....

7 Complete each sentence with a suitable word from the box.

average	~~profit~~	sight	detail	himself	practice	public	whole

a) Harry managed to sell his house at a ..... *profit* ..... .

b) What was he doing here all by .... ?

c) Larry is so famous that he doesn't appear in .... very often.

d) That was a terrible shot! I'm rather out of ....

e) How many cars do you sell, on .... , every week?

f) The police are coming! Stay out of .... until they leave.

g) I suppose I enjoyed my holiday on the ....

h) Can you tell me about the plans in .... ?

8 Complete each sentence with a suitable phrase from the box.

by heart	in difficulties	out of work	by sight	in pain
~~in two~~	on sale	without a doubt		

a) When I sat on the pencil, it broke ...... *in two* ....

b) This is .... the best washing machine on the market.

c) Graham has been .... ever since he came to London.

d) I know her .... , but I don't know her name.

e) The lifeguard dived in to save a swimmer ....

f) John learned his first speech ....

g) You could tell he was .... because he kept groaning.

h) Cigarettes and ice cream are .... in the foyer.

9 Complete each sentence with one of the phrases from the box.

at any rate	in person	out of danger	out of tune
from now on	in private	out of order	~~under orders~~

a) Jim's excuse was that he was acting .... *under orders* .... from his boss.

b) Things have changed. .... , no-one leaves before 5.00.

c) Thank goodness. All the passengers are now ....

d) The President would like to meet you and thank you ....

e) Your violin sounds awful! I think it's ....

f) It's a warm country. We won't need our pullovers, ...

g) Excuse me, but I'd like to have a word with you ....

h) You can't use the phone. It's ....

10 Look carefully at each line. Some of the lines are correct, and some have a word which should not be there. Tick each correct line. If a line has a word which should not be there, write the word in the space.

The psychology of accidents

Most people are under the impression that	..........✓..........
doing something by a mistake is quite different	..........*a*..........
from doing something on purpose. In the fact,	1) ....
according to by some psychologists, many	2) ....
accidents do not, on the whole, really happen	3) ....
to by chance. There may be good reasons for	4) ....
actions which seem to be accidental. For an	5) ....
example, someone who fails to arrive on time	6) ....
as for a meeting at work may be worried about	7) ....
his or her job, or be in with difficulties at home.	8) ....
In other words, there are often good reasons for	9) ....
behaviour which seems at the first to be	10) ....
accidental. Of this course, some people are	11) ....
involved in more accidents than others. These	12) ....
people are called 'accident prone'. In the general	13) ....
they either suffer from stress, or could have in	14) ....
a physical illness without knowing about it.	15) ....

Key points

1 There is a group of prepositions used with verbs of motion.
    across, along, around, down, into, out of, past, to, towards, up

2 Some prepositions can be used without an object.
    *Jean lives **opposite**.*

3 A sentence can end with a preposition.
    *Paul didn't have a chair to sit **on**.*

 → SEE ALSO

Grammar 14: Time expressions
Grammar 15: Consolidation 3

Linking words 1

Explanations

Purpose

■ *So (that)*

We can use *so that* to express purpose (the reason why someone does something). *So that* is usually followed by *can, could, will or would*.

> *The police locked the door **so (that)** no-one could get in.*

■ Infinitive of purpose

We can also use *to* to express purpose. The subject of the main clause and of the purpose clause must be the same.

> *Jack went to England **so that he could study** engineering.*
> *Jack went to England **to study** engineering.* (NOT ~~for to study~~)

If the two subjects are different, we can't use *to*. We have to use *so that*.

> ***Jack** went to England **so that his brother** would have some help working in the restaurant.*

■ *In order to, so as to*

These are more formal ways of expressing purpose.

> *Scientists used only local materials, **in order to** save money.*

There are also negative forms: *in order not to, so as not to*.

> *The soldiers moved at night, **so as not to** alarm the villagers.*

■ *For*

This describes how something is used.

> *This button is **for starting** the engine.*
> *This is **for the lights**.*

Result

■ *So, such a*

So is used with an adjective or adverb.

> *Jim was **so tall (that)** he hit his head on the ceiling.*
> *Jim drove **so quickly (that)** they reached the station twenty minutes early.*

Such a is used with adjective + singular noun.

> *Helen is **such a busy person (that)** she never feels bored.*

■ *So many, so much, so few, so little*

So many/few are used with plural nouns. *So much/little* are used with uncountable nouns.

> *There were **so many passengers (that)** we couldn't find a seat.*
> *There was **so much noise (that)** I didn't get to sleep until 3 a.m.*

■ *Too/Not enough + to*

Too means *more than is necessary or good*. *Not enough* means *less than is necessary or good*. They can both be used with an adjective + *to*. Compare:

> *The bookcase was **too big to** get down the stairs.*
> *The bookcase was **not small enough to** get down the stairs.*

Contrast

■ *Although, though, even though*
Although often becomes *though* in speech. *Though* can come at the end of a sentence, *although* cannot.

> **Although** *I asked her, she didn't come.*   (speech and writing)
> **Though** *I asked her, she didn't come.*   (speech)
> *I asked her, (but) she didn't come,* **though**.   (speech)

Even though gives a stronger contrast than *although*.

> **Even though** *I asked her, she didn't come.*   (which was really surprising)

■ *While, whereas*
While and *whereas* are used in formal speech and writing. They compare two facts and emphasize the difference between them.

> **While** *United were fast and accurate, City were slow and careless.*

■ *However, nevertheless*
However is a way of expressing contrast in formal speech or writing. It can go at the beginning, middle or end of the sentence, and is separated by a comma (or a pause in speech).

> *Normally we don't refund money without a receipt.* **However**, *on this occasion I'll do it.*
> *Normally we don't refund money without a receipt. On this occasion,* **however**, *I'll do it.*

Nevertheless is a very formal way of expressing *however*.

> *I'm not happy with your work.* **Nevertheless**, *I'm going to give you one last chance.*

■ *Despite* and *in spite of*
These expressions are followed by a noun (including the *-ing* form used as a noun), and not by a clause (subject + verb).

> **In spite of the rain**, *we went out.*   (Although it was raining, we went out.)
> **Despite losing**, *we celebrated.*   (Although we lost, we celebrated.)

Practice

1 Underline the most suitable word or phrase in each sentence.

a) Janet went out *so that she bought/to buy* Harry a present.

b) This food is much too hot *to eat/to be eaten*.

c) *However/Though* it was late, I decided to phone Brian.

d) *Although/Despite* the car was cheap, it was in good condition.

e) Let's check once more, *for being/so as to be* sure.

f) We could go to the club. Is it worth it, *even though/though*?

g) It was *so windy/such a windy* that half the trees had blown down.

h) The batteries were *not enough small/too small* to fit the radio.

i) Despite *of the weather/the weather*, we went sailing.

j) Bill had *so much/so that* fun that he stayed another week.

2 Complete the second sentence so that it has a similar meaning to the first sentence, using the word given. Do not change the word given. You must use between two and five words, including the word given.

a) Sue went shopping so she could buy herself a new television.

to

Sue ...*went shopping to buy herself*........................ a new television.

b) You use this to open wine bottles.

for

This .... wine bottles.

c) I put the food in the fridge because I wanted it to get cold.

would

I put the food in the fridge .... cold.

d) Harry left early because he didn't want to miss the bus.

as

Harry .... to miss the bus.

e) I saved up some money to buy a motorbike.

could

I saved up some money .... a motorbike.

f) Jane gave up smoking because she wanted to save money.

order

Jane gave up smoking .... money.

g) I came here so that I could see you.

to

I .... you.

3 Rewrite each sentence, beginning as shown. Do not change the meaning.

a) Sam lost his job because he was lazy.
Sam was ......*so lazy that he lost his job.*..

b) I couldn't buy the house because it was expensive.
The house was too ....

c) The book was so interesting that I couldn't put it down.
It was ....

d) There was too much noise, so we couldn't hear the speech.
There was so ....

e) The house was too small to live in comfortably.
The house wasn't ....

f) We can't eat now because there isn't enough time.
There is too ....

g) I can't come to your party because I'm too busy.
I'm too ....

h) The class was cancelled because there weren't enough students.
There were so ....

4 Complete each sentence with one suitable word.

a) I couldn't run fast ......*enough*...... to catch the shoplifter.

b) They were .... good roads that we could drive at high speed.

c) It was .... dark that I couldn't see a thing.

d) The trousers were .... long enough to fit Jean.

e) We had .... a good time that we decided to go there again.

f) It was .... late that we couldn't get a bus home.

g) I took a taxi as it was .... far to walk.

h) The ladder wasn't tall .... to reach the window.

i) There are .... lovely fish that you don't feel like eating meat.

j) There were .... many dishes that I couldn't make up my mind.

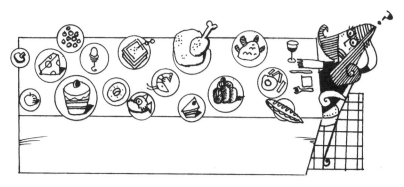

5 Rewrite each sentence, beginning as shown. Do not change the meaning. Two sentences should be rewritten as one.

a) Despite the cold weather, we all went for a walk.

Although ...*it was cold, we all went for a walk.*...........................

b) John has done well in French, but not so well in Maths.

While ....

c) I tried to persuade her. I didn't succeed, however.

Although ....

d) It was raining, but I went swimming anyway.

In spite of ....

e) Ann felt ill, but insisted on going to work.

Despite ....

f) In spite of his early lead, Hudson lost the race.

Although ....

g) I'm not going to pay, although I know that I should.

While ....

h) We expected Larry to accept the job, but he didn't.

Even though Larry ....

6 Explain what each object is for, using one of the verbs in the box.

lock	~~paint~~	stick	clean	keep	open	put	wash

a) brush

...*It's for painting things.*....................................

b) glue

....

c) fridge

....

d) sink

....

e) dustbin

....

f) toothbrush

....

g) corkscrew

....

h) key

....

7 Look carefully at each line. Some of the lines are correct, and some have a word which should not be there. Tick each correct line. If a line has a word which should not be there, write the word in the space.

Goodwriters... A course for you!

Jane was one of those students who has problems	.........✓.........
with writing. First, her handwriting it was so bad	.........*it*.........
that most teachers couldn't to read it. The letters were	1) ....
so small, that the words were extremely difficult to	2) ....
read. Even though she tried to change her handwriting,	3) ....
she felt discouraged. Secondly, she made so the many	4) ....
mistakes in spelling and punctuation, so that her work	5) ....
always gave a bad impression. As well as this, she	6) ....
had problems with organizing her writing, in despite	7) ....
making plans and writing notes. One day, though, she	8) ....
took a Goodwriter writing course, so to learn how to	9) ....
be an effective writer. At Goodwriters we taught her	10) ....
how to organize her ideas. Although however she found	11) ....
it difficult at first, so she soon made progress. She	12) ....
learned to revise her writing, so as to improve it.	13) ....
She started reading so too much that her spelling	14) ....
improved, so while her handwriting became clearer too.	15) ....

Key points

1   The infinitive of purpose must have the same subject as the main clause.
      I went to the shops. I wanted to buy some fruit.
      I went to the shops **to buy** *some fruit.*
   We do not use *for* in examples like this.

2   *In order to* is more common in formal speech and writing. In normal conversation we just use *to*.

3   Contrasts with *while, whereas* and *nevertheless* are used in formal speech and writing.

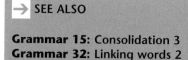

→ SEE ALSO

Grammar 15: Consolidation 3
Grammar 32: Linking words 2

Explanations

The Explanations section focuses on problem areas only. Other time expressions are included in the Practice section.

Present time

Nowadays and *these days*
Both contrast the present with the past.
> ***Nowadays** more women have careers.*
> *What are you up to **these days?***

Notice that the word *actually* is not used with a time reference, as it is in many European languages. *Actually* means *in fact* or *really*.

Future time

■ *In*
In can refer to future time. When we use it like this, it refers to the end of a period of time.
> *I'll be there **in a moment**.*
> *I'll be back **in a week**.*

■ Calendar references
If today is Monday:
> *Wednesday is **the day after tomorrow** or **the day after next**.*
> *Wednesday is also **in two days' time**.*
> *Next Monday is **this time next week**.*

■ *At the end, in the end, at last*
At the end refers to a point in time.
> *I left at the end of the film.*
In the end means *after a lot of time* or *eventually*.
> *I think that our side will win **in the end/eventually**.*
> *We waited for ages, and **in the end/finally** we left.*
At last shows that we are pleased because a long wait has ended.
> *At last you have arrived!*

■ *Presently*
This means in a few moments. It is a formal use.
> *Just a minute. I'll be with you **presently**.*

Past time

■ *Once*
This can mean *in the past*. It can also mean *from the time when*.
> *I lived here **once**. (in the past)*
> ***Once** she gets here, we can leave. (when)*

■ Periods of the day
Last is used with *night*, but not with *morning, afternoon* or *evening*.
> *They left **yesterday morning** and came back **last night**.*

■ Calendar references
If today is Monday:
> Saturday night was **the night before last.**

■ *In those days* and *at that time*
Both refer to a past time we have already mentioned.
> I met Janet in 1980. **In those days** I was a keen dancer.

■ *After, later* and *afterwards*
After is followed by an object.
> I'll see you **after the holidays.**

Later means *after some time*. It is not followed by an object.
> I'm busy now. I'll call you back later.

Afterwards means *after something has happened.*
> The film is starting now. I'll tell you **afterwards**.

Other problems

■ *In:*   *In January, In 1968, In the morning/afternoon/evening*
On: *On Thursday, On my birthday*
At: *At six o'clock, At night, At midday/midnight, At the weekend*

■ *For:*   *I lived there for ten years.*   (*for* + a period of time)
Since: I have lived here since 1999.   (*since* + a point in time)
Ago: *Edward died two years ago.*   (how far back in the past)

■ *By:*   *I need your homework by next week.*   (not later than next week)
Until: I'll be away until next week.   (all the time up to next week)

■ *On time: Bill is never late, he's always on time.*   (not late)
In time: Luckily the police arrived in time to help.   (early enough)

Practice

1 <u>Underline</u> the most suitable word or phrase in each sentence.

a) I haven't seen Jim *before/since* we worked together in London.

b) I'll finish the letter now and you can post it *after/later*.

c) What were you doing *last evening/yesterday evening* when I called?

d) Did you live here *in/since* 1987?

e) Diana hasn't finished her course *already/yet*.

f) What do you usually do *in the afternoon/this afternoon*?

g) Have you seen Jean and Chris *nowadays/recently*?

h) Helen arrived here *at Thursday night/on Thursday night*.

i) It's really ages *since/when* I saw you last.

j) Ann is going to be famous *once/one day*.

2 Put one word in each space.

a) Graham came to see us over a week ago, the Friday before ...... *last* ....

b) Is it very warm here .... the winter?

c) No thanks, I've had some tea ....

d) Don't worry, it won't hurt and I'll .... be finished.

e) I liked the book. I didn't know what was going to happen ....

f) I think that people had much more spare time in the ....

g) This is very urgent. Please send it at ....

h) Harry isn't here. He left about five minutes ....

i) The film doesn't start until 7.30. We're half an hour ....

j) Would you mind waiting for .... a moment, please?

3 Complete each sentence with a word or phrase from the box.

afterwards	eventually	in the end	~~nowadays~~	soon
immediately	lately	once	yet	

a) There is far too much traffic on the roads ...... *nowadays* ....

b) Never mind. I'm sure we'll find what we are looking for ....

c) I haven't seen you for ages. What have you been doing .... ?

d) Jack hasn't left. He hasn't finished his work ....

e) Take some notes in the meeting, and we'll discuss them ....

f) If you don't mind waiting, Brenda will be back ....

g) I considered taking a new job, but decided against it ....

h) Norman and I worked for the same company ....

i) You didn't fool me! I recognised you ....

4 Complete each sentence with the most suitable word or phrase.

a) We ran into the station and caught the train ....*B*.......... in time.

    A) right   B) just   C) early   D) already

b) Lunch will be ready .... the time you get back.

    A) at   B) during   C) in   D) by

c) I haven't been feeling well .... , doctor.

    A) recently   B) afterwards   C) suddenly   D) at last

d) Long .... , the valley you can see was actually a lake.

    A) past   B) ago   C) since   D) before

e) Jean bought an expensive watch, but regretted it ....

    A) at the end   B) later   C) then   D) after

f) I haven't had a Chinese meal for ....

    A) long   B) it's ages   C) years   D) the summer

g) I've cleaned all the parts, but the motor .... doesn't work.

    A) at last   B) now   C) always   D) still

h) .... you get used to the job, it won't seem so bad.

    A) since   B) while   C) once   D) as

i) I haven't .... decided where to go on holiday.

    A) yet   B) already   C) still   D) just

j) The first time I noticed something was wrong was .... I got home.

    A) since   B) when   C) for   D) until

5 Complete each sentence with one of the phrases from the box.

> all night long   from time to time   one at a time   all the time
> in a few moments   over and over again   all the year round
> in the nick of time   the other day   for hours on end
> once and for all   this time next week

a) Don't carry the boxes all together. We'll move them ...*one at a time*... .

b) I've told you .... , don't leave it here!

c) It's time you stopped biting your nails ....

d) Sheila grabbed Bill .... before he fell.

e) Hurry up! The bomb will go off ....

f) We shouldn't have trusted Michael. He was lying ....

g) Gerry sits staring at the television ....

h) .... I'll be lying on the beach, not working in the office!

i) The swimming pool on the common is open ....

j) I met your friend Janet in the café ....

k) Dave isn't a keen fisherman, but he goes fishing ....

l) The party finished at dawn after we had danced ....

6 Put one word in each space.

a) You will receive your salary ....*at*........ the end of the month.

b) I feel really tired. I think I'll go to bed early ....

c) The weather has been terrible so far .... month.

d) I'll see what David says, and .... I'll come back and tell you.

e) I'm a bit busy .... , but I can talk to you later.

f) If you haven't finished .... , don't worry.

g) Are you doing anything .... Friday evening?

h) Where's Brian? He should be here .... now.

i) We cannot accept applications sent .... the closing date.

j) .... upon a time, there were three bears.

7   Replace the word or phrase in *italics* with one of the words or phrases given (A–C), so that the meaning stays the same.

a)   The weather was bad at first, but it cleared up *in the end*. ....B..........

A) at last   B) eventually   C) lately

b)   Jane was leading the race, but *all at once* she fell over. ....

A) suddenly   B) one by one   C) after that

c)   Have you been swimming *recently*? ....

A) lately   B) already   C) yet

d)   I enjoy going skiing *every now and again*. ....

A) frequently   B) immediately   C) occasionally

e)   I saw Terry in the street *the other day*. ....

A) recently   B) yesterday   C) last night

f)   I think we've solved this problem *once and for all*. ....

A) in the end   B) forever   C) temporarily

g)   Kath told Martin that she was leaving *for good*. ....

A) for ever   B) for a while   C) early

h)   We arrived for the train *in good time*. ....

A) on time   B) at the right moment   C) with time to spare

i)   I believe we met *on a previous occasion*. ....

A) once before   B) the last time   C) completely by chance

j)   The political situation seems to be changing *minute by minute*. ....

A) from time to time   B) time after time   C) very rapidly

Key points   1   Some time expressions are connected with particular tenses.

*Claire **arrived** an hour **ago**.*

*I've **been living** here **since 1977**.*

*John **worked** there **for two years**.*

*Sally **has been studying** French **for six months**.*

*I **haven't been** to the theatre **for ages**.*

*Terry **will have left** the café **by then**.*

2   *For* can sometimes be left out.

*Sandra **waited three hours** in freezing weather.*

→ SEE ALSO

Grammar 1 to 5: Past time, Present perfect, Future time, Present time
Grammar 15: Consolidation 3

1 Put one suitable word in each space.

An old school friend

When John saw the large crowd (1) .....*which*..... had gathered (2) ....
the street, he wasn't sure (3) .... first what had happened. There were
(4) .... many people blocking the entrance to the hotel, that he had to
push his way (5) .... them to get (6) .... the door. At the
door he found two policemen (7) .... were trying to hold the crowd
back. 'What (8) .... earth is going on?' he asked them. Then John
noticed that some of the crowd were holding placards (9) .... read:
'We love you Sally.' (10) .... course, that was it. Sally Good was a
footballer, the first woman to play for England. (11) .... John wasn't
really interested in sport he decided to join the crowd and wait
(12) .... she appeared. About ten minutes (13) .... , a smiling
woman appeared and waved to the crowd. John was taken completely
(14) .... surprise when she took his arm and said, 'Remember me? I'm
the girl (15) .... used to sit next to you at school.'

2 Put one suitable word in each space.

a) ....*By*........ the time you've done the shopping, I'll be ready.

b) I'm going home now, but I'll phone you ....

c) Harry has been working very hard ....

d) I'll write to you .... the end of the week.

e) I waited for you .... 6.00, but then I left.

f) Peter sometimes goes walking .... hours.

g) I won't be long. I'll be ready .... a moment.

h) .... upon a time, there was a beautiful princess.

i) Guess who I saw the .... day. My old English teacher!

j) I'm not a regular swimmer but I go .... and again.

3 **Put one suitable word in each space.**

a) This is the book I told you ...... *about* ..... .

b) There's someone outside .... car has broken down.

c) Sue won the gold medal .... having a bad leg.

d) I suppose I agree with you .... a great extent.

e) The police, from .... I learned nothing, are being secretive.

f) Excuse me, but your bicycle is .... my way.

g) She bought me a present, ... I told her not to bother.

h) Tony knows most of Shakespeare .... heart.

i) The letter was addressed: 'To .... it may concern.'

j) There are no letters today. The post office is .... strike.

4 **Rewrite each sentence so that it contains the word given in capitals. Do not change the meaning.**

a) I bought my car from that man.   WHOM

...... *That is the man from whom I bought my car* ......

b) That boy's sister sits behind me at school.   WHOSE

....

c) Bill's computer had broken and he had to use a pencil.   WHOSE

....

d) The girls were hungry and decided to have a meal.   WHO

....

e) I live in Croydon – it's near London.   WHICH

....

f) Did you borrow this book?   THAT

....

g) This is Brenda – she lives upstairs.   WHO

....

h) You gave me a very useful present.   WHICH

....

i) The car was in good condition and wasn't expensive.   WHICH

....

j) Someone found the money and was given a reward.   WHO

....

5   **Put a suitable preposition in each space.**

a) We landed ....*at*........ Athens Airport, which is ....*by*........ the sea.

b) He was cold .... bed so his mother put a blanket .... him.

c) I'm not .... favour of nuclear power in .... of accidents.

d) When I sheltered .... a tree, an apple fell .... my head.

e) Quite .... chance I noticed that the house was .... sale.

f) Can we discuss this .... private? Alone, ... other words.

g) If you're .... difficulties with money, I'll help you .... all means.

h) Hearing she was .... of work took me .... surprise.

6   **Complete the second sentence so that it has a similar meaning to the first sentence, using the word given. Do not change the word given. You must use between two and five words, including the word given.**

a) We were in Venice a week ago today.

time

We were in Venice ......*this time last*.................................. week.

b) Joe had financial problems, but bought a new motorbike.

despite

Joe bought a new motorbike .... financial problems.

c) I couldn't drink the soup, as it was too hot.

to

The soup .... drink.

d) Susan was tired, so she decided to go to bed.

that

Susan was .... decided to go to bed.

e) We spoke in whispers as we didn't want to wake the baby.

not

We spoke in whispers .... to wake the baby.

f) I kept looking for my missing watch, but I knew it was no use.

even

I kept looking for my missing watch .... it was no use.

g) There were a lot of people, and I couldn't see the screen properly.

that

There were .... I couldn't see the screen properly.

h) The weather is fine, but my flowers haven't come out.

of

My flowers haven't come out .... weather.

7 Decide which answer (A, B, C or D) best fits each space.

Arriving in Bluffville

Stephen arrived in Bluffville (1) ....*B*......... the early evening, and walked (2) .... the bus station through the town centre, looking for somewhere to stay. There was a huge old-fashioned hotel, (3) .... it was obviously closed. The windows (4) .... street level were covered (5) .... sheets of corrugated iron. (6) .... there must have been many travellers passing (7) .... Bluffville, but now the motorway (8) .... the south passed the town several miles (9) .... , and so very few people stopped. Stephen found a telephone (10) .... a run-down bar, and called the nearest motel (11) .... turned out to be seven miles away on the motorway. He asked the barman, (12) .... was reading a comic book, how (13) .... a taxi would cost to take him (14) .... the motel. The man stared hard at Stephen (15) .... he said, 'No taxis here – haven't been any for more than ten years.'

1)	A at	B in	C after	D and
2)	A down	B with	C from	D away
3)	A though	B which	C that	D despite
4)	A at	B the	C under	D across
5)	A and	B with	C from	D up
6)	A over	B so	C soon	D once
7)	A out	B into	C through	D from
8)	A in	B of	C by	D to
9)	A away	B out	C far	D long
10)	A and	B which	C in	D box
11)	A it	B which	C who	D this
12)	A although	B why	C he	D who
13)	A far	B much	C many	D often
14)	A to	B in	C at	D out
15)	A who	B since	C before	D eventually

8 Look carefully at each line. Some of the lines are correct, and some have a word which should not be there. Tick each correct line. If a line has a word which should not be there, write the word in the space.

The electronic age

I recently learned how to use a computer, and	✓
I have many friends who they play computer games	*they*
at home. However, although recently I have begun to worry	1) ....
that in nowadays we rely too much on electronic gadgets.	2) ....
Once before people managed to write and think using	3) ....
their brains, but now many people have become so	4) ....
accustomed to using machines, so that they can't do	5) ....
anything without them. There are many people who	6) ....
they depend on electronic gadgets completely. For	7) ....
an instance, many of my friends sit at home in the	8) ....
evening and watch television, and instead of going	9) ....
out so to meet people. I think that this makes everybody	10) ....
feel more lonely, even though they learn a lot about	11) ....
people all over in the world. Of course there are many	12) ....
electronic gadgets that save us time, though not all	13) ....
of them are really necessary. I am in favour of some	14) ....
gadgets, but I am against of having everything in life	15) ....
depending on pushing a button.	

Modal verbs: present and future

Explanations

Ability

Can and *be able to*
Can, like all modal verbs, cannot be used in an infinitive or continuous form.
We use *be able to* in situations where we need these forms.

> *I'd like to **be able to** swim.*
> ***Not being able to** swim is annoying.*

Certainty and uncertainty

■ *Must* and *can't*
These words have a meaning related to certainty – they are used to make deductions. This is when we are sure or almost sure about something because it is logical. This usage is especially common with the verb *be*.

> *You **must be** tired after your long journey.*   (I'm sure you are)
> *That **can't be** Sue. She's in Brazil.*   (I'm sure it's not possible)

These words are also used in other ways: *must* for obligation (see next section) and *can('t)* for ability (see above).

■ *May, might* and *could*
These words all express uncertainty or possibility. *Could* is not used with *not* in this context.

> *I **might** go out, I don't know. I **could** get wet!*

The meaning for all three words is approximately 50 per cent probability. But if we stress the modal verb strongly in speech the probability is reduced.

> *I **might** see you later if I finish my work, but don't count on it.*
> (*might* is strongly stressed in speech)

■ *Should* and *ought to*
These words are both used for obligation (see next section).
But they also have a meaning related to certainty – they are used when we expect that something will happen.

> *Brenda **should be** home by now.*   (I expect that she is)

■ *Be bound to*
This is used to say that something is certain to happen in the future.

> *You're **bound to see** Paula if you go there.*   (I'm sure you will)

Obligation

■ *Must* and *have to*
In writing there is no real difference between these words. In speech there is sometimes a small difference. *Must* is used when the speaker personally feels something is important and *have to* is used when the situation makes something necessary.

> *You **must start** working harder!*   (I say so)
> *You **have to turn** left here.*   (it's the law)
> *Sorry, I **must leave/have to leave** now.*   (in this example there is no difference)

- *Mustn't* and *don't have to*
  Be careful: *must* and *have to* are very similar in their affirmative forms (see previous paragraph) but they are completely different in their negative forms.
  Mustn't describes something which is prohibited. *Don't have to* describes something which is not necessary.

  > *You **mustn't** leave now.*   (It's not allowed. It's against the rules.)
  > *You **don't have to** leave now.*   (It's not necessary. You have a choice.)

- *Should* and *ought to*
  These words have the same meaning. They are used to say what is the best thing to do. They can be used to give an opinion, some advice, or polite instructions.

  > *We **should** do something different for our holidays this year.*
  > *I think you **should** see a doctor.*
  > *You **ought not to** smoke if you're pregnant.*
  > *You **should** send in your application by July 18th.*

- *Had better*
  This phrase gives strong advice about how to stop something going wrong. It can refer to present or future time.

  > *I think you**'d better** leave now.*   (before it is too late)
  > *You**'d better not** drive.*   (it might be dangerous)

- *Is/Are to*
  This is used in formal instructions. *Not* is stressed.

  > *No-one **is to** leave the room.*
  > *You **are not to** leave the room.*

Practice

1 <u>Underline</u> the correct word or phrase in each sentence.

a) There's someone at the door. It *can/<u>must</u>* be the postman.

b) Don't worry, you *don't have to/mustn't* pay now.

c) I think you *had better/would better* take a pullover with you.

d) Jones *could/must* be president if Smith has to resign.

e) Sorry, I can't stay any longer. I *have to/might* go.

f) It was 5 o'clock an hour ago. Your watch *can't/mustn't* be right.

g) It's a school rule, all the pupils *have to/must* wear a uniform.

h) I suppose that our team *must/should* win, but I'm not sure.

i) Let's tell Diana. She *could/might* not know.

j) In my opinion, the government *might/should* do something about this.

2 Complete the second sentence so that it has a similar meaning to the first sentence, using the word given. Do not change the word given. You must use between two and five words, including the word given.

a) I think you should give up smoking immediately.

   had

   I think you ....*had better give up*.......................... smoking immediately.

b) I expect we will get there by 5.00, if there isn't too much traffic.

   should

   We .... 5.00, if there isn't too much traffic.

c) Is it necessary for me to bring my passport?

   have

   Do .... my passport?

d) I am sure that the cat is in the house somewhere.

   be

   The cat .... in the house somewhere.

e) An aerial is not required with this radio.

   have

   You don't .... an aerial with this radio.

f) It is very inconvenient if you can't drive.

to

It's very inconvenient if .... drive.

g) I am sure that John is not the thief.

be

John .... the thief.

h) I am certain that Norman will be late.

bound

Norman .... late.

i) All students should report to the main hall at 9.00.

are

All students .... to the main hall at 9.00.

j) I thought that you would know better!

ought

You .... better!

3 <u>Underline</u> **the most suitable word or phrase in each sentence.**

a) We can't be lost. *It isn't allowed/<u>I don't believe it.</u>*

b) Jane is bound to be late. *She always is/She must be.*

c) Late-comers are to report to the main office. *It's a good idea/It's the rule.*

d) You don't have to stay *unless it's necessary/if you don't want to.*

e) Astronauts must feel afraid sometimes. *They're supposed to/It's only natural.*

f) You can't come in here. *It isn't allowed/I don't believe it.*

g) All motorcyclists have to wear crash helmets. *It's a good idea/It's the rule.*

h) I ought not to tell Jack. *It's not a good idea/It's the rule.*

i) We should be there soon. *I expect so/It's absolutely certain.*

j) You'd better leave now. *That's my advice/That's an order!*

4 **Complete each sentence so that it contains** *might, might not, must, mustn't, can* **or** *can't.* **More than one answer may be possible.**

a) Don't stand up in the boat! You ....*might*........ fall in the river!

b) Sue says she's stuck in traffic and she .... be late.

c) You really .... start spending more time on your work.

d) Tell Peter he .... stay the night here if he wants to.

e) That's a really stupid idea! You .... be serious, surely!

f) You .... realise it, but this is very important to me.

g) Don't be silly. You .... expect me to believe you!

h) We're not sure but we .... go to Prague for Christmas this year.

i) Me learn to fly! You .... be joking!

j) Bill cooked the lunch, so you .... expect anything special!

5 Rewrite each sentence so that it contains *can, could, must, have to* or *should* (including negative forms).

a) I'm sure that Helen feels really lonely.
....*Helen must feel really lonely.*...

b) You're not allowed to park here.
....

c) It would be a good idea if Harry took a holiday.
....

d) I'm sure that Brenda isn't over thirty.
....

e) Do I need a different driving licence for a motorbike?
....

f) What would you advise me to do?
....

g) Mary knows how to stand on her head.
....

h) You needn't come with me if you don't want to.
....

i) It's possible for anyone to break into this house!
....

j) The dentist will see you soon. I don't think he'll be long.
....

6 Choose the most suitable description for each picture.

a)

1) He should be exhausted!
②) He must be exhausted!

b)

1) We mustn't pay to go in.
2) We don't have to pay to go in.

c)

1) I'm afraid we have to operate.
2) I'm afraid we should operate.

d)

1) Mind out, you could drop it!
2) Mind out! You can drop it!

e)

1) Thanks, but I'd better not!
2) I don't have to, thanks.

f)

1) We must be here for hours!
2) We're bound to be here for hours!

Key points

1 Most modal auxiliaries have more than one meaning. You should think carefully about the context, or tone of voice, to understand the meaning.

2 The negative forms *mustn't* and *don't have to* have different meanings.
   *You **mustn't** go.*   (it's against the rules)
   *You **don't have to** go.*   (it isn't necessary)

3 In normal speech *should* is a weaker obligation than *must* and *have to*.
   You should go to the doctor. (I think it's a good idea)
   You must go to the doctor.   (it's necessary)

But in formal speech or writing *should* can be a way of expressing a strong obligation.
   *Passengers for Gatwick Airport **should** change at Reading.*

→ SEE ALSO

Grammar 17: Modal verbs: past
Grammar 20: Consolidation 4

Modal verbs: past

Explanations

Ability

Could and *was able to*

To talk about general past ability we use *could*.

> *When I was young, I **could run** very fast.*

To talk about one specific past action we use *was able to*.

> *Luckily, Mary **was able to help** us.*

Certainty and uncertainty

■ *Must have* and *can't have*

These are used to make logical deductions about past actions.

> *I **must have left** my wallet in the car.*   (I am sure I did)
> *Jim **can't have noticed** you.*   (I am sure he didn't)

■ *May have, might have* and *could have*

These express possibility or uncertainty about past actions.

> *Jean **might have missed** the train.*   (perhaps she did)
> *He **may not have received** the letter.*   (perhaps he didn't)
> *You **could have been killed**!*   (it was a possibility)

■ *Was/Were to have*

This describes something which was supposed to happen, but didn't. It is formal in use.

> *He **was to have left** yesterday.*   (he was supposed to leave, but he didn't)

Obligation

■ *Had to*

Must has no past form, so we use *had to*.

> *Sorry I'm late, I **had to take** the children to school.*

The question form is *Did you have to?*

> ***Did** you **have to work** late yesterday?*

■ *Should have* and *ought to have*

These express the feeling that a mistake was made. There is a criticism.

> *I **should have posted** this letter yesterday.* (I didn't do the right thing)
> *You **shouldn't have told** me the answer.*   (you were wrong to do so)

■ *Needn't have* and *didn't need to*

There is a slight difference between these two forms. Compare:

> *I **needn't have arrived** at seven.*
>
> (I arrived at seven, but it wasn't necessary)
>
> *I **didn't need to arrive** at seven.*
>
> (we don't know when I arrived – maybe seven or later)

But in everyday speech we often use *didn't need to* for both cases.

Pronunciation and writing	In speech, *have* is often contracted in the forms in this unit. I **must've left** my wallet in the car.
Indirect speech	*Must* and *shall* In indirect speech (see Grammar 6) *must* is reported as *must* or *had to*. *Shall* is reported as *should*.

      'You must go.'   *He told me I must go.*
                 He told me I had to go.
      'Shall I help?'   *He asked if he should help.*

Practice

1 Choose the most suitable response to each comment or question.

a) A: What did I do wrong?
   B: 1) You shouldn't have connected these two wires.
      2) You didn't have to connect these two wires.

b) A: Why is the dog barking?
   B: 1) It should have heard something.
      2) It must have heard something.

c) A: Why are you home so early?
   B: 1) I needn't have worked this afternoon.
      2) I didn't have to work this afternoon.

d) A: Why did you worry about me? I didn't take any risks.
   B: 1) You must have been injured.
      2) You could have been injured.

e) A: You forgot my birthday again!
   B: 1) Sorry, I should have looked in my diary.
      2) Sorry, I had to look in my diary.

f) A: We had a terrible crossing on the boat in a storm.
   B: 1) That didn't have to be very pleasant!
      2) That can't have been very pleasant!

g) A: Where were you yesterday? You didn't turn up!
   B: 1) I had to go to London.
      2) I must have gone to London.

h) A: What do you think about the election?
   B: 1) The Freedom Party had to win.
      2) The Freedom Party should have won.

i) A: There's a lot of food left over from the party, isn't there?
   B: 1) Yes, you couldn't have made so many sandwiches.
      2) Yes, you needn't have made so many sandwiches.

j) A: What do you think has happened to Tony?
   B: 1) I don't know, he should have got lost.
      2) I don't know, he might have got lost.

2 Complete the second sentence so that it has a similar meaning to the first sentence, using the word given. Do not change the word given. You must use between two and five words, including the word given.

a) It wasn't necessary for me to go out after all.

have

I ......*needn't have gone out*.. after all.

b) There was a plan for Jack to become manager, but he left.

was

Jack .... manager, but he left.

c) It was a mistake for you to buy that car.

bought

You .... that car.

d) I don't think that Sally enjoyed her holiday.

have

Sally .... enjoyed her holiday.

e) It's possible that Bill saw me.

may

Bill .... me.

f) I'm sure that Karen was a beautiful baby.

been

Karen .... a beautiful baby.

g) Perhaps Alan didn't mean what he said.

meant

Alan .... what he said.

h) It's possible that I left my wallet at home.

could

I .... my wallet at home.

i) I think you were wrong to sell your bike.

shouldn't

You .... bike.

j) The only thing I could do was run away!

had

I .... run away!

3   Underline the most suitable phrase in each sentence.

a) We should have turned left. <u>We've missed the turning</u>/We followed the instructions.

b) We didn't have to wear uniform at school. *But I never did/That's why I liked it.*

c) The butler must have stolen the jewels. *He was ordered to/There is no other explanation.*

d) You could have phoned from the station. *I'm sure you did/Why didn't you?*

e) You needn't have bought any dog food. *There isn't any/There is plenty.*

f) Ann might not have understood the message. *I suppose it's possible/She wasn't supposed to.*

g) You can't have spent all the money already! *You weren't able to/I'm sure you haven't.*

h) I shouldn't have used this kind of paint. *It's the right kind/It's the wrong kind.*

4   Rewrite each sentence so that it contains *can't, might, must, should* or *needn't.*

a) I'm sure that David took your books by mistake.
   David must have taken your books by mistake.

b) It was a mistake to park outside the police station.

   ....

c) It was unnecessary for you to clean the floor.

   ....

d) I'm sure that Liz hasn't met Harry before.

   ....

e) Ann possibly hasn't left yet.

   ....

f) I'm sure they haven't eaten all the food. It's not possible!

   ....

g) Jack is supposed to have arrived half an hour ago.

   ....

h) Perhaps Pam and Tim decided not to come.

   ....

i) I think it was the cat that took the fish from the table!

   ....

j) It was a waste of time worrying, after all!

   ....

5 **Choose the most suitable description for each picture.**

a)

1) You must have read the notice.
2) You should have read the notice.

b)

1) We can't have worn our raincoats.
2) We needn't have worn our raincoats.

c)

1) He must have hit him in the right spot!
2) He should have hit him in the right spot!

d)

1) You must have caused an accident!
2) You might have caused an accident!

e)

1) Sorry, I had to go to the dentist's.
2) Sorry, I should have gone to the dentist's.

f)

1) You shouldn't have stroked the lion!
2) You didn't have to stroke the lion!

6   Look carefully at each line. Some of the lines are correct, and some have a word which should not be there. Tick each correct line. If a line has a word which should not be there, write the word in the space.

Zoo escape shocks residents

Residents in the Blackwood area complained last	.........✓.........
night that they should have had been warned about	.......*had*......
the escape of a dangerous snake. The snake, a python	1) ....
is three metres long, and can to kill pets. 'I heard	2) ....
about it on the radio,' said Mrs Agnes Bird. 'I had gone	3) ....
to lock my dog in the kitchen this morning, because	4) ....
I thought the snake could easily have attack it. Now	5) ....
I am not sure what I ought to be do.' The snake, called	6) ....
Lulu, disappeared from the Blackwood Zoo. 'It must be	7) ....
have found a hole in the wall, or it might have been	8) ....
slipped out while the door was open,' said zoo director	9) ....
Basil Hart. Mr Hart said that people didn't needn't have	10) ....
been alarmed. 'A local radio station must have had	11) ....
mixed up its reports,' he went on. 'We found Lulu a	12) ....
few minutes after we missed her. We have had to climb	13) ....
a tree and bring her down. So you see, you should have	14) ....
never believe silly stories you hear on the radio!	15) ....

Key point   In speech, *have* is often contracted with modals used in the past.
*You shouldn't***'ve** *done it.*

→ **SEE ALSO**

Grammar 20: Consolidation 4

Explanations

■ What are functions?

We can describe language by using words to talk about grammar (grammatical description). But we can also describe language by saying how it is used. This is the function of the language (functional description).

> *If I were you, I'd leave now.* grammatical description: second conditional
> functional description: giving advice

■ Choosing what to say

Our choice of words can be influenced by the situation we are in, by the person we are talking to, and by what we are talking about. Compare these different phrases for asking permission.

Asking permission from a friend:

> *Is it all right if I use the phone?*

Asking permission from the same person, but about a more serious topic:

> *Do you think I could possibly phone Australia?*

Asking permission from a stranger:

> *Do you mind if I open the window?*

The first example was informal and friendly. The second two examples were more formal and polite. There are no exact rules about when to use an informal phrase and when to use a polite phrase, but usually we use polite language when we:

- talk to strangers or people we don't know well.
- talk to people who have higher status.
- talk about sensitive topics.

■ This unit practises the following functions and possible responses.

Asking for and giving advice
Agreeing and disagreeing
Apologising
Complaining
Ending a conversation
Asking for and giving directions
Greeting
Asking how someone is
Asking for information
Introducing yourself and others
Inviting
Accepting and declining invitations
Offering something
Offering to do something

Practice

1 **Match each sentence (a–j) with a function from 1–10.**

a) That's very kind of you, I'd love to. ....4.........

b) Well, it's been nice talking to you, but I'm afraid I have to go. ....

c) Could you tell me how to get to the post office? ....

d) You might have told me you were having a party! ....

e) Shall I carry this bag for you? ....

f) What do you think I should do? ....

g) Actually, I don't think that's right. ....

h) Would you like to come round for a drink later? ....

i) Jack, this is my brother, Mark. ....

j) Could you tell me what time the bank opens? ....

1 Complaining
2 Inviting
3 Asking for information
4 Accepting an invitation
5 Asking for advice

6 Asking for directions
7 Introducing other people
8 Offering to do something
9 Disagreeing
10 Ending a conversation

2 **Match each sentence (a–j) with a function from 1–10.**

a) Would you like some more tea? ....6.........

b) I think you'd better phone the police. ....

c) I'd love to come, but I'm already going out that evening. ....

d) Good morning, I'm Brenda Watson, the Marketing Manager. ....

e) I'm sorry I'm late – it won't happen again. ....

f) Would you like me to do the washing-up? ....

g) Excuse me, but is the bus station anywhere near here? ....

h) Hi, Sally, how are you? ....

i) I think that's the point exactly. ....

j) It's at the end of this street, opposite the church. ....

1 Declining an invitation
2 Introducing yourself
3 Greeting a friend
4 Offering to do something
5 Asking for directions

6 Offering something
7 Agreeing
8 Apologising
9 Giving directions
10 Giving advice

3 **Choose the most suitable response.**

a) Do you feel like going to the cinema this evening?

    ① That would be great.

    2) Thank you very much for your kind invitation.

b) More coffee anybody?

    1) Would it be all right if I had some more?

    2) I'd love some.

c) I wish you wouldn't smoke in here!

    1) I don't agree, I'm afraid.

    2) Sorry, shall I open the window?

d) Well, it was nice talking to you, but I have to dash.

    1) Yes, I enjoyed talking to you too.

    2) OK, see you.

e) Could you tell me whether this train stops at Hatfield?

    1) I believe I could.

    2) I believe it does.

f) Shall I collect the tickets for you?

    1) That would be a real help.

    2) Yes, I think you shall.

g) What would you do in my situation?

    1) I think you should ask for a loan from the bank.

    2) I thought you would ask for a loan from the bank.

h) How do you do. I'm Bill Thompson.

    1) Very well thank you.

    2) How do you do.

4   Complete the second sentence so that it has a similar meaning to the first sentence, using the word given. Do not change the word given. You must use between two and five words, including the word given.

a) Can I offer you a lift home?

   like

   Would .... *you like a lift* .... home?

b) What time does the next train leave?

   tell

   Could .... the next train leaves?

c) I think you should sell the car.

   I'd

   If I .... the car.

d) Shall I mow the lawn?

   to

   Would .... mow the lawn?

e) Am I going the right way for Downwood?

   this

   Is .... Downwood?

f) Do you have to make so much noise!

   wouldn't

   I .... so much noise!

g) What's your advice?

   should

   What do .... do?

h) Let's go for a pizza.

   going

   How .... a pizza?

Key points   1   Our choice of words depends on the situation, our relationship with the person we are talking to, and what we are talking about.

2   We should respond in an appropriate way, informally or politely (see point 1) and in accordance with how the other person speaks to us first.

3   If we do not use polite forms, there is a risk that the other person will think we are being rude. We may not get the result from the conversation that we want.

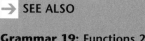

→ SEE ALSO

Grammar 19: Functions 2
Grammar 20: Consolidation 4

Functions 2

Explanations

This unit practises the following functions and possible responses.

Things to say on special occasions or at special moments
Asking for and giving an opinion
Pausing to think
Asking for permission
Giving and refusing permission
Expressing preferences
Promising
Reassuring
Recommending
Refusing to do something
Making and responding to a request
Suggesting
Thanking

Practice

1 **Match each sentence (a–j) with a function from 1–10.**

a) Wait a minute, let me see. ....5..........

b) What did you think of the film, then? ....

c) I'll definitely bring your camera back tomorrow. ....

d) Would it be all right if I left a bit early today? ....

e) Sorry, no, I won't do it. ....

f) Could you possibly turn on the air conditioning? ....

g) I think I'd rather have fish, actually. ....

h) Why don't we have a party next weekend? ....

i) That's very kind of you, I appreciate it. ....

j) Don't worry, everything will turn out all right. ....

1 Promising	6 Making a request
2 Refusing	7 Thanking
3 Suggesting	8 Asking for an opinion
4 Expressing a preference	9 Reassuring
5 Pausing to think	10 Asking permission

2 **Match each sentence (a–j) with a function from 1–10.**

a) Congratulations! ....4..........   f) Excuse me! ....

b) Look out! ....   g) Pardon? ....

c) Oh bother! ....   h) Bless you! ....

d) Whoops! ....   i) Cheers! ....

e) Well done! ....   j) You poor thing! ....

1 Praising someone's performance

2 Expressing annoyance

3 Wishing someone good health when drinking

4 Expressing happiness at someone's success

5 Attracting attention or asking someone to move out of your way

6 Expressing sympathy

7 Expressing that something has/has nearly gone wrong

8 Giving a warning

9 Showing that you have misheard or misunderstood

10 Said when another person sneezes

3   **Choose the most suitable response.**

a) What do you think of my new car?

    (1) It's all right I suppose.

    2) I think a lot.

b) Do you promise to pay me back at the end of the month?

    1) I'll pay.

    2) I promise.

c) Can I use your phone?

    1) You may not.

    2) Of course.

d) Where do you suggest I stay?

    1) I recommend the Hilton.

    2) Let's stay at the Hilton.

e) Do you want beer or wine?

    1) I'd prefer beer, please.

    2) I'd rather beer, please.

f) I can't stop worrying about my exam tomorrow.

    1) That's all right, never mind.

    2) I'm sure you'll do well.

g) Janet, make us some tea, will you?

    1) No I won't, I'm afraid.

    2) I can't, I'm afraid.

h) Would you mind moving your bag from the seat?

    1) Oh, sorry.

    2) No, I wouldn't.

i) How kind, you really shouldn't have bothered.

    1) It was nothing, really.

    2) Don't worry, I didn't bother.

j) Is it all right if I use your bike?

    1) Please accept it with my best wishes.

    2) Sure, go ahead.

4 Complete the second sentence so that it has a similar meaning to the first sentence, using the word given. Do not change the word given. You must use between two and five words, including the word given.

a) What's your opinion of Roger's new book?

   think

   What do ....*you think of*........................ Roger's new book?

b) Thank you very much for your help.

   am

   I .... for your help.

c) May I leave my bag here?

   if

   Is it .... leave my bag here?

d) Let's go to the beach tomorrow.

   we

   Why .... to the beach tomorrow?

e) I like going sailing more than swimming.

   rather

   I'd .... swimming.

f) Could you open a window?

   think

   Do .... the window?

g) Is it all right if you take care of the children?

   mind

   Do .... care of the children?

h) I recommend going by train.

   go

   I think you .... by train.

i) Excuse me, I can't get past you!

   in

   Excuse me, you .... way.

j) 'You've passed your driving test, Ron! Well done!' said Carol.

   on

   Carol congratulated .... driving test.

5 Look carefully at each line. Some lines are correct, but some have a word which should not be there. Tick each correct line. If a line has a word which should not be there, write the word in the space.

Say one thing, mean another

Do you ever get annoyed by people who say one	.......✓........
thing but mean another? For example, they say you,	........you.......
'That's a very kind of you, I'd love to,' when you	1) ....
are invite them to the cinema, but really they	2) ....
are thinking of an excuse so they can avoid you!	3) ....
People who ask for an advice also annoy me. They	4) ....
say things like 'What do you think I should do?'	5) ....
but then they don't listen to what you tell with them.	6) ....
Sometimes they don't even let you answer, but	7) ....
answer themselves! This really gets on to my nerves.	8) ....
Politeness is also a problem. When people ask to you	9) ....
to open a window, they say 'Excuse me, but it could	10) ....
you possibly open the window for me?' I prefer to	11) ....
be more direct. Why shouldn't we just ever say	12) ....
'Can you to open the window?' or something like that?	13) ....
I've tried this a few times, but people either look	14) ....
annoyed, or they don't do it what I ask them to. I	15) ....
wonder why?	

Key points

1 Our choice of words depends on the situation, our relationship with the person we are talking to, and what we are talking about.

2 We should respond in an appropriate way, informally or politely, depending on all the things mentioned in point 1, and also on how the other person speaks to us first.

3 If we do not use polite forms there is a risk that the other person will think we are being rude. We may not get the result from the conversation that we want.

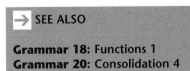

→ SEE ALSO

Grammar 18: Functions 1
Grammar 20: Consolidation 4

1 **Put one suitable word in each space.**

Asking for directions

Have you ever tried asking people for directions? I (1) ......*had*...... to go to London on business recently, and I soon realised that I (2) .... have bought a street map. Whenever I followed the directions of passers-by, I got lost. 'You can't (3) .... it,' they would say. 'Carry straight (4) .... , it's opposite the bank.' After walking for half an hour, I would realise that I (5) .... have gone wrong somewhere. '(6) .... you tell me where the bank (7) .... , please?' I would ask someone. I (8) .... to have known that this was a mistake. 'Which bank do you mean? I think you (9) .... go back to the station ...' I now see that I (10) .... have taken a taxi. After all, London taxi drivers (11) .... to pass a test on their knowledge of its streets. But of course, whenever I thought of this, I (12) .... not find a taxi. In the end I found a solution. I went up to the first tourists I saw and asked if I (13) .... look at their tourist map. They turned out to be from Scotland, and they (14) .... me very detailed instructions. The only problem was that I wasn't (15) .... to understand exactly what they said.

2 **Complete the second sentence so that it has a similar meaning to the first sentence, using the word given. Do not change the word given. You must use between two and five words, including the word given.**

a) I'm sorry I broke your keyboard.

   apologise

   I do .....*apologise for breaking*..................... your keyboard.

b) Can you give me directions for the station?

   how

   Could you tell .... the station?

c) You must be thirsty, so can I offer you some tea?

   like

   You must be thirsty, so .... tea?

d) If I were you, I wouldn't buy a dog.

   should

   I don't .... dog.

e) I'm sure that Jack hasn't left home yet.

have

Jack .... home yet.

f) I suppose that this is Trafalgar Square.

be

This .... Trafalgar Square.

g) Perhaps Jean's plane was delayed.

been

Jean's plane .... delayed.

h) It was unnecessary for you to come early today.

have

You .... come early today.

3 Look carefully at each line. Some of the lines are correct, and some have a word which should not be there. Tick each correct line. If a line has a word which should not be there, write the word in the space.

Putting up a friend

Dear Brenda,

Thanks for replying so quickly to my last letter.	............✓............
You must to have been surprised when you received	............*to*............
a letter from me. I'm glad you will be able	1) ....
to have put me up when I come to London.	2) ....
Could you be possibly give me some directions	3) ....
for your flat? I'm bound to get lost. Do I	4) ....
have to take a taxi from the station, or is it	5) ....
near enough to walk? Perhaps if I should buy	6) ....
a street map of Birmingham when I am arrive. And	7) ....
is it all right if I can bring my little brother, Tim?	8) ....
By the way, congratulations on your new job.	9) ....
You must not be very happy. Do you think that	10) ....
you made the right decision, though? I think	11) ....
you should or have gone to university like me.	12) ....
I'm sure that you would have been enjoyed it. I	13) ....
have done to study a lot, but with any luck I should	14) ....
get a good job when I finish. I'd be better post	15) ....
this letter now.	

Best wishes,

Sheila

4   Choose the most suitable expression for each situation.

a) You want to invite someone you have just met to go to the theatre with you.
    1) May I go to the theatre?
    2) Would you like to come to the theatre?
    3) Do you think you should go to the theatre?

b) You are recommending a new restaurant to a friend.
    1) You really must try the new Italian restaurant in Green Street.
    2) You had better try the new Italian restaurant in Green Street.
    3) You would try the new Italian restaurant in Green Street.

c) Your boss suggests that you work overtime on Saturday, but you don't want to.
    1) You must be joking!
    2) It's nice of you to ask, but I refuse.
    3) Sorry, but I have something already arranged.

d) You want to ask the waiter to bring you another drink.
    1) I'd like another beer, please.
    2) Excuse me, but do you think I could take another beer?
    3) You can bring me a beer if you like.

e) You want someone to move out of the way.
    1) Look out!
    2) Excuse me!
    3) Pardon!

f) You greet a friend you haven't seen for a few weeks.
    1) Hello Pauline, how do you do?
    2) Hello Pauline, what's going on?
    3) Hello Pauline, how are you?

g) You are sitting on a bus and want the person in front of you to shut the window.
    1) Could you shut the window, please?
    2) May I shut the window, please?
    3) Do you want to shut the window, please?

h) You want to know how to get to the station, and you ask a stranger.
    1) Tell me, where is the station?
    2) Do you mind telling me where the station is?
    3) Could you tell me the way to the station, please?

i) You want some advice from a friend.
    1) What do you think I should do?
    2) Tell me what I must do.
    3) What could you do if you were me?

j) You ask your boss for permission to leave work early.
    1) Do you mind leaving early?
    2) Is it all right if I go now?
    3) I'm off now, bye!

5 Decide which answer (A, B, C or D) best fits each space.

The lost property office

Recently I read a magazine article about the things (1) ....*C*.......... people lose when they travel on the London Underground. I (2) .... believe it at first. (3) .... you are a violinist, and when you (4) .... off at your station, you leave your violin (5) .... the train. It seems strange that nobody says, '(6) .... me, but I think you have forgotten something.' I suppose the violinist (7) .... have been thinking of something else, and there might (8) .... have been any other (9) .... on the train. Still, why didn't the violinist go (10) .... the lost property office? All the lost property on the underground system (11) .... to be sent to this office, so if you lose anything you (12) .... easily get it back. In this case, the violinist must have (13) .... very absent minded. Perhaps he or she didn't (14) .... to play the violin ever again after this journey. Or perhaps they were just too embarrassed (15) .... go to the office.

1)	A who	B whose	C that	D a
2)	A wasn't	B haven't	C shouldn't	D couldn't
3)	A If	B Suppose	C Why	D Sometimes
4)	A get	B go	C fall	D are
5)	A at	B for	C on	D by
6)	A Help	B It's	C Excuse	D Correct
7)	A who	B might	C should	D to
8)	A not	B then	C often	D so
9)	A pedestrians	B customers	C audience	D passengers
10)	A in	B at	C to	D for
11)	A should	B must	C needs	D has
12)	A can	B can't	C don't	D are
13)	A been	B or	C had	D because
14)	A know	B like	C have	D used
15)	A and	B to	C must	D so

Countable and uncountable nouns

Explanations

■ Countable nouns
A countable noun has a singular and a plural form. We can use a singular or plural verb with it. We can use numbers with it.

> *Where **is** my shirt?*
> *Where **are** my shirts?*
> *a shirt, shirts, some shirts, four shirts*

■ Uncountable nouns
An uncountable noun has only one form. We can only use a singular verb with it. We cannot use numbers with it.

> *Here **is** some **advice** for you.*
> *advice, some advice*

However, we can count an uncountable noun indirectly by using a phrase like *a piece of, a bit of.*

> *When I left home my mother gave me **two** useful **bits of** advice.*
> *I've found out **several** interesting **pieces of** information.*

A few uncountable nouns end in *-s*, but they follow the normal rules for uncountable nouns and have a singular verb.

> *The news **is** very bad today.*
> *Billiards **is** an interesting game.*

■ Typical uncountable nouns

Substances:	*water, air, coffee, plastic, iron, paper*
Abstract ideas:	*life, fun, freedom, health, time, progress*
Activities:	*work, travel, sleep, football, help, research*
Human feelings:	*happiness, anger, honesty, hope, respect, courage*
Groups of items:	*furniture, luggage*

Other words are found in the Practice section. Note the words below which are uncountable in English but countable in many other languages:

> *accommodation, advice, behaviour, business, cash, equipment, furniture, health, homework, information, knowledge, luggage, money, permission, rubbish, scenery, traffic, travel, weather, work*

■ Uncountable nouns that describe a category
Some uncountable nouns can be used in a countable way when they describe a category.

Uncountable use:	*Would you like **some fruit** after your coffee?*
Use as a category:	*There are **two** main **fruits** exported from Madeira, bananas and pineapples.*

■ Change of meaning

Some words have different meanings in countable and uncountable forms.

Countable:	*an iron*	(domestic appliance)
	a wood	(small area of trees)
	a paper	(newspaper)
	a chicken	(the animal)
Uncountable:	*some iron*	(a substance/material)
	some wood	(a substance/material)
	some paper	(a substance/material)
	chicken	(the meat)

There is a similar contrast between:

Item:	*a coffee* (a cup of coffee)
Material:	*coffee*

■ Other examples with a change of meaning:

business (in general)	*a business* (a company)
gossip (talking)	*a gossip* (a person)
hair (all together)	*a hair* (a single strand)
help (in general)	*a help* (a helpful person/thing)
toast (grilled bread)	*a toast* (formal words said before drinking)
work (in general)	*a work* (a work of art/engineering)

■ Plural nouns

These nouns only have a plural form and take a plural verb.

> *My trousers **are** too tight.*

> *The stairs **are** very steep.*

Other common examples are:

> *clothes, contents, feelings, goods, jeans, means, outskirts, surroundings, thanks*

■ Group nouns

Some nouns can be followed by either a singular or plural verb.

> *I think the government **is/are** wrong.*

It depends whether we think of the group as a whole (singular verb), or its individual members (plural verb). Other common examples:

> *army, audience, class, company, crew, crowd, data, family, group, media, press, public, staff, team*

Some group nouns only take a plural verb: *cattle, police, people*

Practice

1 Underline the most suitable word in each sentence.

a) Different countries have different *weather/weathers*.

b) All areas of the skin are in fact covered in tiny *hair/hairs*.

c) We've looked at the menu and we'd all like *chicken/chickens*.

d) Jack is a millionaire and owns a lot of *business/businesses*.

e) Have you a copy of the complete *work/works* of Dante?

f) None of the passengers had insured their *baggage/baggages*.

g) Students must pass their *paper/papers* to the front.

h) I'm afraid we can't find cheap *accommodation/accommodations* for all of you.

2 Complete each sentence with *a/an, some* or by leaving the space blank.

a) When the play ended, there was ..../........... lengthy applause.

b) I can't come out tonight. I have .... homework to do.

c) Sue received .... excellent education.

d) The inside is strengthened with .... steel frame.

e) My friends bought me .... coffee maker for my birthday.

f) David has just bought .... new furniture.

g) Let me give you .... advice.

h) My trousers need pressing. Can you lend me .... iron?

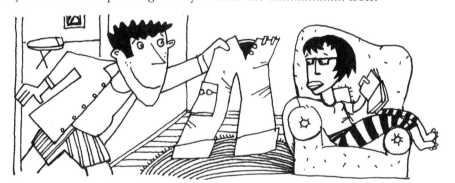

3 Underline the most suitable word in each sentence.

a) I would love to go on a long *journey/travel* by train.

b) What's the latest news? Can I look at your *paper/journal*?

c) Here's your ticket. Do you have any *luggage/suitcase*?

d) Don't forget to buy a sliced *bread/loaf*.

e) Why don't we leave the car in this *car park/parking*.

f) I can't come to work today. I have a bad *cold/flu*.

g) Excuse me sir, but do you have a *licence/permission* for this gun?

h) Brighton has quite a good *beach/seaside*.

4 **Put one suitable word in each space.**

a) I'm looking for ..*accommodation*... . Do you know anywhere I can stay?

b) Take my .... , don't go out alone after dark.

c) The government plans to improve .... by paying teachers more.

d) Can you lend me some .... ? I want to print out a letter.

e) I need some .... about language schools. Can you help me?

f) Richard is unemployed, and he is looking for a ....

g) Could I have some .... ? Those apples and oranges look nice.

h) I used to have long .... , but I had it cut.

i) I can't do this on my own. Could you give me some .... ?

j) If you can't undo the knot, cut the string with some ....

5 **Complete each sentence with the most suitable word or phrase.**

a) I like your new trousers. Where did you buy ....*B*........ ?

    A) it   B) them   C) them both   D) them all

b) There is always a very large .... at the church I go to.

    A) congregation   B) audience   C) spectator   D) company

c) The local .... has agreed to repair the road outside our house.

    A) government   B) people   C) council   D) jury

d) When the police arrived, we were pleased to see ....

    A) him   B) him or her   C) it   D) them

e) The car turned over, but luckily it didn't suffer serious ....

    A) damage   B) injury   C) damages   D) injuries

f) Sorry, I'm late, but I had a lot of .... to do.

    A) job   B) work   C) task   D) labour

g) Julie bought herself a complete new .... for winter.

    A) outfit   B) cloth   C) clothing   D) wear

h) I feel like going out tonight. Let's go to a/an ....

    A) dancing   B) night   C) club   D entertainment

i) Thanks for a great weekend! We really had a/an ....

    A) fun   B) enjoyment   C) hospitality   D) good time

j) In order to prove Smith is guilty, we must find some ....

    A) information   B) evidence   C) knowledge   D) means

6 Choose the most appropriate meaning for each sentence.

a) You mustn't lose heart.

1) Don't have an operation.   ②) Don't give up hope.

b) Where's my glass?

1) I need a drink.   2) I can't see.

c) Jack has a new post.

1) The postman has delivered a letter.   2) He has a different job.

d) All goods must be paid for in advance.

1) Nothing enjoyable in life is free.   2) You have to pay for these things first.

e) I've joined a new company.

1) I have a new job.   2) I have some new friends.

f) This hotel has class.

1) You can study hotel management here.   2) It is a good quality hotel.

g) I don't have the means to help you.

1) I'm not able to help.   2) I can't understand what help you need.

h) I'd like some china.

1) I want to go abroad.   2) I need some cups and plates.

i) Do you have any cash?

1) Do you only have a cheque?   2) Isn't there a place to pay in this shop?

j) They have a business in Leeds.

1) They have to go there to do a job.   2) They own a company there.

7 Complete the second sentence so that it has a similar meaning to the first sentence, using the word given. Do not change the word given. You must use between two and five words, including the word given.

a) This island has a large population.

   people

   There .... *are a lot of people* .... on this island.

b) Do you own these things?

   your

   Are .... belongings?

c) The weather was good on our holiday.

   had

   We .... on our holiday.

d) There were a lot of cars on the road to Manchester.

   traffic

   There .... on the road to Manchester.

e) Gerry is a very strong person, in my opinion.

   strength

   Gerry .... in my opinion.

f) There are pieces of paper all over the floor!

litter

There .... all over the floor.

g) Can I park my car here?

allowed

Is .... here?

h) I know these machines are very expensive.

machinery

I know .... very expensive.

8 Complete each sentence with a suitable word from the box.

| flight | item | ~~piece~~ | sheet | clap | head | set | slice |

a) Let me give you a ......*piece*...... of advice.

b) There is an interesting .... of news in the paper.

c) A .... of stairs takes you to the top of the house.

d) Could I have another .... of paper, please?

e) Helen has a lovely .... of hair.

f) Do you want another .... of toast?

g) We bought Mike and Lynn a .... of cutlery for a wedding present.

h) The lightning was followed by a .... of thunder.

9 Complete each sentence with a suitable word from the box.

| accommodation | ~~bread~~ | cookery | lightning | spelling | advice |
| cash | information | luggage | parking | | |

a) I can't cut this loaf. Do you have a proper ......*bread*...... knife?

b) I'm afraid that 'neice' is a .... mistake.

c) There's usually a/an .... space opposite the cinema.

d) We need a/an .... box to keep the money in.

e) The tourist board have built a/an .... centre near the castle.

f) We decided to put a/an .... conductor on the roof.

g) Marjorie used to write a/an .... column in a magazine.

h) These suitcases are very heavy. We must find a/an .... trolley.

i) I must rush. I'm going to a/an .... lesson.

j) Julie found her flat through a/an .... agency.

10   Decide which answer (A, B, C or D) best fits each space.

Food habits

Breakfast is one of those (1) ....*B*.......... that varies from person to person, and country to country. For some (2) .... it means a (3) .... of toast and some coffee. In various places I've also been offered (4) .... or fruit. (5) .... executives might eat breakfast at the (6) .... , while for many schoolchildren breakfast is a (7) .... of milk at home, and then a long wait (8) .... the first break of the morning, when they eat (9) .... or (10) .... chocolate bar. Some families sit down and eat together (11) .... the morning, and listen to (12) .... news on the radio or (13) .... early morning television. For other people, the early morning is a rush (14) .... work or school, and there just simply isn't (15) ....

1) A times	B meals	C foods	D plates
2) A people	B persons	C breakfasts	D us
3) A sheet	B loaf	C slice	D sandwich
4) A a cheese	B the cheese	C cheese	D cheeses
5) A Business	B A business	C Business's	D Businessmen
6) A train	B street	C morning	D office
7) A glass	B piece	C warm	D box
8) A to	B is	C until	D which
9) A sandwich	B the sandwich	C a sandwiches	D sandwiches
10) A a	B some	C a piece	D a glass of
11) A for	B in	C at	D while
12) A a	B what	C some	D the
13) A look	B watch	C see	D regard
14) A to	B from	C at	D and
15) A there	B it	C enough	D time

Key points   1   Check in a dictionary to be sure that a noun is countable or uncountable.

2   The meaning of a noun may change depending on whether it is used in a countable or uncountable sense.

3   Note that some nouns ending in *-s* take a singular verb:

   *The news **is** bad today*

And that some nouns only have a plural form:

   *The police **are** arriving shortly.*

 SEE ALSO

Grammar 22: Articles
Grammar 25: Consolidation 5

Explanations

Indefinite article
(*a/an*)

- With something we refer to for the first time.

  *I've just had **a great idea**.   I'll give you **a call** next week.*

- With one of a group of things.

  *Shall we choose **a book** from this catalogue?*

- Where we use an adjective to describe a noun.

  *Cairo is **a very big city**.   It's **a beautiful day**.*

- With someone's job.

  *Peter is **a truck driver**.*

- With singular fractions, group numbers and large numbers.

  *one and **a half** kilos   **a dozen** eggs   **a hundred** envelopes*

- Meaning *per*.

  *He was doing ninety miles **an hour**.*
  *Julie earns £500 **a week**.*

Definite article
(*the*)

- With nouns we have mentioned previously.

  *There is a bedroom and a living room. **The bedroom** is quite large.*

- With nouns we mention for the first time, but where it is clear which person or thing we are talking about.

  *Can you pass **the marmalade**?*
  *My life changed completely after **the war**.*

- Where there is only one of something. It is clear which one we are talking about.

  ***The moon** is full tonight.*

- With nouns followed by a descriptive phrase, which makes them definite.

  *This is **the man I told you about**.*

  See also the examples in brackets in the next section, paragraphs 4 and 7.
  This category includes proper names with a descriptive phrase. Compare
  with the next section, paragraph 2:

  London Bridge BUT ***the** Tower of London*

- With national groups.

  ***The British** drink far too much tea.*

- With classes of people.

  ***The rich** get richer and **the poor** get poorer.*

- With individual items which represent a class.
    The lion is fast disappearing.

- With names of musical instruments that we can play.
    I can't play the piano but I can play the guitar.

- With some geographical names. In particular: oceans, seas, rivers, canals and regions.
    The Thames flows into the North Sea.   *the Arctic*
    Also with plural countries, or where the country name contains a noun.
    the Netherlands   *the People's Republic of China*

- With superlatives, ordinals, *the same, the only.*
    This is the best.   *You are the first.*   *This is the only one.*

- With media.
    What's on (the) television?   *I went to the cinema.*

Zero article (no article)

- With uncountable nouns and plural countable nouns when we are talking generally.
    Give peace a chance.   *Football is life.*
    I hate wasps.   *All he talks about is cars.*

- With most continents, countries, states, islands, mountains, lakes, cities, parks, roads and streets, squares, bridges, palaces, castles, cathedrals, stations and airports.
    We live in France.   *We took the train from Paddington Station to Bath.*
    But see previous section, paragraph 9, for geographical names that use the definite article.

- With company names, years, months, days and special times of the year.
    She works for Lufthansa.   *I'll see you in January.*

- With names of meals when we are talking generally.
    It's time for lunch.   (BUT *The lunch I had at Café Sol was good value.*)
    What's for dinner?   (BUT *The dinner Sue gave us last night was delicious.*)

- With unique jobs or roles (the definite article is also possible in these cases).
    Jim is (the) chairman of the company.

- With prepositions of place with certain buildings, where the purpose of the building is more important than the place itself.
    Sally is in prison.   (she's a prisoner)
    Sally is in the prison.   (she's a visitor to that specific building)
    Similar are: *bed, church, class, court, hospital, school, university*

- With means of transport when we are talking generally.
    We went there by car.   (BUT *We went there in the car that Alex borrowed.*)
    Note that if we use *in* or *on*, we need an indefinite article.
    We went there in a car/on a bus.

Practice

1 Put *a/an* or *the* in each space, or leave the space blank.

a) We went by ..../........ – train to ....*the*........ west of England.

b) .... people who live in .... Netherlands are called .... Dutch.

c) .... judge sent me to .... prison for .... ten years.

d) .... Columbus was one of .... first people to cross .... Atlantic.

e) As .... captain of .... ship, I have .... complete authority.

f) David learned to play .... violin when he was at .... university.

g) .... Trafalgar Square is near .... Charing Cross Station.

h) Did you read .... book I lent you .... last week?

i) We'll put up .... shelves and then go to .... café for .... something to eat.

j) Is that .... present Bill gave you for .... Christmas?

2 <u>Underline</u> the most suitable phrase in each sentence.

a) Is this *a person/the person* you told me about?

b) This is *the only cinema/an only cinema* in the area.

c) Philip has just bought *the Thames barge/a Thames barge*.

d) I'm going to *the British Museum/British Museum* this afternoon.

e) Are you going to *church/the church* on Sunday?

f) Do you have *a milk jug/milk jug*?

g) *The Prime Minister/Prime Minister* will give a speech this afternoon.

h) *The computer/Computer* has already changed our lives dramatically.

i) I haven't been to *an open-air theatre/open-air theatre* before.

j) Here is *a thousand pounds/the thousand pounds* I owe you.

3 **Complete each sentence with the most suitable word or phrase.**

a) The butler was .... *C* .... I suspected.

   A) last person   B) a last person   C) the last person   D) some last person

b) Where .... you borrowed last week?

   A) is scissors   B) are the scissors   C) is some scissors   D) are scissors

c) Why don't we go to the park .... ?

   A) in the car   B) with a car   C) with car   D) by the car

d) Too much rubbish is being dumped in ....

   A) sea   B) the sea   C) a sea   D) some sea

e) This is exactly .... I was looking for.

   A) job   B) a job   C) some job   D) the job

f) Of all these cars, I think I prefer ....

   A) a Japanese   B) some Japanese   C) the Japanese one   D) a Japanese one

g) I try to go jogging at least four times ....

   A) the week   B) of the week   C) a week   D) of a week

h) Sally spent six months out of ....

   A) work   B) a work   C) the work   D) some work

4 **Complete each sentence (a–i) with one of the endings from 1–9. More than one answer may be possible.**

a) Some people say that the .... *8* ....

b) Most people think that a/an ....

c) I don't agree that ....

d) I feel that a ....

e) I don't believe that a/an ....

f) I didn't realise that the ....

g) It's incredible to think that a/an ....

h) I didn't know that ....

i) I think it's quite unfair that the ....

1 good job is an important part of life.

2 single injection can protect you from so many diseases.

3 hundred miles an hour is too fast even on a motorway.

4 the unemployed should receive more help from the state.

5 queen of England doesn't pay any income tax.

6 tiger may well become extinct very soon.

7 third of a person's income should be paid in tax.

8 English are difficult to get to know at first.

9 the Tower of London was built by William the Conqueror.

5   Put *a/an* or *the* in each space, or leave the space blank.

a) Neil Armstrong made ....*the*.......... first footprint on ....*the*.......... Moon.

b) There was .... accident yesterday at .... corner of
.... street.

c) I need .... time to think about .... offer you made me.

d) .... recipe for .... success is .... hard work.

e) .... people who live in .... glass houses shouldn't throw
.... stones.

f) .... worst part of .... living in a caravan is ....
lack of space.

g) .... book you ordered .... last week is now in
.... stock.

h) .... dancing is .... more interesting activity than
.... reading.

i) .... people we met on .... holiday in ....
north of England sent us .... postcard.

j) .... little knowledge is .... dangerous thing.

6   Complete the second sentence so that it has a similar meaning to the first
     sentence, using the word given. Do not change the word given. You must use
     between two and five words, including the word given.

a) There is one problem here, and that's the weather.

   only

   The ....*only problem here is*........................... the weather.

b) There are no good films on this week.

   cinema

   There is nothing .... this week.

c) Can't you swim faster than that?

   fastest

   Is .... can swim?

d) I haven't been here before.

   time

   This is .... been here.

e) A lot of wine is drunk in France.

   French

   The .... a lot of wine.

f) If you drive faster, it is more dangerous.

   the

   The .... dangerous it is.

g) It is difficult to discover what is true.

   truth

   The .... discover.

h) Are you a good pianist?

   piano

   Can you .... well?

7   Underline the most suitable phrase in each sentence.

a) I was *under an impression/under the impression* that you had left.

b) I have to go. I'm *in a hurry/in hurry*.

c) I managed to sell the old painting *at a profit/at profit*.

d) I think I prefer the other restaurant *on the whole/on whole*.

e) How many hours do you work, *on average/on the average*, every week?

f) I was *in pain/in a pain* after I twisted my ankle.

g) Jack recovered from his accident and is now *out of danger/out of the danger*.

h) Excuse me, but you're *in the way/in a way*.

i) Sue felt seasick on *the cross-channel ferry/a cross the channel ferry*.

j) The burglar hit me on *my back of the neck/the back of my neck*.

8   **Put *a/an* or *the* in each space, or leave the space blank.**

a) What's the use in taking ..../.......... – medicine for ....a.......... cold?

b) Is .... happiness of .... majority more important than
    .... rights of .... individual?

c) It's .... long way by .... train to .... north of
    .... Scotland.

d) .... philosophers seem to think that .... life is
    .... mystery.

e) .... most cars start badly on .... cold mornings.

f) There was .... time when I enjoyed .... skating.

g) Do you have .... reason for .... arriving late?

h) When I arrive .... home I feel .... sense of ....
    relief.

i) .... end of .... book is .... by far
    .... best part.

j) .... friend always tells me .... answers to ....
    homework we have.

Key points   1   With some types of building, the meaning can change depending on the use of
the article.

> *Helen is **at school**.* (the purpose of the school is important – Helen is a
> student or a teacher)
>
> *Helen is **at the school**.*   (the building itself is important – it is the place
> where we can find Helen)

2   The use of the article can show something about the context of a short piece of
text. In particular, whether an item has or has not been mentioned before.

> *The BBC reported that **the** two men have since been recaptured.*

Use of *the* shows that the two men have been mentioned before, and so this is
an extract from a longer text.

3   Many uses of articles are idiomatic, and should be learned as part of a phrase.

> *Diana works as **a** graphic designer.*

 SEE ALSO

Grammar 21: Countable and
uncountable nouns
Grammar 23: *All, no, none,
each, every, either, neither*

Explanations

All

■ When *all* is used to show the quantity of something, it can be followed by *of*.
   *Jim was there **all (of)** the time.*

■ *All* can be used for emphasis. Note the position.
   ***They all** wore white shorts and shirts.*
   ***Those stamps you bought me** have **all** disappeared.*

■ *All* means *the only thing* when it is used in the construction *all* + subject + verb.
   ***All I want** is some peace and quiet.*
   It is unusual to use *all* as a single-word subject or object. Instead we use *everything* to mean *all the things*.
   ***Everything** has gone wrong!*   (NOT ~~All has gone wrong!~~)

No

■ When *no* is used to show the quantity of something, it can mean *not any*.
   *There are **no** plates left.*   ***No** new students have joined the class.*

■ *No* can also be used with a comparative adjective.
   *It's **no worse** than before.*
   *There were **no less** than 500 applications for the job.*

■ *No* is not normally used alone before an adjective. Compare:
   *This book **doesn't** have **any** interesting parts.*   (usual)
   *There are **no** interesting parts in this book.*   (unusual – very emphatic)
   *It is **not** interesting.*
   But there is an idiomatic use of *no* with *good*.
   *I tried hard but it was **no good**, I couldn't reach.*   (no good = useless)
   Another common idiomatic use is with *-ing* forms.
   *Remember, **no cheating**!*   ***No smoking**, please.*

None

■ We do not use *no of*. Instead, we use *none of* or *none* on its own.
   ***None of** the films that are showing in town look very interesting.*
   *I've checked all the films that are showing in town. **None** look very interesting.*
   In everyday speech *none* is often followed by a plural verb form. In formal speech or writing it can be followed by a singular verb form.
   ***None** of these telephones **work**.*
   ***None** of the members of the committee **has** arrived yet.*

■ To emphasize the idea of *none* we can use *none at all* or *not one*.
   A: *How many people came to the party?*
   B: ***None!/None at all!/Not one!***

Each, every

- The meaning of *each* and *every* is very similar and often either word is possible.

   ***Each/Every** time I come here I go to my favourite restaurant.*

   But sometimes there is a small difference. We use *each* when we think of the single items in a group, one by one. We use *every* when we think of the items in a group all together. Compare:

   *They gave a medal to **each** member of the team.*

   *I believe **every** word he says.*

- *Each* is more usual with a smaller group, and can mean *only two*. *Every* is more usual with a larger number, and cannot mean *two*.

   *She kissed him on **each** cheek.*

- We can use *each of*, but we cannot use *every of*.

   *When the team won the cup, **each of** them was given a medal.*

- *Each* can be used after the subject, or at the end of a sentence.

   ***The members each** received a medal.*

   *The members received a medal **each**.*

- Repeated actions are generally described with *every*.

   *I practise the violin **every** day.*

Either, neither

- *Either* and *neither* both refer to choices between two items. *Either* means *the one or the other*. *Neither* means *not the one or the other*.

   *Monday or Tuesday? Yes, **either day** is fine.*

   *Monday or Tuesday? I'm sorry, but **neither day** is convenient.*

   So *not + either* is the same as *neither*.

   *I did**n't** like **either** of those films.*

   ***Neither** of the films was any good.*

- *Either* can also mean *both*. Note that *either* is followed by the singular form of the noun.

   *On **either side** of the house there are shops.*   (on both sides)

Practice

1   Rewrite each sentence so that it contains the word given in capitals, and the meaning stays the same. Do not change the word in any way.

a)   This is the only money I have left.   ALL
   ...*This is all the money I have left.*...

b)   There wasn't anyone at the meeting.   NO
   ....

c)   Both singers had bad voices.   NEITHER
   ....

d)   All of the cups are dirty.   NONE
   ....

e)   Everyone was cheering loudly.   ALL
   ....

f)   You both deserve promotion.   EACH
   ....

g)   I read both books, but I liked neither of them.   EITHER
   ....

h)   Whenever I cross the Channel by boat I feel seasick.   EVERY
   ....

2   Rewrite each sentence, beginning as shown, so that the meaning stays the same.

a)   Everyone in the office was given a personal parking space.
   Each ...*person in the office was given a personal parking space.*...

b)   This town doesn't have any good hotels.
   There are ....

c)   Love is the only thing that you need.
   All ....

d)   These two pens don't write properly.
   Neither ....

e)   We are all responsible for our own actions.
   Each ....

f)   All of us feel lonely sometimes.
   We ....

g)   All of the shops are closed.
   None ....

h)   Both jobs were unsuitable for Helen.
   Neither ....

3 Complete each sentence with the most suitable word or phrase.

a) Jack walked into the room with a gun in either .... *C* ....

    A) side   B) door   C) hand   D) one

b) I had .... a hundred offers for my house.

    A) neither   B) each   C) all   D) no less than

c) I feel so tired this evening. I've been working hard ....

    A) all day   B) every day   C) each day   D) day by day

d) The two cars for sale were in poor condition, so I didn't buy ....

    A) either of them   B) both of them   C) neither of them   D) each of them

e) I tried to lift the heavy trunk but it was ....

    A) not good   B) no less than good   C) neither good   D) no good

f) The room was full of people and .... were speaking.

    A) neither of them   B) all of them   C) none of them   D) each of them

g) .... spent more time walking a century ago.

    A) People all   B) All persons   C) each people   D) All

h) My friend Jonathan has a gold earring in ....

    A) his two ears   B) each ear   C) every year   D) the ears

i) I looked everywhere for my pen and it was here ....

    A) none of the time   B) every time   C) all the time   D) each time

j) People say that there is .... like show business.

    A) all business   B) no business   C) not business   D) all business

4 Complete each sentence with the most suitable word from the box.

all   each (x2)   ~~either~~ (x2)   every (x2)   no (x2)   none

a) Is ......*either*..... of you interested in working on Saturday this week?

b) I am afraid there are .... vacancies in the company at present.

c) I think we should be given at least £50 ....

d) .... other Saturday we watch our local hockey team.

e) Let's start now. There's .... time like the present!

f) .... you are interested in doing is going to the café!

g) There are two beds. You can sleep in .... one, it doesn't matter.

h) Sally gave a present to .... and every one of us!

i) And the star of our show is .... other than Dorothy Rogers!

j) My boss has given me .... chance to succeed.

5 Complete the second sentence so that it has a similar meaning to the first sentence, using the word given. Do not change the word given. You must use between two and five words, including the word given.

a) I always go to the cinema on Thursdays in winter.

   Thursday

   I go to the cinema .... *every Thursday* .... in winter.

b) This has nothing to do with you!

   none

   This is .... business!

c) I'm afraid there aren't any empty seats at the front.

   all

   I'm afraid .... at the front are taken.

d) From today, lorries are not allowed to go through the town centre.

   no

   From today .... to go through the town centre.

e) The days get colder and colder.

   it

   Each .... colder.

f) Both questions were impossible to understand.

   couldn't

   I .... question.

g) You only want to listen to rock music!

   is

   All you .... to rock music.

h) As many as 20,000 people are thought to have attended the concert.

   than

   No .... are thought to have attended the concert.

i) Each child was given £100.

   were

   The .... £100 each.

j) We cannot waste any time!

   no

   There .... waste.

6 Look carefully at each line. Some of the lines are correct, and some have a word which should not be there. Tick each correct line. If a line has a word which should not be there, write the word in the space.

Supermarkets

The every time I go to a supermarket I ask	........*The*........
myself why I go shopping there so often.	........✓........
Last time I ended up buying all the kinds of things	1) ....
when the all I really wanted was a packet of	2) ....
rice and a small loaf, but could find neither	3) ....
of them. I looked in every one corner of the shop	4) ....
but there was simply no a sign of these products.	5) ....
I looked carefully on either side of the aisles	6) ....
but it was no any good. I ought to confess here	7) ....
that I had forgotten my glasses! All of I could see	8) ....
was rows of colourful shapes of all sizes. I decided	9) ....
to ask an assistant. They were all a busy of course	10) ....
and none of them was anywhere nearby in any	11) ....
case. Meanwhile I had been filling my basket with	12) ....
all the kinds of things I thought I wanted. After I	13) ....
had paid, I had no money left for the weekend,	14) ....
but I hadn't bought the either of the things I wanted!	15) ....

Key points

1   In the construction *all* + subject + verb, *all* means *the only thing*.

All we need now *is a new car.*

But we do not use *all* by itself as a subject. Instead we use *everything*.

Everything *is missing, I'm afraid.*   (NOT ~~All is missing~~)

2   Note these idiomatic uses of *no*.

No *parking.*   **No** *smoking.*

It's **no** *use.*   *It's* **no** *good.*

3   *Each* refers to the single items in a group, one by one. *Every* refers to all the items of a group together. It is usual for larger numbers.

Make sure that **each** *letter* **has** *a stamp.*

Every *Manchester United fan will be celebrating tonight.*

Both words are followed by a singular verb (*has* not *have* in the example above). We can use *each of*, but not *every of*.

Each of *these books has its interesting points.*

4   *Either* and *neither* refer to two items, separately.

Both hotels look good to me. **Either** *one would be OK.*

Neither *of these hotels* **is** *very comfortable.*

Both words are followed by a singular verb (*is* not *are* in the example above).

5   *None* (= not one) is often followed by a plural verb form in everyday speech, but a singular verb in formal speech and writing.

None *of the students* **have/has** *answered the question correctly.*

→ SEE ALSO

Grammar 25: Consolidation 5

Making comparisons

Explanations

Comparative adjectives

■ Comparatives with *-er*
One-syllable adjectives, and two-syllable adjectives ending in *-y*, generally add *-er* to make the comparative form (with *y* changing to *i*). Adjectives ending in *-e* add only *-r*.

> *small, smaller*   *early, earlier*   *late, later*

■ Comparatives with *more*
Other two-syllable adjectives, and adjectives of more than two syllables, use *more* or *less*.

> *more/less modern*   *more/less interesting*

■ Comparatives with *-er* or *more*
A small group of two-syllable adjectives have both forms. Examples are:
clever, common, narrow, polite, quiet, simple, tired.

> *polite, politer/more polite*

■ Irregular comparatives
Irregular comparatives are:

> *good, better*   *bad, worse*   *far, farther/further*

Note that *further* has two meanings: a normal meaning of *more far*, and another meaning of just *more*.

> *How much **further** do we have to go?*   (more far)
> *I can't really advise you any **further**.*   (more)

Old has a regular form *older*, and an irregular form *elder* that is used as an adjective.

> *This is my **elder** sister.*

Superlatives

Superlatives follow similar rules to comparatives in paragraphs 1 and 2 above.
One-syllable adjectives use *(the) -est* and longer adjectives use *(the) most*.

> *small, smaller, the smallest   early, earlier, the earliest   late, later, the latest*
> *modern, more modern, the most modern*
> *interesting, more interesting, the most interesting*

Irregular forms are:

> *good, the best*
> *bad, the worst*

Comparatives of adverbs

■ Adverbs follow the same rules as adjectives.

> One syllable: *fast, faster, the fastest*
> Two syllables ending *-y:* *early, earlier, the earliest*
> Two or more syllables: *efficiently, more/less efficiently, the most/least efficiently*

■ The adverbs *well* and *badly* are irregular.
    well, better, the best   *bad, worse, the worst*

Making comparisons

■ The simplest kind of comparison uses *than*.
    *You look **younger than** your brother.*

■ Comparatives can be repeated to suggest continuing change.
    *This lesson seems to be getting **longer and longer**.*
    *Jim started feeling **more and more tired**.*

■ Comparatives can be made stronger or weaker by using these words:
    stronger: *much*   *far*   *a lot*
    weaker: *a bit*   *a little*
    *This book is **much/a little** more expensive.*

■ Note this construction that repeats the word *the*.
    ***The faster** you drive, **the more** petrol you use.*

■ Expressions with *best*.
    *Sorry, but this is **the best** I can do.*
    *I tried **my best**.*
    *May **the best** man win.*   (this can refer to two or more people)

Comparative clauses

■ With *than*.
    *Food here is more expensive **than** I thought.*

■ With *not as/so ... as*.
    *Being a nurse is **not as** interesting **as** being a doctor.*

■ With *(just) as ... as*.
    *Living in the country is **just as** expensive **as** living in London.*

■ With *such ... as*.
    *I've never been to **such** a good party **as** that one.*

■ When we compare actions we can use an auxiliary at the end of the sentence.
    I can swim a lot better than Jack. OR *I can swim a lot better than Jack **can**.*
    You paid more for your car than me. OR *You paid more for your car than I **did**.*
Note how modals like *can* are repeated, but other verbs use a form of *do*.

Practice

1   **Put one suitable word in each space.**

a) My brother is two years older ....*than*...... me.

b) The train takes just .... long as the bus.

c) I thought the second hotel we stayed in was .... more friendly.

d) Unfortunately we are .... well-off than we used to be.

e) Do you think you could make a .... less noise?

f) These exercises seem to be getting harder and ....

g) Jean doesn't need as much help as Harry ....

h) David didn't enjoy the match as much as I ....

2   **Rewrite each sentence beginning as shown. Do not change the meaning.**

a) Jill can run faster than Peter.
    Peter ....*can't run as fast as Jill (can)*.....................

b) I thought this journey would last longer than it did.
    This journey didn't ....

c) I didn't arrive as early as I expected.
    I arrived ....

d) You are working too slowly.
    You'll have to ....

e) I have a brother who is older than me.
    I have an ....

f) Martin thought the second part of the film was more interesting.
    Martin didn't think the first ....

g) Paula's work is less careful than before.
    Paula has been working ....

h) There aren't any trains earlier than this one.
    This is ....

i) All other cafés are further away.
    This café ....

j) Is this the best price you can offer?
    Can't you ....

3   Complete each sentence with the most suitable word or phrase.

a)   I really think that apologising is ....*C*.......... you can do.

A) not as much as   B) a little   C) the least   D) as far as

b)   I can't stand this weather. It's getting ....

A) more and more   B) worse and worse   C) coldest and coldest

D) further and further

c)   Although Brenda came last, everyone agreed she had .... her best.

A) done   B) made   C) had   D) got

d)   I wish Charles worked as hard as Mary ....

A) did   B) can   C) will   D) does

e)   The more you water this plant, the .... it will grow.

A) best   B) tall   C) wetter   D) faster

f)   From now on, we won't be able to go out as much as we ....

A) were   B) had   C) used to   D) will

g)   I've never owned .... independent cat as this one!

A) a more than   B) such an   C) a so   D) as much an

h)   Brian has been working .... since he was promoted.

A) much harder   B) as harder   C) just as hardly   D) more hardly

i)   I've been feeling .... tired lately, doctor.

A) such a   B) the most   C) more and more   D) much

j)   This exercise will give you .... practice.

A) farther   B) much more   C) as better   D) a lot

4   Put one suitable word in each space, beginning with the letter given.

a)   Is William feeling any b.*etter*.......... today?

b)   Everyone ate a lot, but Chris ate the m...................... .

c)   What's the l...................... news about the situation in India?

d)   I'd feel a lot h...................... if you let me help.

e)   Graham has been sinking d...................... into debt lately.

f)   It's 35 degrees today! It must be the h...................... day so far this year.

g)   Only £45? Is that all? Oh well, it's b...................... than nothing.

h)   He had to wait a f...................... two months before he got his promotion.

i)   Ruth wore her b...................... dress to her sister's wedding.

j)   Harry has got over the w...................... of his cold.

5 Rewrite each sentence, beginning as shown. Do not change the meaning.

a) That's the best meal I've ever eaten.

   I've never eaten a ......*better meal.*..

b) Fish and meat are the same price in some countries.

   Fish costs just ....

c) I've never enjoyed myself so much.

   I've never had ....

d) If you run a lot, you will get fitter.

   The more ....

e) The doctor can't see you earlier than Wednesday, I'm afraid.

   Wednesday is ....

f) I must have a rest. I can't walk any more.

   I must have a rest. I can't go ....

g) Home computers used to be much more expensive.

   Home computers aren't ....

h) I don't know as much Italian as Sue does.

   Sue knows ....

i) I thought that learning to drive would be difficult, but it isn't.

   Learning to drive is ....

j) Barbara can skate just as well as John can.

   John isn't ....

6   Complete the second sentence so that it has a similar meaning to the first sentence, using the word given. Do not change the word given. You must use between two and five words, including the word given.

a)   Your car was cheaper than mine.

   cost

   Your car ....*cost less than mine* .... did.

b)   I'm not as good at maths as you are.

   better

   You .... I am.

c)   Keith is slightly taller than Nigel.

   little

   Keith .... Nigel.

d)   Bill was growing angrier all the time.

   and

   Bill .... angrier.

e)   Sally tried as hard as she could.

   did

   Sally .... best.

f)   I thought this film would be better.

   as

   This film .... I expected.

g)   This is the bumpiest road I've ever driven along!

   such

   I've never .... road.

h)   When you eat a lot, you get fat.

   more

   The .... you get.

i)   George said he couldn't do any better.

   could

   George said it .... do.

j)   This year's exam and last year's exam were equally difficult.

   just

   This year's exam .... last year's exam.

7 Look carefully at each line. Some of the lines are correct, and some have a word which should not be there. Tick each correct line. If a line has a word which should not be there, write the word in the space.

Transport solutions

First of all, walking is obviously the cheapest ....✓............

means of travelling, and can be the quicker ....*the*............

in a city centre. Of course, the further you have 1) ....

to go, the more so tired you will become. 2) ....

In some ways walking is more healthier than 3) ....

travelling by bus or car, but it can be just as the 4) ....

unhealthy because cities are the much more 5) ....

polluted than they used to be. Cars are faster 6) ....

of course and more than convenient, but as cities 7) ....

become more of crowded, parking is getting 8) ....

harder. Sometimes public transport is better, 9) ....

even though buses don't go as fast as cars do it. 10) ....

Cars are a lot more and convenient but as they 11) ....

cause most pollution, it is the better to avoid 12) ....

using them if possible. In a city the fastest way 13) ....

of travelling is on a bike, which keeps you fitter 14) ....

and is not so that noisy as a motorbike or a car. 15) ....

Key points

1   Check spelling rules for comparative and superlative adjectives.
In one syllable adjectives ending with one consonant, double the final consonant.

> *big   bigger   the biggest*

In one/two syllable adjectives ending with -*y*, change *y* to *i*.

> *happy   happier   the happiest*

2   Adverbs form comparatives and superlatives like adjectives.

> *fast   faster   the fastest*

3   Auxiliaries are often used at the end of a comparative clause to avoid repeating the verb.

> *Wendy works twice as hard **as I do**.*   (NOT ... ~~as I work~~)

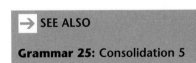

→ SEE ALSO

Grammar 25: Consolidation 5

1 **Put one suitable word in each space.**

Holiday problems

Somehow I always have problems when I go away on holiday. (1) ......*Every*...... year my travel agent promises me that my holiday will be (2) .... best I have ever had, but none of these promises has ever (3) .... true. This year I got food poisoning (4) .... day I arrived. It must have been the fish I ate at the hotel (5) .... evening. In (6) .... morning I felt terrible, and I was seen by two doctors. I tried to explain my problem to them, but (7) .... of them spoke English, (8) .... didn't help. It took me (9) .... of the first week to recover, and I spent three or four days sitting next to (10) .... hotel swimming pool reading newspapers. By the time I felt better, (11) .... weather had changed, but I was determined to go sight-seeing, and do (12) .... swimming. Unfortunately (13) .... of the museums were open, as there was (14) .... strike. I would have enjoyed myself (15) .... if I had stayed at home.

2 **Complete the second sentence so that it has a similar meaning to the first sentence, using the word given. Do not change the word given. You must use between two and five words, including the word given.**

a) That's the worst film I've ever seen.
   worse
   I've ......*never seen a worse*...... film.

b) There aren't any sandwiches left, I'm afraid.
   all
   I'm afraid .... eaten.

c) I thought that Martin's last novel was more interesting.
   latest
   Martin's .... interesting as his last one.

d) I talked to neither of Harry's sisters.
   either
   I didn't .... Harry's sisters.

e) Bob is a much better swimmer than George.

swim

George .... as Bob.

f) If you walk slowly, it takes longer to get there.

longer

The more .... it takes to get there.

g) Calling the police isn't any good.

no

It's .... the police.

h) I phoned Norman last of all.

person

Norman .... phoned.

i) This is the best party I've ever been to.

a

I've .... good party as this.

j) I thought this meal would cost more than it did.

less

This meal .... thought.

3 Complete each sentence with one suitable word. Do not use the word *piece*.

a) Would you like another ....*slice*........ of cake?

b) There is another .... of stairs after this one.

c) What a lovely .... of hair you have.

d) Put up your hand if you need another .... of paper.

e) There was an interesting .... of news about Japan in the paper.

f) Could you put a few .... of coal on the fire?

g) Pour me a .... of water, would you?

h) They gave me a very large .... of potatoes with my dinner.

i) There was a terrible flash of lightning and a .... of thunder.

j) Oh bother, I've split my new .... of shorts.

4 Rewrite each sentence so that it contains the word given in capitals, and the meaning stays the same. The word cannot be changed in any way.

a) You are not allowed to park here. PARKING

...... *Parking is not allowed here.* ......

b) There aren't any tables, chairs or beds in the house. FURNITURE

....

c) This room seems very crowded. PEOPLE

....

d) Can you tell me about guided tours of the city? INFORMATION

....

e) The people in the theatre were enthusiastic. AUDIENCE

....

f) I like maths best. SUBJECT

....

g) There are a lot of cars on this road today. TRAFFIC

....

5 Complete the second sentence so that it has a similar meaning to the first sentence, using the word given. Do not change the word given. You must use between two and five words, including the word given.

a) Jim teaches French.

works

Jim ...... *works as a French* ...... teacher.

b) Can't you do better than that?

the

Is .... do?

c) I haven't eaten lobster before.

ever

This is the .... eaten.

d) Is Julia a good violinist?

play

Can Julia .... well?

e) Actually, the only thing you need is a screwdriver.

all

Actually .... a screwdriver.

f) Both of the lifts were out of order.

of

Neither .... working.

6 Put one word in each space.

a) My trousers are creased. I must iron ......*them*...... .

b) Could you give me .... information about the Arts Festival?

c) I can't come out tonight. I have .... work to do.

d) Look at your hair! You must have .... cut!

e) I've decided to buy .... new furniture.

f) Thank you very much. You've been .... great help.

g) Is this .... café you told me about?

h) Chris was .... last person to leave the room.

7 Look carefully at each line. Some of the lines are correct, and some have a word which should not be there. Tick each correct line. If a line has a word which should not be there, write the word in the space.

The house painters

Last week some painters came round to	......✓......
paint my house. I usually do this kind of a job	......*a*......
myself, but I've been here very busy for the last	1) ....
month. So I called a more local decorating firm,	2) ....
and they agreed to do it for a reasonable price.	3) ....
Three men arrived on Monday the morning to	4) ....
paint the outside walls. Of course, they were used	5) ....
the wrong colour and spilt paint all over the	6) ....
front door. Some one of the windows	7) ....
upstairs were open, and some of paint went	8) ....
inside the house and ruined both the carpet in	9) ....
the living-room. They also broke a window.	10) ....
I phoned their company, and the manager	11) ....
assured me that they would repaint than the	12) ....
walls. Then I went away on a business.	13) ....
I've just come back, and the walls are a different	14) ....
colour, but it is still such the wrong colour.	15) ....
If I had done the job myself, I would have	
finished it by now.	

Explanations

Understanding phrasal verbs

■ Verbs are often followed by particles like *back, off, through, up*, etc (the word *particle* means *adverb* or *preposition*). Sometimes both verb and particle have their normal meaning. At other times there is a new meaning when they are put together. Compare:

*Can you **bring up** the radio from downstairs?*　(normal meaning)
*She has **brought up** two children on her own.*
(new meaning = *look after until adult*)

The term 'phrasal verb' is used for the second case, where the verb + particle together has a special meaning. Phrasal verbs are common in informal English.

■ Often one phrasal verb can have several different meanings and the correct one is only clear from the context.

■ There are four types of phrasal verbs. These are covered in Grammar 26 and 27.
　Grammar 26: • phrasal verbs with two particles.
　　　　　　　• phrasal verbs with one particle; there must be an object; the particle is inseparable.
　Grammar 27: • phrasal verbs with one particle; there must be an object; the particle can be separated from the verb.
　　　　　　　• phrasal verbs with one particle; there is no object.

Verbs with two particles

A selection of phrasal verbs is listed here with examples. Others, and other meanings of those listed here, are included in the Practice section.
Most of the verbs in the list need an object, and the object can only come at the end (so the verbs are inseparable).

*I'm **looking forward to** my holidays.*

But some verbs are marked with an asterisk *. With these verbs there is another form: there is no object, and the final particle is not used.

*I've decided to **cut down on** smoking.　I've decided to **cut down**.*

Cut down on*
　*I've decided to **cut down on** smoking.*　(reduce the amount of)
Catch up with*
　*They are too far ahead for us to **catch up with** them.*　(reach the same place as)
Come up against
　*I'm afraid we've **come up against** a problem we can't solve.*　(meet, find)
Come up with
　*Have you **come up with** an answer yet?*　(think of)

Drop in on*

> *I **dropped in on** Bill and Sheila on my way home.* (visit for a short time)

Face up to

> *You must **face up to** reality!* (accept, deal with)

Feel up to

> *You must **feel up to** going to work.* (have the strength and energy to do)

Get away with

> *Jack stole the money and **got away with** it.* (do something bad and not be punished)

Get along/on with*

> *Do you **get along/on with** your new boss?* (have good relations with)

Get on with

> *Stop talking and **get on with** your work!* (continue with)

Get out of

> *I managed to **get out of** working late.* (avoid a responsibility)

Get round to

> *I haven't **got round to** decorating yet.* (find time to do)

Get up to

> *What has young Bill been **getting up to**?* (do something bad)

Go in for

> *Do you **go in for** sailing?* (have as a hobby)

Grow out of

> *Julie has **grown out of** playing with dolls.* (become too old for)

Keep up with*

> *You're going too fast! I can't **keep up with** you!* (stay in the same place as)

Look down on

> *Our neighbours **look down on** anyone without a car.* (feel superior to)

Look up to

> *I really **look up to** my teacher.* (respect)

Look forward to

> *We are **looking forward to** our holiday.* (think we will enjoy)

Make up for

> *This wonderful dinner **made up for** the bad service.* (compensate for)

Put up with

> *I can't **put up with** these screaming children!* (accept without complaining)

Run out of*

> *Oh dear, we've **run out of** petrol!* (have no more of)

Stand up for

> *You must learn to **stand up for** yourself!* (defend)

Verbs with one particle: transitive and inseparable

These phrasal verbs take an object, and the object must come after the particle. It cannot go between the verb and the particle.

> *I love coffee. I can't **do without** it in the morning!* (NOT ~~do it without~~)

Ask after

> *Jim **asked after** you yesterday.*   (ask for news of)

Call for

> *I'll **call for** you at six.*   (come to your house and collect you)

Call on

> *I **called on** some friends in Plymouth.*   (visit for a short time)

Come across

> *Joe **came across** this old painting in the attic.*   (find by chance)

Come into

> *Sue **came into** a large sum of money.*   (inherit)

Count on

> *I'm **counting on** you to help me.*   (depend on)

Deal with

> *How can we **deal with** the traffic problem?*   (take action to solve a problem)

Do without

> *We'll have to **do without** a holiday this year.*   (manage without having)

Get at

> *What are you **getting at?***   (suggest)

Get over

> *Barry has **got over** his illness now.*   (recover from)

Go over

> *Let's **go over** our plan once more.*   (discuss the details)

Join in

> *Try to **join in** the lesson as much as you can.*   (take part in, contribute to)

Live on

> *They **live on** the money her father gives them.*   (have as income)

Look into

> *The government is **looking into** the problem.*   (investigate)

Look round

> *Let's **look round** the town today.*   (look at everything)

Make for

> *Where are you **making for** exactly?*   (go in the direction of)

Pick on

> *My teacher is always **picking on** me.*   (choose a person to punish)

Run into

> *I **ran into** Steve in the supermarket yesterday.*   (meet by chance)

See about

> *Well have to **see about** getting you an office.*   (make arrangements)

See to

> *Can you **see to** the dog's food?*   (attend to, take care of)

Stand for

> *I won't **stand for** such rudeness!*   (tolerate)

> *Andrew is **standing for** parliament.*   (be a candidate for)

Take after

> *Helen **takes after** her mother.*   (have the same characteristics as)

Practice

1 **Rewrite each sentence so that it contains the phrasal verb in brackets. You may have to change the form.**

a) Sorry, but I haven't found time to fix your bike yet. (get round to)

......*Sorry, but I haven't got round to fixing your bike yet.*......

b) Oh bother, we don't have any milk left. (run out of)

....

c) It took me a long time to recover from my illness. (get over)

....

d) Julie must be too old to bite her nails. (grow out of)

....

e) I think we've found an answer to the problem. (come up with)

....

f) I don't think I'm well enough to play football today. (feel up to)

....

g) Ann is someone I really respect. (look up to)

....

h) I must arrange to have the kitchen painted. (see about)

....

i) Please help me. I'm relying on you. (count on)

....

j) Peter is just like his father! (take after)

....

2 Complete the second sentence so that it has a similar meaning to the first sentence, using the word given. Do not change the word given. You must use between two and five words, including the word given.

a) Quite by chance, Brenda met Philip at the station.

   ran

   Brenda .... *ran into Philip* .... at the station.

b) You'll just have to learn to accept the facts!

   face

   You'll just .... the facts.

c) How can you bear so much traffic noise?

   put

   How can you .... traffic noise?

d) Charles cheated in his exams, and didn't get caught.

   got

   Charles cheated in his exams, and .... it.

e) I visited a few friends while I was in Manchester.

   called

   I .... while I was in Manchester.

f) What are you trying to say?

   getting

   What .... at?

g) I must go to the dentist, and get my teeth taken care of.

   seen

   I must go to the dentist .... to.

3 Complete each sentence with one of the words from the box.

across	against	~~for~~	in	into	on	round	to	up	with

a) I'll send someone to call .... *for* .... the parcel on Thursday.

b) You'll have to work hard to keep .... with the rest of the class.

c) Jean didn't expect to come up .... such difficulties.

d) It's not fair. You're always picking .... me.

e) Terry sang the first verse and then everyone joined ....

f) I came .... one of your novels in a second-hand bookshop.

g) I'm not interested in buying anything. I'm just looking ....

h) Don't you think the manager should deal .... this problem?

i) George came .... a lot of money when his uncle died.

j) You look very guilty! What have you been getting up .... ?

4 Complete each sentence with the most suitable word or phrase.

a) The weather was fine, and everyone was .... *B* .... the coast.

   A) going in for   B) making for   C) joining in   D) seeing about

b) How much money do you manage to .... ?

   A) come into   B) go in for   C) deal with   D) live on

c) There isn't any sugar, I'm afraid. You'll have to ....

   A) run out   B) put up with   C) do without   D) make for

d) I was passing their house, so I .... Claire and Michael.

   A) dropped in on   B) came up with   C) got on with   D) ran into

e) I don't really .... winter sports very much.

   A) deal with   B) face up to   C) go in for   D) get round to

f) Losing my job was a great shock, but I think I'm .... it.

   A) seeing to   B) putting up with   C) standing for   D) getting over

g) Sheila's gone to .... having a new phone installed.

   A) see about   B) deal with   C) get round to   D) ask after

h) I've had to .... a lot of insulting behaviour from you!

   A) look down on   B) put up with   C) stand up for   D) get on with

i) The hotel was terrible, but the wonderful beach .... our disappointment.

   A) got over   B) faced up to   C) saw to   D) made up for

j) Jack has decided to .... the time he spends watching television.

   A) run out of   B) see to   C) cut down on   D) come up with

5   Choose the most suitable ending for each sentence. Note that some of the phrasal verbs have a different meaning to the one given in the Explanations section.

a) I can't put up with ....*B*...............

   A) you if you should come to London.   B) people who smoke all the time.
   C) the plates onto the top shelf.

b) The chairperson of the committee then called on Tony ....

   A) but his line was engaged.   B) to make a speech in reply.
   C) so that his voice could be heard above the crowd.

c) Mary has been chosen to stand for ....

   A) the bad behaviour of her colleagues.   B) herself in future.
   C) Parliament in the next election.

d) After my holidays it takes me a few days to catch up with ....

   A) the people running in front of me.   B) all the news I've missed.
   C) a really bad cold.

e) Small children soon grow out of ....

   A) their shoes.   B) all the good food they eat.
   C) the habits they have when they get older.

f) I've decided to go in for ....

   A) eating fruit for breakfast.   B) a few days rest in the country.
   C) a photography competition in *Photographer's Weekly*.

g) I'm afraid that our plans to open a new factory have run into ....

   A) some old friends.   B) a tree by the side of the road.
   C) a few unexpected difficulties.

h) We find that this type of tyre makes for ....

   A) safer driving in wet weather.   B) the first place it can stop.
   C) all smaller types of cars.

i) I saw my old friend John last week. I couldn't get over ....

   A) my cold before I saw him, though.   B) near enough to talk to him though.
   C) how young he looked.

j) Here people are only worried about keeping up with ....

   A) others who are faster.   B) late-night television programmes.
   C) the Joneses.

Key points   1   Check any new phrasal verb in a dictionary, to see how it is used.
2   Remember that many phrasal verbs have more than one meaning.
3   Phrasal verbs tend to be more common in spoken language and informal written language.

→ SEE ALSO

Grammar 30: Consolidation 6

Phrasal verbs 2

Explanations

Verbs with one particle: transitive and separable

These phrasal verbs take an object. This object can come after the particle or between the verb and the particle (so the verbs are separable).

*We **brought up** this child.   We **brought** her **up**.*

In general, as in the examples above, object phrases tend to be put after the particle while pronouns are often put between the verb and the particle.

Two exceptions in the list below are *call back* and *show around* where the object is always put between the verb and the particle.

Verbs marked with an asterisk * have a second meaning. With this meaning they have an intransitive form.

Bring up
*We **brought up** this child.*   (look after until adult)

Carry out
*You haven't **carried out** my instructions.*   (act upon)

Call off
*We have decided to **call off** the match.*   (cancel)

Clear up*
*Could you **clear up** your room please?*   (make tidy)
*The weather is **clearing up***.*   (improve)

Fill in*
*Can you **fill in** this form please?*   (complete by writing)
*Our teacher was ill, so Mrs Frost **filled in***.*   (take someone's place)

Find out
*I want to **find out** what happened.*   (learn about, discover)

Give away
*The millionaire **gave** all his money **away**.*   (make a gift of)
*Jill asked me not to **give** her secret **away**.*   (make something known)

Give up*
*I've decided to **give up** eating meat.*   (stop doing something)
*Jorge finally **gave up** teaching me Portuguese*.*   (stop trying to do something)

Hold up
*Two masked men **held up** the bank.*   (rob)

Knock out
*The blow on the head **knocked** me **out**.*   (make unconscious)

Leave out
*I always **leave out** the difficult exercises.*   (not include)

Look up*
*I have to **look** this word **up** in my dictionary.*   (find information)
*Things are **looking up***.*   (appear better)

Make up*

*I think you **made** this story **up**.* (invent)

*The couple quarrelled but then **made up***. (become friends again)

Pick up

*I'll **pick** you **up** at six.* (collect)

Put aside

*Harry **puts** money **aside** every week for his holiday.* (save)

Put off

*They **put** the meeting **off** until Thursday.* (postpone)

*The smell of fish **put** me **off** my tea.* (make someone not want to do something)

Put up

*If you come to Florence I can **put** you **up**.* (provide accommodation)

Show around

*Let me **show** you **around** the new building.* (give a guided tour)

Take over*

*A German company **took** us **over** last year.* (buy a company)

*If you are tired, I'll **take over***. (take someone's place)

Take up

*I've decided to **take up** tennis.* (start a hobby)

Tear up

*Wendy **tore up** Alan's letters.* (tear into pieces)

Think over

*Please **think over** our offer.* (consider)

Try out

*Have you **tried out** the new computer?* (use for the first time)

Turn down

*Paul was offered the job but he **turned it down**.* (refuse an offer)

Wear out

*All this work has **worn me out**.* (make tired)

Work out

*This is a difficult problem. I can't **work** it **out**.* (find a solution)

| Verbs with one particle: intransitive | These phrasal verbs have no object. Verbs marked with an asterisk * have a second meaning. With this meaning they have a transitive form. There are other meanings not included here. |

Break down

*The car **broke down** on the motorway.* (stop working)

Break out

*The war **broke out** unexpectedly.* (begin suddenly)

Come out

*Her new book **came out** last week.* (be published)

Draw up*

    *Suddenly an ambulance **drew up** outside.*   (come to a stop)

    *My lawyer is **drawing up** a contract for us*.*   (write a legal document)

Fall out

    *Charles and Emily have **fallen out** again.*   (quarrel)

Get away

    *The bank robbers **got away** in a stolen van.*   (escape)

Give in

    *She pleaded with me, and I finally **gave in**.*   (stop fighting against)

Go off

    *Everyone panicked when the bomb **went off**.*   (explode)

Look out

    ***Look out!** There's a car coming!*   (beware)

Set in

    *I think the rain has **set in** for the day.*   (to arrive and stay)

Show off

    *You always **show off** at parties.*   (behave to attract attention)

Take off

    *Your plane **takes off** at 6.00.*   (leave the ground)

Turn up*

    *Guess who **turned up** at our party?*   (arrive, often unexpectedly)

    *Can you **turn up** the sound*?*   (increase)

Wear off

    *When the drug **wears off** you may feel pain.*   (become less strong or disappear)

Practice

1 Rewrite each sentence using a verb from the box so that the meaning stays the same. You may have to change the form.

call off	draw up	give in	look up	put aside	put up
turn down	~~turn up~~	wear off	work out		

a) Jack always arrives late for work.
.....*Jack always turns up late for work.*.....................................

b) See if their number is in the phone directory.
....

c) I'm saving up to buy a new bike.
....

d) After a few days the pain in Dave's leg went away.
....

e) I'm afraid the match has been cancelled.
....

f) The government refused to yield to the demands of the terrorists.
....

g) We offered them £250,000 for the house but they refused our offer.
....

h) You can stay with us if you come to Cambridge.
....

i) I can't calculate how much the whole trip will cost.
....

j) A large silver limousine stopped outside the house.
....

2 **Put one word in each space.**

a) Why don't you let me show you .....*round*..... London?

b) Jane is coming to pick us .... after work.

c) Have you found .... what time the train leaves?

d) We had to wait for an hour before the plane took ....

e) Harry was brought .... by his grandparents.

f) A shelf fell on my head and knocked me ....

g) I was so angry when I saw the parking ticket that I tore it ....

h) A fire has broken .... in an office block in central London.

i) Julian always talks loudly and shows ....

j) If you don't like this part you can leave it ....

3 **Complete the second sentence so that it has a similar meaning to the first sentence, using the word given. Do not change the word given. You must use between two and five words, including the word given.**

a) I think it's going to rain all day.

in

I think the .... *rain has set in for* .... the day.

b) I don't know what to write on this form.

in

I don't know .... this form.

c) I started doing this job when Janet left.

over

I .... when Janet left.

d) This story of yours isn't true!

up

You .... story!

e) We believe that it was you who robbed the post office.

up

We believe that .... the post office.

f) Tina's car stopped working on the way to Scotland.

down

Tina's car .... on the way to Scotland.

g) It would be a good idea to stop drinking coffee.

up

It would be a good idea .... coffee.

h) Ruth's party has been postponed until next month.

off

Ruth's party .... next month.

4 **Put one suitable word in each space.**

a) In the army, all orders have to be .....*carried*.... out!

b) Why don't you .... up golf? It's a good pastime.

c) If I won a lot of money, I would .... some of it away.

d) Let's .... out the new food processor.

e) This room is a mess. Why don't you .... it up?

f) Joe is very quarrelsome, he .... out with everyone.

g) Where were you exactly when the bomb .... off?

h) Can you .... in for me while I go to the bank?

5 **Complete each sentence with the most suitable word or phrase.**

a) Brian ....*C*......... at our dinner party wearing a pink bow tie.
   A) wore out   B) showed off   C) turned up   D) tried out

b) You don't have to decide now, you can ....
   A) put it aside   B) call it off   C) tear it up   D) think it over

c) Pat was caught by the police, but Martin ....
   A) gave in   B) gave up   C) got away   D) held up

d) After the quarrel, we kissed and ....
   A) cleared up   B) looked up   C) made up   D) put up

e) Why exactly did war .... between the two countries?
   A) break out   B) set in   C) go off   D) call off

f) After a long day at work most people feel ....
   A) broken down   B) worn out   C) knocked out   D) turned down

g) I've just been offered a new job! Things are ....
   A) turning up   B) clearing up   C) making up   D) looking up

h) In the end I .... the form in disgust, and threw it away.
   A) filled in   B) worked out   C) tore up   D) put off

6 **Replace the words in *italics* with a suitable phrasal verb.**

a) I think that you *invented* this story. ..*made up*..

b) When do you think your book will *be published*? ....

c) I think that the weather is *improving*. ....

d) I can't *find an answer to* this problem. ....

e) *Be careful!* You're going to fall! ....

f) I'm afraid William tends to *stop trying*. ....

g) The plane is going to *leave the ground*. ....

h) I think that Sue and Neil have *quarrelled*. ....

7 Choose the best meaning for the words in *italics*. Note that some of the phrasal verbs have a different meaning to the one given in the Explanations section.

a) At half past six, the alarm clock *went off*. ....B..........

A) exploded   B) rang   C) disappeared

b) Jim is very good at *taking off his teacher*. ....

A) flying with his teacher   B) getting rid of his teacher

C) imitating his teacher

c) Please don't *bring up that subject* again! ....

A) start shouting about it   B) mention it   C) talk about it for hours on end

d) There is one small matter I would like to *clear up*. ....

A) find an explanation for   B) make clean and tidy

C) get rid of once and for all

e) Jean is really good at *picking up languages*. ....

A) choosing languages   B) learning languages by being in a country

C) learning languages by heart

f) All my old clothes need *taking up*. ....

A) taking to the cleaners   B) to be replaced   C) to be made shorter

g) The whole cost of the equipment *works out at £450*. ....

A) comes to   B) can be reduced to   C) will involve an extra

h) Jackie *broke down* and everyone felt sorry for her. ....

A) injured herself   B) caused an accident   C) started crying

Key points 1 Check any new phrasal verb in a dictionary, to see how it is used.
2 Remember that many phrasal verbs have more than one meaning.
3 Phrasal verbs are common in spoken and informal written language.

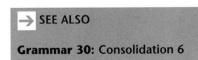

→ SEE ALSO

Grammar 30: Consolidation 6

Explanations

- Verbs followed by *-ing* or a noun

  Some verbs can be followed either by another verb in an *-ing* form or a noun.

  > Try to **avoid walking** as much as possible.
  >
  > I managed to **avoid an argument**.

  Verbs in this list include:

  > *avoid, be worth, dislike, enjoy, fancy, help, keep, mind, miss, practise, risk, can't stand*

  > It's not **worth waiting** for a bus at this time of day.
  >
  > I **dislike having** to get up early.
  >
  > Do you **enjoy meeting** people from other countries?
  >
  > I don't **fancy going out** this evening.
  >
  > George can't **help laughing** when he sees you!
  >
  > I wish you wouldn't **keep interrupting**.
  >
  > I don't **mind helping** you do the washing-up.
  >
  > Jane **misses going** for long country walks.
  >
  > You should **practise introducing** yourself.
  >
  > We can't **risk starting** a fire in the forest.
  >
  > I **can't stand going** to office parties.

- Verbs followed by *-ing*, or a noun, or a *that*-clause

  Some verbs can be followed either by another verb in an *-ing* form, or a noun, or a *that*-clause.

  > Jack **admitted stealing** the money.
  >
  > When accused of stealing the money, Jack **admitted it**.
  >
  > Jack **admitted that** he had stolen the money.

  Verbs in this list include:

  > *admit, consider, deny, imagine, recollect, report, suggest*

  > Have you **considered taking up** jogging?
  >
  > You must **consider that** Jim has never driven abroad before.
  >
  > Peter **denied stealing** the money.
  >
  > Can you **imagine living** in California?
  >
  > I don't **recollect meeting** you before.
  >
  > Suddenly I **recollected that** I had another appointment.
  >
  > Helen **reported losing** her watch to the director.
  >
  > I **suggested going** to the beach.
  >
  > I **suggested that** we went to the beach.

■ Verbs followed by -*ing* or infinitive: little change of meaning
Some verbs can be followed either by an -*ing* form or an infinitive and there is little or no change in meaning. Verbs in this list include:

attempt, begin, continue, dread, not bear, hate, intend, like, love, prefer, start
*I **attempted to leave/leaving** but the police stopped me.*

The forms *would like, would love* and *would prefer* are followed by an infinitive.

*I'd **like to come** to your party, but I'll be away then.*

Like to can have its normal meaning of something that gives pleasure. But it has a second meaning which is to talk about a habitual action, whether or not it gives us pleasure.

*On Sundays I **like to get up** early and go for a swim.*

■ Verbs followed by -*ing* or infinitive: change of meaning
Some verbs can be followed either by an -*ing* form, or by the infinitive, and there is a change in meaning. Study the examples below carefully and check more examples in a dictionary.

forget and *remember*
We use *forget/remember doing* for memories of the past (the action happens before the remembering). We use *forget/remember to do* for actions someone is/was supposed to do (the remembering happens before the action).

*I won't **forget meeting** you.*	(meet → forget)
*I **forgot** that I **had invited** ten people to lunch.*	(invite → forget)
*I **forgot to buy** any coffee.*	(forget → buy)
*I won't **forget to go** there.*	(forget → go)
*I **remember locking** the door.*	(lock → remember)
*I **remembered** that I **had left** my keys behind.*	(leave → remember)
*Please **remember to lock** the door.*	(remember → lock)

go on
We use *go on doing* when we continue doing something. We use *go on to do* when we move on to do something else.

*Diana **went on working** all night.*	(did the same thing)
*The director **went on to say** that the strike was over.*	(did something else)

mean
We use *mean doing* when one thing results in or involves another. We use *mean to do* to express an intention.

*This **means leaving** at 6.00.*	(involves)
*This **means** that we will have to leave at 6.00!*	(has a result)
*I **meant to phone** you but I forgot.*	(intended)

regret

We use *regret doing* when we are sorry about something that happened in the past.

> Kate **regretted not buying** the house.
> Kate **regretted that** she hadn't bought the house.

We use *regret to inform/to tell* when we are giving bad news. This use is formal.

> I **regret to tell** you that you have failed.

stop

We use *stop doing* when we end an action. We use *stop to do* when we give the reason for stopping.

> I **stopped going** to evening classes.   (gave up going)
> I **stopped to buy** some coffee.   (in order to buy)

try

We use *try doing* when we do something and see what happens. We use *try to do* when we make an effort to do something, but don't necessarily succeed.

> Why don't you **try getting up** early?   (suggesting an action)
> I **tried to get up** early, but I couldn't.   (try and fail)

- Verbs followed by the infinitive
  Some verbs can only be followed by the infinitive. These include:
  afford, appear, ask, choose, fail, happen, help, long, manage, offer, prepare, refuse, tend, wait, want

  > I can't **afford to go** on holiday abroad this year.
  > The car **appears to have broken down**.
  > David **asked me to give** this to you.
  > I **chose not to go** to university.
  > Gerry **failed to arrive** on time.
  > I **happened to be passing** so I dropped in.

- Verbs followed by the infinitive, or a *that*-clause
  Some verbs can be followed by the infinitive or a *that*-clause. These include:
  agree, arrange, decide, demand, desire, expect, hope, intend, learn, plan, pretend, promise, seem, threaten, wish

  > Tom **agreed to meet** us outside the cinema.
  > Tom **agreed that** he would meet us outside the cinema.
  > We **arranged that** we would leave at 5.30.
  > John **decided to take** the bus.
  > John **decided that** he would take the bus.

■ Verbs followed by *-ing*, or infinitive without *to*

Some verbs can be followed by an object + *-ing*, or an infinitive without *to*. There is a change in meaning. These verbs are sometimes called 'verbs of perception' and include:

feel, hear, listen to, notice, see, watch

If we see or hear only part of the action, or it continues, we use the *-ing* form. If we see or hear the whole action from beginning to end, we use the infinitive without *to*. Compare:

*I **felt** the train **moving**.*   (continuing action)

*I **felt** the train **move**.*   (one completed action)

Some of these verbs can be used with a *that* clause with a change of meaning.

*I **feel that** you should look for another job.*   (believe)

*I've just **heard that** the match is off.*   (receive news)

***See that** you lock up when you leave.*   (make sure)

Practice

1 **Complete each sentence with a suitable form of the verb in brackets.**

a) I really miss (play) ....*playing*........ tennis like I used to.

b) I'm sorry. I meant (write) .... to you, but I've been busy.

c) Martin failed (pay) .... the rent on time yet again.

d) It's not worth (buy) .... a return ticket.

e) Have you ever considered (work) .... as a teacher?

f) I promise I won't forget (feed) .... the cat.

g) We've arranged (meet) .... outside the school at 4.30.

h) If you've got a headache, try (take) .... an aspirin.

2 **Complete the second sentence so that it has a similar meaning to the first sentence, using the word given. Do not change the word given. You must use between two and five words, including the word given.**

a) Jack said that he hadn't cheated in the exam.

cheating

Jack ....*denied cheating*.. in the exam.

b) It was difficult for me not to laugh at Wendy's letter.

help

I .... at Wendy's letter.

c) I'm sorry but you have not been appointed to the post.

regret

I .... you have not been appointed to the post.

d) I needed a drink of water and so I stopped running.

to

I stopped running .... water.

e) I think it would be a good idea to take the train.

taking

I .... the train.

f) Don't forget the lights when you leave.

off

Don't forget .... when you leave.

g) I think Derek has forgotten the meeting.

appears

Derek .... the meeting.

h) My neighbour said he would call the police!

threatened

My neighbour .... the police.

168

3 **Complete each sentence with a suitable form of the verb in brackets.**

a) Pauline couldn't manage (eat) ....*to eat*............ all the ice cream.

b) I've decided (not sell) .... my bike after all.

c) A witness reported (see) .... Terry at the scene of the crime.

d) William pretended (not notice) .... the 'No Parking' sign.

e) I suppose I tend (buy) .... more books than I used to.

f) Sometimes I regret (move) .... to this part of the country.

g) Did you notice anyone (wait) .... outside when you left?

h) Mark expects (finish) .... work round about 6.00.

4 **Complete each sentence with a suitable form of one of the verbs in brackets.**

a) Mary was so angry that she ....*demanded*............ to see the manager.

(demand, hope, risk, stop)

b) The weather is so awful that I don't .... going out this evening.

(fancy, like, try, want)

c) The children could hardly .... to leave their pets behind.

(bear, forget, regret, seem)

d) John .... to let his children go to the concert.

(afford, avoid, refuse, stop)

e) If I give you the information, I .... losing my job!

(expect, mean, prepare, risk)

f) What do you .... to be doing in ten years time?

(begin, expect, remember, suggest)

g) Do you .... to tell the police about the missing money?

(admit, confess, deny, intend)

Key points 1 Check new verbs in a good dictionary as it will show how they should be used.

2 Note that some verbs can be used in different ways with changes of meaning.

→ SEE ALSO

Grammar 30: Consolidation 6

Verb/Adjective + preposition

Explanations

Prepositions following verbs

■ *About*
> *agree about, argue about, boast about, dream about, know about, laugh about, read about, talk about*

■ *At*
> *guess at, laugh at, look at*

■ *For*
> *apply for, arrange for, ask for something, blame someone for, care for, forgive someone for, look for, pay for something, search for, vote for, wait for*

■ *In*
> *believe in, confide in someone, involve someone in something, specialise in, succeed in, take part in*

■ *Of*
> *accuse someone of something, (dis)approve of, die of something, dream of, remind someone of something, rob someone of something, smell of, taste of, warn someone of something*

■ *On*
> *blame something on someone, concentrate on, congratulate someone on something, depend on, insist on, rely on*

■ *To*
> *add something to, admit to, apologise to someone for something, be accustomed to, be used to, belong to, confess to, explain something to someone, lend something to someone, listen to, object to, reply to, talk to someone about something*

■ *With*
> *agree with, argue with, begin with, charge someone with a crime, deal with, discuss something with someone, provide someone with something, share something with someone, trust someone with something*

Prepositions following adjectives

■ *About*
> *annoyed about, anxious about, certain about, excited about, happy about, pleased about, right about, sorry about, upset about*

■ *At*
> *angry at, annoyed at, bad/good at, surprised at*

■ *By*
> *bored by, shocked by, surprised by*

- *For*

    famous for, late for, ready for, sorry for

- *From*

    absent from, different from, safe from

- *In*

    interested in

- *Of*

    afraid of, ashamed of, aware of, capable of, fond of, full of, it is good of you (to do something), jealous of

- *On*

    keen on

- *To*

    grateful to, kind to, married to

- *With*

    angry with, annoyed with, bored with, happy with, pleased with

Practice

1 **Put one suitable word in each space.**

a) A lot of people I know really believe ....*in*.......... ghosts.

b) Martin grew to be very fond .... his pet snake.

c) This bread tastes .... fish!

d) Everyone was shocked .... Susan's strange appearance.

e) The company blamed the drop in sales .... the economic situation.

f) Brenda decided to discuss her problems .... a psychiatrist.

g) When Harry made his speech, everyone laughed .... him.

h) Robert has been married .... Deborah for over a year.

i) You were right after all .... the result of the election.

j) The woman who lived next door admitted .... the robbery.

2 **Rewrite each sentence beginning as shown. Do not change the meaning.**

a) Two men stole the old lady's handbag.
   The old lady was ....*robbed of her handbag.*.....................................

b) John finds photography interesting.
   John is ....

c) Helen has a good knowledge of car engines.
   Helen knows a lot ....

d) The food in France is famous.
   France is ....

e) I'd like to thank your brother for his help.
   I am very grateful ....

f) Can you and Stephen share this book, please?
   Can you share this book ....

g) I find studying all night rather difficult.
   I'm not used to ....

h) Harry feels frightened when he sees a snake.
   Harry is afraid ....

i) I'm sorry about breaking your camera.
   Please forgive me ....

j) Peter knows how to draw well.
   Peter is good ....

3 **Put one suitable word in each space.**

a) David was ...*ashamed*... of what he had done, and he blushed.

b) I'm not very .... on the idea of going climbing.

c) Mary is always .... about all the famous people she has met.

d) Jim was often .... for work, and lost his job as a result.

e) There were no empty seats on the train, which was .... of soldiers.

f) Bill decided not to .... Bob with his secrets.

g) The two boys were .... of stealing a sports car.

h) We .... in persuading Carol to lend us her boat.

i) You have worked very hard! I am very .... with you!

j) I can't remember her name, but it .... with 'J'.

4 **Complete the second sentence so that it has a similar meaning to the first sentence, using the word given. Do not change the word given. You must use between two and five words, including the word given.**

a) William could do better work.

   capable

   William ....*is capable of*........................... doing better work.

b) I own this car.

   belongs

   This car .... me.

c) The job received over a hundred applications.

   applied

   Over a hundred people .... the job.

d) Mrs Jones' death was caused by old age.

   died

   Mrs Jones .... old age.

e) 'Well done, Tony, you have passed the exam,' said Joe.

   congratulated

   Joe .... the exam.

f) Jean borrowed Shirley's camera.

   lent

   Shirley .... camera.

g) Graham found the film very boring.

   by

   Graham .... the film.

h) We all pitied Stephen.

   sorry

   We all .... Stephen.

5 **Put one suitable word in each space.**

a) My boss shouted at me – he was really .....*angry*...... with me!

b) I can see your point, but I just don't .... with you.

c) Terry doesn't .... of his children going to rock concerts.

d) George and I .... about politics all night!

e) Can I have a .... at the evening paper?

f) This story .... me of a novel by Dickens.

g) Peter feels .... of anyone who talks to his girlfriend.

h) I didn't expect you to behave like that! I'm .... at you!

i) Oh dear, I forgot to .... any baking powder to the cake.

j) I think you should .... your boss for a rise.

6 **Complete each sentence with the most suitable word or phrase.**

a) Thank you very much. It's very ....*B*......... you to help me.

A) good with   B) good of   C) good for   D) good about

b) The bad weather was .... the series of power cuts.

A) blamed for   B) blamed on   C) blamed with   D) blamed by

c) I'm sorry, but I .... seeing the manager at once!

A) arrange for   B) look for   C) agree with   D) insist on

d) Why do you spend all your time .... your sister!

A) arguing about   B) arguing for   C) arguing with   D) arguing at

e) Helen is very .... going to work in Germany.

A) excited about   B) excited for   C) excited with   D) excited to

f) The tourists were not .... the danger of bandits in the hills.

A) known about   B) aware of   C) provided with   D) guessed at

g) I understood the problem after it had been .... me.

A) explained to   B) admitted to   C) confessed to   D) replied to

h) I wish you wouldn't show off and .... your success so much!

A) full of   B) bored by   C) boast about   D) congratulate on

i) If you listen to music, you can't .... your homework.

A) read about   B) arrange for   C) specialise in   D) concentrate on

j) Will we be .... the storm if we shelter under a tree?

A) happy about   B) safe from   C) depended on   D) cared for

7 Look carefully at each line. Some of the lines are correct, and some have a word which should not be there. Tick each correct line. If a line has a word which should not be there, write the word in the space.

Brothers and sisters

When I was young I had argued with my	.... *had* ....
brothers and sisters all the time. I used to	.... ✓ ....
share with most of my toys with my brother,	1) ....
but he specialised in to keeping them for	2) ....
himself. When I asked about him for anything	3) ....
he simply used to refuse to give it to me, and	4) ....
then I became and very angry with him. Our	5) ....
sisters blamed for everything on us when our	6) ....
parents accused us of quarrelling all the time.	7) ....
My brother and I got up annoyed about this,	8) ....
but only succeeded them in making matters	9) ....
worse. Our parents didn't approve of our	10) ....
quarrelling so much, and insisted us on	11) ....
not taking sides. They either laughed about	12) ....
it, or told us to forgive and each other for	13) ....
everything. Soon we became ashamed of	14) ....
quarrelling, and became good at last getting	15) ....
on well with each other.	

Key points

1 Check verbs and adjectives in a dictionary to be certain which prepositions follow them.

2 In some cases different prepositions give different meanings.

3 Note the difference between *used to* (see Grammar 1) and *be used to*.

   *I **used to go** to the beach every weekend when I was a child.*

This is a habit in the past which is no longer true. *To* is part of the infinitive *to go* in this sentence.

   *I **am not used to getting up** so early in the morning.*

If you *are used to* something you have done it many times so that it no longer seems surprising or difficult. In this case *to* is a preposition, and *getting up* is the noun form of the verb (gerund).

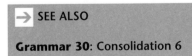

→ SEE ALSO

Grammar 30: Consolidation 6

1 Put one suitable word in each space.

Parents and children

I was reading an article last week in which the writer describes how her children
had changed as they (1) ......*grew*....... up. When they were small, she had to
(2) .... up with noisy games in the house, or (3) .... in
their interminable games of football in the garden which (4) .... her
out. If the house went quiet, she wondered what the monsters were
(5) .... up to, or what crisis she would have to (6) .... with
next. She dreaded the fact that they might (7) .... after her husband,
who admitted having been an uncontrollable child who (8) .... most
of the time (9) .... off to his friends by breaking things or
(10) .... into fights. What was worse was that everyone else thought
he was a sweet child, and he (11) .... away with terrible things!
However, she had experienced an even greater shock with her children. They
had (12) .... out of all their naughty behaviour, and
(13) .... up serious hobbies such as chess and playing the piano. They
never did anything without (14) .... it over first, and coming to a
serious decision. She had to (15) .... up to the fact that they made
her feel rather childish, and that in some ways she preferred them when they
were young and noisy!

2 Complete each sentence with an expression with *get*.

a) When are you going to ......*get round*...... to writing to the bank?

b) I'm afraid I don't .... very well with my teacher.

c) I don't understand what you are .... What do you mean?

d) How are you feeling? Have you .... your cold yet?

e) Jim chased the burglar, but unfortunately the burglar ....

3 Complete each sentence with an expression with *come*.

a) Has the new book of tests ......*come out*...... yet?

b) It's a difficult situation and we haven't .... a solution yet.

c) I .... these old photographs in my desk yesterday.

d) Julie became rich when she .... a fortune.

e) I'm afraid we've .... a lot of problems in this project.

4 Complete the second sentence so that it has a similar meaning to the first sentence, using the word given. Do not change the word given. You must use between two and five words, including the word given.

a) I wish I could work in the evenings as I used to.

   miss

   I ....*miss working*.. in the evenings.

b) If I take the job, I'll have to move to London.

   mean

   Taking the job .... London.

c) Neil wishes he hadn't sold his car.

   having

   Neil .... car.

d) Please see that you post all the letters.

   to

   Please don't .... all the letters.

e) Sheila has decided to take driving lessons.

   how

   Sheila has decided .... drive.

f) Jim said he hadn't stolen the jewels.

   stealing

   Jim .... the jewels.

g) How about going to the theatre tonight?

   like

   Would .... the theatre tonight?

h) Peter will look after the children – he has no objection.

   looking

   Peter doesn't .... children.

i) 'I'll definitely be here by eight,' Ann promised.

   would

   Ann .... by eight.

j) We first met in 1978. Do you remember?

   our

   Do you remember .... 1978?

5 Decide which answer (A, B, C or D) best fits each space.

I don't believe in ghosts!

Last year I stayed for a few days in an old house in Scotland which was famous
(1) ......*B*......... its ghost. I don't really believe (2) .... ghosts, so I'm
not afraid (3) .... them of course. So when my hosts suggested
(4) .... up all night to see their ghost, I simply laughed
(5) .... them. Then they told me (6) .... the woman who
haunted their house. She had been accused (7) .... murdering her
husband in the eighteenth century because she had been jealous
(8) .... him, but she had avoided (9) .... tried, and had
disappeared. She appeared quite regularly, walking through the house as if she
was searching (10) .... something. I agreed to watch that night,
although it would (11) .... sitting for hours in the cold. I expected
one of my friends to appear dressed (12) .... the ghost, and so when
the figure of a woman finally came (13) .... me, I (14) ....
to be terrified. You can imagine my surprise when the figure took a knife from
her dress, and then vanished. I decided to disappear myself, and drove home to
London as (15) .... as I could.

1)	A with	B for	C from	D as
2)	A for	B to	C at	D in
3)	A with	B for	C of	D by
4)	A waking	B getting	C staying	D coming
5)	A at	B with	C about	D to
6)	A for	B that	C with	D about
7)	A that	B of	C for	D while
8)	A of	B by	C to	D for
9)	A and	B being	C but	D having
10)	A like	B after	C with	D for
11)	A mean	B be	C have	D uncomfortable
12)	A with	B for	C as	D in
13)	A about	B towards	C round	D through
14)	A wanted	B imagined	C pretended	D supposed
15)	A quickly	B then	C well	D though

6 **Put one suitable word in each space.**

a) Don't go so fast! I can hardly ....*keep*....... up with you.

b) Don't be such a coward! .... up for yourself!

c) Please don't let me down. I'm .... on you.

d) We don't know who started the fire, but we're .... into it.

e) I must go to the dentist's and have my teeth .... to.

7 **Complete each sentence with an expression containing *of*.**

a) Jim's boss didn't think he was .....*capable of*....... working on his own.

b) Mrs White is very .... animals, and has six cats.

c) I know I shouldn't have stolen the money. I'm .... myself.

d) It was very .... you to help me carry my shopping.

e) Georgina is very .... anyone who dances with her husband.

8 **Complete each sentence with an expression containing *about*.**

a) I knew I'd really seen a ghost. I was ...*certain about*... it!

b) Bill was very .... missing my birthday party.

c) You were .... the film. It was awful, just as you said.

d) I always get worried at airports. I feel .... missing the plane.

e) Poor Lucy has lost her job. She's very .... it.

9 **Complete each sentence with a word ending in *-ing*.**

a) That's all right, I don't mind ....*washing*... up the dirty dishes.

b) Most people try to avoid .... up words in the dictionary.

c) Can you imagine .... up six small children?

d) I was considering .... up golf, actually.

e) We're rather hard up. It means .... without a holiday this year.

10 **Put one suitable word in each space.**

a) Have you ever thought of .....*taking*..... up cycling?

b) Harry had a serious illness, but he has .... over it now.

c) We have decided to .... off our holiday until next month.

d) I think that you .... up the whole story!

e) What are the children .... up to in the garden?

f) Everyone says that Chris .... after his father.

g) You'll never guess who .... up at the end-of-term party!

h) Please .... over our offer before you make a decision.

i) After the party, John had to .... up all the mess.

11 **Complete the second sentence so that it has a similar meaning to the first sentence, using the word given. Do not change the word given. You must use between two and five words, including the word given.**

a) The minister responsible has promised to investigate the problem.

   into

   The minister responsible has promised ....*to look into*........ the problem.

b) Sorry, we must end there, as there is no more time.

   run

   Sorry, we must end there, as .... time.

c) All passengers are asked to complete this immigration form.

   in

   All passengers are asked to .... this immigration form.

d) The war began when the army crossed the border.

   out

   The war .... when the army crossed the border.

e) I don't understand what Ann is trying to say in this letter.

   at

   I don't understand what Ann is .... in this letter.

f) Your behaviour is intolerable! I won't tolerate it!

   for

   Your behaviour is intolerable! I .... it!

g) I always omit the garlic from this recipe.

   out

   I always .... the garlic from this recipe.

h) Have you ever discovered a writer called Jack Common?

   across

   Have you ever .... a writer called Jack Common?

i) I'll do some of the driving, when you feel like a rest.

   over

   I'll .... , when you feel like a rest from driving.

j) I'll do the garden soon, but I just haven't found the time yet.

   got

   I'll do the garden soon, but I just haven't .... yet.

Inversion and question tags

Explanations

Inversion after negative adverbs

In formal speech and writing there is a special construction when the sentence begins with a negative adverb (or one with negative meaning). The subject and the verb are inverted from the normal form to a question form. Study the examples below.

- *Not only*
  - *Harry **not only missed** the train, but also lost his case.* (normal form)
  - ***Not only did** Harry **miss** the train, but (he) also lost his case.* (inversion)

- *No sooner*
  - With *no sooner* the main verb is always in the past perfect.
  - *Tim **had no sooner left**, than the phone rang.* (normal form)
  - ***No sooner had** Tim **left**, than the phone rang.* (inversion)

- *Under no circumstances*
  - *You **shouldn't** touch these wires **under any circumstances**.* (normal form)
  - ***Under no circumstances should** you touch these wires.* (inversion)

- *Seldom*
  - *I **have seldom watched** a better match.* (normal form)
  - ***Seldom have** I **watched** a better match.* (inversion)

- Other expressions which are followed by an inversion are:
  - *little, never, not once, only then, only after, rarely*

Inversion to emphasize an adverb

With some expressions we can begin the sentence with an adverb and then put the verb before the subject.

- With *come* and *go* we can start the sentence with an adverb of place. This construction is used with exclamations. It is an informal usage.
  - ***Here comes** Jack!*   ***There goes** my money!*
  - ***Up went** the plane into the clouds!*   ***Along the road came** Jim.*

- With *live* and *stand* we can start the sentence with an adverb of place. This is a formal usage.
  - ***In this house lived** Charles Dickens.*
  - ***On a hill outside the town stands** the castle.*

- With *be* we can begin the sentence with *now*.
  - ***Now is** the best time to visit the Channel Islands.*

Question tags

■ Sometimes a simple statement is too short and does not help the conversation to develop in a friendly way.

You're French.

The other person does not know what to say. We can add a tag to the end of the statement so that it becomes a question.

You're French, aren't you?

Now the other person knows that they have to reply and the conversation can continue.

If the intonation of the tag rises it is a genuine question. The other person will probably continue the conversation.

A: *You're French, aren't you? (_____↗)*

B: *Yes, that's right. I was born in a town in the north of France although now I live ...*

If the intonation falls, it is just checking information. The first speaker will probably continue.

A: *You're French, aren't you? (_____↘)*

B: *Yes, that's right.*

A: *I thought you were. Have you met Pierre? He's from France as well.*

■ Tags are formed using auxiliaries (*do, be, have* or a modal).

*Helen **lives** here, **doesn't** she?*

*You **left** early, **didn't** you?*

*Jack **was** born in Italy, **wasn't** he?*

*You **will** help me, **won't** you?*

*Someone's got to pay, **haven't** they?*

■ A positive statement has a negative tag, and expects the answer *Yes.*

A: *You **agree** with me, **don't** you?*

B: *Yes, I do.*

A negative statement has a positive tag, and expects the answer *No.*

A: *You **don't** take sugar, **do** you?*

B: *No, I don't.*

It is possible for a positive tag to follow a positive statement, to express interest, or ask for confirmation. This is less common.

*So **you like** working here, **do you?***

Tags with *will* and *won't* can be used after imperatives.

*Don't drive too fast, **will you?***

■ *Let's* ... has a tag formed with *shall.*

*Let's have a drink, **shall we?***

Practice

1 <u>Underline</u> the most suitable words in each sentence.

a) Let's go to London next weekend, <u>*shall we*</u>/*won't we*?

b) You shouldn't have told me, *did you/should you*?

c) Jim hasn't been waiting long, *was he/has he*?

d) You won't tell anyone about this, *do you/will you*?

e) You're not doing what I told you, *do you/are you*?

f) Answer the phone for me, *will you/do you*?

g) George can't have noticed, *can he/has he*?

h) You've got to leave now, *don't you/haven't you*?

i) Pam and Tim got married last year, *didn't they/haven't they*?

j) I don't think John's very friendly, *does he/is he*?

2 Add suitable question tags. (Do not use positive tags for positive statements.)

a) Don't leave anything behind, ...*will you*... ?

b) David is bringing some wine, ... ?

c) You'll be home before midnight, ... ?

d) Harry was working in Bristol then, ... ?

e) Nobody knows who invented the wheel, ... ?

f) You don't need me any more, ... ?

g) The ticket to London doesn't cost a lot, ... ?

h) Let's invite the Smiths from next door, ... ?

i) You aren't too busy to talk, ... ?

j) Jean owns a restaurant, ... ?

3 Rewrite each sentence, beginning as shown, so that the meaning stays the same.

a) Tony was not only late, but he had left all his books behind.
Not only *was Tony late, but he had left all his books behind.*

b) I had no sooner gone to bed than someone rang my doorbell.
No sooner ....

c) I have seldom stayed in a worse hotel.
Seldom ....

d) I have never heard such nonsense!
Never ....

e) I realised only then that I had lost my keys.
Only then ....

f) The economic situation has rarely been worse.
Rarely ....

g) The manager not once offered us an apology.
Not once ....

h) You should not send money to us by post under any circumstances.
Under no circumstances ....

i) I understood *Hamlet* only after seeing it on the stage.
Only after seeing *Hamlet* ....

j) The embassy staff little realised that Ted was a secret agent.
Little ....

4 Rewrite each sentence so that it begins with the word or words in *italics*.

a) The best time to buy a house is *now*.
Now is the best time to buy a house.

b) The bus came *round the corner*.
....

c) The price of petrol went *up*.
....

d) The Parthenon stands *on the top* of the Acropolis.
....

e) The wheels of the engine went *round and round*.
....

f) Winston Churchill lived *in this house*.
....

g) The flag went *down*.
....

h) The best part of the story comes *now*.
....

5 Decide which answer (A, B, C or D) best fits each space.

Asking for advice

You don't happen to know how this computer works, (1) ....*C*.......... ?
(2) .... had I bought it (3) .... I regretted spending so much
money! I haven't even got an instruction manual. (4) .... did I
completely fail to understand the instructions, (5) .... then I
accidentally threw the manual away. Now I'll never understand it,
(6) .... , I said to myself. (7) .... my weekend, I thought, but
then I remembered you. You've done a course on computers, (8) .... ?
Let's look at it together, (9) .... , and try to understand it. You press
this button first, (10) .... ? Then (11) .... this little light,
and a message that says 'Error'. It shouldn't do that, (12) .... ? You
can fix it, (13) .... ? Don't do that! This label says: '(14) ....
should an unqualified person remove this panel'. Well, you are unqualified,
(15) .... ? What do you mean, do it yourself!

1)	**A** are you	**B** is it	**C** do you	**D** isn't it
2)	**A** No sooner	**B** After	**C** Not only	**D** As soon as
3)	**A** that	**B** but	**C** and	**D** than
4)	**A** Not only	**B** Seldom	**C** Not once	**D** Only then
5)	**A** than	**B** but	**C** so	**D** and
6)	**A** can't I	**B** won't I	**C** will I	**D** can I
7)	**A** It goes	**B** Goes it	**C** Goes there	**D** There goes
8)	**A** isn't it	**B** haven't you	**C** didn't you	**D** don't you
9)	**A** do we	**B** don't it	**C** shall we	**D** aren't we
10)	**A** don't you	**B** isn't it	**C** can't you	**D** won't you
11)	**A** on comes	**B** comes on	**C** it comes on	**D** comes it on
12)	**A** does it	**B** should it	**C** shouldn't it	**D** won't it
13)	**A** isn't it	**B** don't you	**C** can't you	**D** can't it
14)	**A** Not only	**B** Only then	**C** Never	**D** Under no circumstances
15)	**A** isn't it	**B** are you	**C** don't you	**D** aren't you

Key points

1 In formal speech and writing it is possible to use inversion after negative
adverbs. The adverb has to be at the beginning of the sentence or clause.

2 Intonation carries important meaning in question tags. Rising tags are
questions, falling tags are checking information.

> *Your name's Pauline, isn't it?* (question)
>
> *Your name's Pauline, isn't it?* (checking)

3 Inversion with *come* and *go* is informal.
> *Look out, here comes the teacher!*

 SEE ALSO

Grammar 35: Consolidation 7

185

Explanations

Reason

■ *Because, as* and *since*

As and *since* have the meaning of *because* and can begin a sentence.

> ***As/since** it was late, we decided to go home.*

In formal, written language we can use *for* to mean *because*, but it cannot begin a sentence.

> *Peter has given up sailing, **for** he doesn't have the time.*

■ *Because of, on account of, due to* and *owing to*

We can use all these words in place of *because of*.

> *Everyone was depressed **on account of/due to/owing to** the bad weather.*

Note this difference:

> *Sue's **success** was **due to** her hard work.*   (noun + *be* + *due to*)
>
> *Sue **succeeded owing to** her hard work.*   (verb + *owing to*)

Text organizers

Grammar 13 and the first part of this unit cover linking words that join clauses within a sentence. There are also linking words that join ideas across sentences and paragraphs. These are sometimes called 'text organizers' because they make clear the organization of what we say or write. They are more common in writing or formal speech. They usually come at the start of a sentence and have a comma afterwards, but can come after a comma in the middle of a sentence.

■ Sequencing

We often number or order the points we are making.

> *First (of all) ..., Secondly ..., Next ..., Then ..., Finally/lastly/last of all ...*

In narrative, the sequence of events can be introduced by:

> *First ..., Then ..., After that ..., Finally/in the end ...*

■ Adding

We can introduce additional points.

> *Furthermore ..., Moreover ..., In addition to ..., As well as this ...,*
> *Besides this ...*

■ Giving opinions

We can introduce personal opinions.

> *Personally ..., In my own opinion/view ...*

■ Giving examples

We can introduce examples.

> *For example ..., For instance ...*

We can also use *such as* to give an example, but it is not used at the beginning of a sentence.

> *The factory produces electrical goods, **such as** food mixers and other kitchen appliances.*

■ Showing a result

Grammar 13 gave some informal ways to show a result. Formal ways include:

Consequently ..., As a result ..., Thus ...

■ Making a contrast

Grammar 13 gave some informal ways to make a contrast. Formal ways include:

On the other hand ..., However ..., Nevertheless ..., In contrast ...,
In comparison ...

■ Summarizing

We can summarize all the points we have made.

In conclusion ..., To sum up ...

Practice

1 <u>Underline</u> the most suitable word or phrase in each sentence.

a) Many people feel nervous about flying, and worry about the possibility of an accident. *Furthermore/<u>However</u>*, according to statistics, flying is actually safer than walking down the street.

b) Our local supermarket no longer opens every day, *as/on account of* very few people live in our village.

c) There are a number of objections to the planned motorway. *As well as this/First of all*, the new road will destroy valuable farming land. *In contrast/In addition to this*, it will bring thousands of vehicles and tourists. *As a result/For example*, our peaceful way of life will be destroyed forever.

d) We conducted a survey of accommodation in the town, and came up with some interesting results. The hotels we saw were rather expensive, and *consequently/moreover* the actual facilities on offer were not always impressive. *Besides this/In contrast*, there were many guest houses, offering just bed and breakfast, which were not only good value but also had much better rooms than the hotels did. *Finally/Personally*, I would recommend The Oaks, a particularly impressive guest house in Long Harbour Road.

e) *Owing to/Since* the increased demand for parking spaces, the company has decided to enlarge the car park. *Consequently/Nevertheless* the exit road on the west side of the car park will be closed from Monday to allow building work to begin.

2 Put one suitable word in each space.

a) ....*In*........ conclusion, I would like to thank you all for your help.

b) .... it's too late to finish the work today, we'll come back tomorrow.

c) The flight was delayed .... a result of the high winds.

d) This radio is expensive, but .... the other hand it has very good reception.

e) First .... all, I would like to welcome you to our annual dinner.

f) John is a hard worker. As .... as this, he is completely reliable.

g) Science has not entirely changed the way we think. .... instance, we still speak of the 'sunrise' although we know it is the Earth that is moving.

h) Although this building project seems attractive, in my .... it would be a mistake to spend so much money on it.

3 Decide which answer (A, B, C or D) best fits each space.

Owning a car

Owning a car has several advantages. (1) ....A......... you can go wherever you want, whenever you want. You don't have to depend on public transport and (2) .... you feel more independent. (3) .... you are able to give lifts to friends, or carry heavy loads of shopping. (4) .... , there can be problems, especially if you live in a city. Running a car can be expensive, and you have to spend money on items (5) .... petrol, servicing the car, and repairs. You might also have problems with parking, as everywhere is becoming more and more crowded with cars. (6) .... , most people feel that the advantages of owning a car outweigh the disadvantages.

   (7) .... most young people of my age start driving as soon as they can. (8) .... , I think that cars nowadays have become essential, but I also feel that they cause a lot of problems, (9) .... they are noisy and dirty. (10) .... , the large numbers of cars on the road means that most towns and cities are organized for the convenience of cars, and the needs of pedestrians are ignored.

1)	A First of all	B As a result	C Personally	D Besides this
2)	A however	B personally	C since	D as a result
3)	A In contrast	B In my view	C Besides this	D However
4)	A On the other hand	B To sum up	C Thus	D For example
5)	A as	B such as	C owing to	D then
6)	A Finally	B Secondly	C However	D As
7)	A For	B Next	C As well as this	D Consequently
8)	A For example	B Personally	C Nevertheless	D In comparison
9)	A for example	B however	C thus	D since
10)	A As a result	B Moreover	C Personally	D In comparison

Key points

1   Text organizers help readers and listeners to follow the development of an argument. Most of the expressions listed are formal in use.

2   Because text organizers make links across sentences, their meaning is only clear when you study the ideas that come before and after them (the whole context).

Pronouns

Explanations

It and *there*

It generally refers to something already mentioned. *There* is used with *be* to say that something exists.

> **There** is **a good film** on tonight. **It** stars Kim Basinger.

It is also used in some phrases which do not have a grammatical subject.

> *It's raining again.   It's half past six.*
> *It doesn't matter.   It's time to go.*

It and adjectives

It is also used in the pattern *it* + adjective + infinitive/-*ing*.

> *It's good to see you.   It was nice meeting you.*

In informal speech, *it* and the verb *be* are often left out.

> **Good** to see you.   **Nice** meeting you.

One

- *One* can be used as a pronoun, and has a plural *ones*.

  > *I don't like **this one**. I only like **green ones**.*

- The phrase *one another* refers to two subjects.

  > *Martin and David can't stand **one another**.*

  This means that Martin can't stand David, and David can't stand Martin.

- In normal conversation we use *you* to refer to *anybody*.

  > *As **you** get older **you** tend to forget things.*

  But in formal speech and writing we can use *one* with this meaning. This is considered over-formal by many speakers.

  > *What does **one** wear to a dinner of this kind?*
  > *It's not pleasant to hear **oneself** described by **one's** employees.*

Someone, everyone, anyone, somewhere, etc

- *-body* can be used instead of *-one* without a change in meaning.

- Words beginning *some* or *any* follow the usual patterns for these words, with *any* words normally used in questions and after negatives.

  > *There's **something** under the desk. Can you see **anything**?*

  But we can use *some* in a question if it is an offer or request.

  > *Are you looking for **somewhere** to stay?*
  > *Could **someone** help me, please?*

  And we use *any* in positive statements where we mean *it doesn't matter which* or *there is no limit to the possibilities*.

  > *Please sit **anywhere** you like.*
  > ***Anyone** who's tall will do.*

What **as a pronoun**	*What* can be used as a pronoun meaning *the thing(s) that.* **What** *we need is a hammer.*

Whatever, whoever,
wherever, whenever,
why ever, however

- These words are used to add emphasis to the question word.
  What you are doing? → **Whatever** *are you doing?* (shows more surprise)

- We also use these words to mean *any at all.*
  Whatever *you say is wrong!* (Anything at all you say ...)

Reflexive
pronouns

- Reflexive pronouns can be used for emphasis.
  Why don't you do it **yourself***?*
  I paid for the tickets **myself***.*

- They are also used for some actions that we do to ourselves.
  Sue **cut herself***. I have* **hurt myself***. Did you* **enjoy yourself***?*
  But other verbs are not normally used with a reflexive pronoun, even though
  they are in other languages. Examples include: *change* (clothes), *complain,*
  decide, dress, feel, meet, relax, remember, rest, sit down, stand up, wake up, wash,
  wonder, worry

Possessives: parts
of the body

When we talk about parts of the body we often use a preposition + *the* rather
than a preposition + a possessive adjective.
    Jack gave Bill a punch **on the nose***. I grabbed him* **by the arm***.*
    Jack punched Bill **on the nose***. I looked him* **in the eyes***.*

Practice

1 Rewrite each sentence, beginning as shown, so that it has the same meaning.

a) The person who stole the painting must have been tall.

Whoever .....*stole the painting must have been tall.*.....

b) I don't mind what you do, but don't tell Jane I was here.

Whatever ....

c) What on earth is the time?

Whatever ....

d) I'd like to know why you told me a lie.

Why ever ....

e) Every time I go on holiday, the weather gets worse.

Whenever ....

f) Tell me where you have been!

Wherever ....

g) How on earth did you know I was going to be here?

However ....

h) I won't believe you, no matter what you say.

Whatever ....

2 Complete the second sentence so that it has a similar meaning to the first sentence, using the word given. Do not change the word given. You must use between two and five words, including the word given.

a) John patted my back.

gave

John .... *gave me a pat on* .... the back.

b) Don't hold a rabbit's ears and pick it up.

by

Don't .... the ears.

c) I'll never be able to look at Tanya's face again.

in

I'll never be able to look .... again.

d) Sue grabbed the thief's arm.

by

Sue .... arm.

e) Helen took the baby's hand.

by

Helen .... hand.

f) The bee stung my arm.

me

The bee .... arm.

g) Somebody gave me a black eye.

punched

Somebody .... eye.

h) Jane patted the dog's head.

on

Jane .... head.

i) 'It's my arm! I'm hit!' said Billy the Kid.

wounded

'I'm .... ,' said Billy the Kid.

j) I felt someone pat my shoulder.

me

I felt someone .... shoulder.

3 Complete each sentence so that it has a similar meaning to the first.

a) The local cinema has a good film on at the moment.

There .....*is a good film on at the local cinema*....... at the moment.

b) I can't drink coffee so late at night.

It's .... so late at night.

c) Don't worry if you can't answer all the questions.

It doesn't .... all the questions.

d) The fridge is empty.

There .... fridge.

e) This journey has been tiring.

It .... journey.

f) The station is far away.

It .... station.

g) Let's have a break now.

It's .... for a break now.

h) I enjoyed seeing you.

It .... you.

4 Rewrite each sentence, beginning as shown. Do not change the meaning.

a) Was it enjoyable at the beach, Joe?

Did you ....*enjoy yourself at the beach, Joe?*..........................

b) We really need a new fridge.

What ....

c) There's a lot of fog today.

It's ....

d) People who believe in ghosts are a bit crazy!

Anyone ....

e) Just call me any time you need me.

Whenever ....

f) I was very interested in what we talked about.

It was interesting ....

g) John is hurt.

John has ....

h) Why did you do that?

Whatever ....

5 Complete each sentence with the most suitable word or phrase.

a) I like this painting but I don't think much of those ....*C*.......... .

A) rest   B) other   C) ones   D) besides

b) What would .... like to do this morning?

A) someone   B) one   C) yourself   D) you

c) Did you enjoy .... ?

A) at the party   B) the party   C) yourself the party

D) with yourself at the party

d) .... nothing much to do in this town.

A) There's   B) It's not   C) There's not   D) It's

e) .... you do, don't tell Harry that we've lost his camera.

A) Anything   B) What   C) Whatever   D) It's better

f) One prefers to shop at Harrods, ... ?

A) doesn't one   B) isn't it   C) don't you   D) isn't one

g) .... didn't you tell me that you felt too ill to work?

A) Whoever   B) Whatever   C) However   D) Why ever

h) Then George punched the police officer .... the face!

A) at   B) on   C) to   D) in

i) Harry shook my hand and said, 'Pleased .... you'.

A) to meet   B) to introduce   C) to shake   D) to acquaint

j) Please invite .... you like to the reception.

A) one   B) anyone   C) ones   D) all

Key points

1   In some cases, *it* does not refer to another noun. Instead, it stands as a subject because the phrase does not have a real subject.

> *It's late.*   *It's a nice day.*   *It's five o'clock.*

2   It is possible to use *some* and words made from it in questions. This is the case with offers and requests.

> *Are you looking for **someone**?*

3   It is possible to use *any* and words made from it in positive statements. This is the case when we mean *no limit*.

> *Call me any time you like.*

4   Some verbs (*cut, enjoy, hurt*) require a reflexive (*myself*, etc) if there is no other object.

> *I enjoyed the party.*   *Martha cut her finger.*
> *I enjoyed **myself**.*   *Martha cut **herself**.*

→ SEE ALSO

Grammar 35: Consolidation 7

Explanations

Common spelling problems

- Words ending in *-ful*
  There is only one *l* when *-ful* is a suffix.
  useful   helpful

- Doubling of consonants
  Adjectives form adverbs by adding *-ly*.
  usefully   helpfully
  Words with one syllable, ending in one vowel and one consonant, double the consonant when adding *-ing, -ed* or *-er*.
  swim swimming   fit fitted   thin thinner
  Most two-syllable words ending in one vowel and one consonant also double the last consonant, especially when the stress is on the second syllable.
  prefer preferred   BUT   **bother bothering**
  A common exception is   *travel   traveller.*

- Words ending in *-y*
  One syllable nouns ending *-y* change *-y* to *-i* in plurals. One-syllable verbs ending *-y* also change *-y* to *-i* in the present simple and past simple.
  spy   spies
  try   tries   tried
  But one-syllable words ending in one vowel and *-y* do not change.
  boy   boys
  One-syllable words do not change when we add *-ful* and *-ness*.
  joy joyful   shy shyness

  Two-syllable words change.
  reply   replies   replied
  happy   happiness
  beauty   beautiful
  But two-syllable words ending in one vowel and *-y* do not change.
  destroy   destroyed

  These rules do not apply when we add *-ing*.
  try   trying   study   studying   annoy   annoying

- Words with *ie* and *ei*
  The general rule is *i* before *e* except after *c*, as long as the sound is /iː/.
  receive   relief
  BUT *feign*   (the sound is not /iː/)

Spelling and pronunciation

In English, one spelling can have different sounds, and the same sound can have different spellings. Note the ways of spelling the underlined sounds in each list below.

If you check the pronunciation of the whole word by looking at the phonetic script in a dictionary you will find that the sound / ə / (called schwa) is very common in English. It is always unstressed. If you beat the rhythm of a word with your hand then / ə / is often the 'up' (unstressed) beat.

- Vowel sounds

/ ʌ /	l<u>o</u>ve	s<u>u</u>dden	bl<u>oo</u>d	c<u>u</u>ff	R<u>ou</u>gh	L<u>o</u>ndon	br<u>o</u>ther
/əʊ/	b<u>oa</u>t	p<u>o</u>st	alth<u>ou</u>gh	kn<u>ow</u>	t<u>oe</u>		
/eə/	<u>air</u>	th<u>ere</u>	b<u>are</u>	w<u>ear</u>			
/ ɑː/	h<u>ear</u>t	p<u>ar</u>t	st<u>a</u>ff	<u>a</u>sk			
/ ɜː/	w<u>or</u>d	h<u>ear</u>d	f<u>ur</u>ther	exp<u>er</u>t	h<u>ur</u>t		
/aʊ/	n<u>ow</u>	sh<u>ou</u>t	pl<u>ough</u>	dr<u>ow</u>n			
/ ɒ /	l<u>o</u>t	st<u>o</u>p	<u>o</u>ff				
/ eɪ /	w<u>ai</u>t	g<u>a</u>te	w<u>ei</u>ght	gr<u>ea</u>t	l<u>ay</u>		
/ aɪ /	br<u>igh</u>t	h<u>eigh</u>t	s<u>i</u>te	<u>eye</u>			
/ ɔː/	d<u>oor</u>	p<u>our</u>	d<u>augh</u>ter				
schwa / ə /	p<u>o</u>tato	<u>a</u>round	s<u>u</u>ggest	p<u>er</u>haps	neckl<u>a</u>ce		

- Consonant sounds

/ ʃ /	<u>sh</u>ame	deli<u>ci</u>ous	posi<u>ti</u>on	in<u>s</u>urance
/ tʃ /	<u>ch</u>urch	furni<u>t</u>ure	wa<u>tch</u>es	
/ ʒ /	lei<u>s</u>ure	confu<u>si</u>on	mea<u>s</u>ure	

- Words ending in -*ough*

Like *now*	*plough*	*bough*	
Like *cuff*	*enough*	*rough*	*tough*
Like *toe*	*though*	*dough*	
Like *off*	*cough*		

- Words containing -*st* where *t* is not pronounced

listen	*glisten*	*hasten*	*fasten*
castle	*whistle*	*bristle*	*mistletoe*

- Words containing -*mb* and -*bt* where *b* is not pronounced

plumber	*thumb*	*comb*	*lamb*	*dumb*	*tomb*
debt	*doubt*	*subtle*			

Practice

1 Correct any words spelled incorrectly.

a) studing   *studying*

b) destroying   ....

c) donkies   ....

d) flys   ....

e) niece   ....

f) hurryed   ....

g) furnichure   ....

h) enough   ....

i) wellcome   ....

j) hotter   ....

k) reciept   ....

l) wonderfull   ....

m) swimming   ....

n) regreted   ....

o) hopefuly   ....

p) applying   ....

q) heard   ....

r) inshurance   ....

s) happily   ....

t) advertisment   ....

2 Find a word from the box which rhymes with each word given.

home	go	white	~~search~~	store	stuff	come	plumber	wait	cow

a) church   *search*

b) hate   ....

c) rough   ....

d) throw   ....

e) comb   ....

f) dumb   ....

g) plough   ....

h) height   ....

i) summer   ....

j) pour   ....

3   Write each word ending in the suffix given.

a) supply (ing)   ...*supplying*...

b) destroy (ed)   ....

c) apply (ed)   ....

d) lonely (ness)   ....

e) employ (s)   ....

f) cry (s)   ....

g) silly (ness)   ....

h) annoy (s)   ....

i) beauty (ful)   ....

j) pretty (ness)   ....

4   Find one word in each group of words which does not have the same vowel sound (sounds are underlined in two-syllable words).

a) become sung company cold flood ....*cold*.......

b) plate treat wait weight great ....

c) lose used choose blouse few ....

d) doubt bough ought now shout ....

e) lost post toast ghost host ....

f) mist missed list iced kissed ....

g) love done gone sunk won ....

h) bird search heart word church ....

i) two show though go owe ....

j) about wonder suppose refer colour ....

5   Correct any words spelled incorrectly.

a) sincerly   ...*sincerely*...   dictionry   ....

b) different   .... intresting   ....

c) loverly   .... necessary   ....

d) writing   .... unninteresting   ....

e) pulover   .... definitly   ....

f) friend   .... responsable   ....

g) holliday   .... quantity   ....

h) likelihood   .... lugage   ....

i) impatient   .... student   ....

j) finaly   .... pavement   ....

1 **Put one suitable word in each space.**

The first day in the job

I will always remember my first day working at the Excelsior Food Company.
First of (1) .... *all* .... , I was given a greasy overall. (2) .... had
worn it before had certainly never washed it! When I mentioned this to the
foreman he said, 'You're not afraid of a bit of dirt, (3) .... you?' I
wanted to say that I thought (4) .... was supposed to be a high
standard of cleanliness in a food factory, but I managed to control
(5) .... Then I was given my first job, (6) .... involved
sweeping the floor. (7) .... only was my overall filthy, but the whole
factory looked as if (8) .... had ever cleaned it properly.

(9) .... were also (10) .... I later discovered to be pigs'
ears scattered around the place. (11) .... it was my first day, I didn't
say anything about this. (12) .... that I had to put pies into boxes for
the rest of the morning. (13) .... was supposed to put them into the
cold-store, but (14) .... this person was, they had obviously forgotten
about it. As a (15) .... , there was soon a huge pile of boxes waiting to
be moved. Then I discovered that I was supposed to be moving them!

2 **Complete the second sentence so that it has a similar meaning to the first
sentence.**

a) Under no circumstances should you press both buttons at once.
You *...should never press both buttons at once under
...... any circumstances.*

b) It was cold, so I decided to wear two pullovers.
As ....

c) Did you have a good time at the party?
Did you enjoy ....

d) Outside the cinema somebody grabbed my arm.
Outside the cinema I ....

e) The army's defeat was due to poor organization.
The army was defeated ....

f) Jean not once offered her boss a word of apology.
Not once ....

g) There's no food in the house, I'm afraid.

There's nothing ....

h) It's pointless going on any further tonight.

There's ....

i) It's difficult to describe what Sally saw.

What ....

j) I have seldom had a more relaxing holiday.

Seldom ....

3   Complete each sentence with the most suitable word or phrase.

a) One really shouldn't drink too much, ...*D*.......... ?

   A) does one   B) should you   C) do you   D) should one

b) .... , I would like to propose a toast.

   A) For example   B) In conclusion   C)   On the other hand   D) Thus

c) Do you think .... could help me choose a pair of trousers?

   A) someone   B) anyone   C) whoever   D) there

d) .... doesn't seem to be anyone at home.

   A) It   B) One   C) There   D) Whenever

e) .... did I realise that the murderer was still in the house!

   A) Seldom   B) Under no circumstances   C) Only after   D) Only then

f) .... , I don't believe that prices will rise next year.

   A) In contrast   B) Personally   C) Not only   D) Whatever

g) You're covered in mud! .... is your mother going to say?

   A) Rarely   B) Furthermore   C) Whatever   D) On account of

h) Oh bother, ... the bus I wanted to catch!

   A) wherever   B) it's left   C) there goes   D) owing to

i) Please help yourselves to .... you like.

   A) whoever   B) nothing   C) everywhere   D) anything

j) Nobody's got to stay late this evening, ... ?

   A) is it   B) have they   C) isn't it   D) don't they

4   **Look carefully at each line. Some of the lines are correct, and some have a word which should not be there. Tick each correct line. If a line has a word which should not be there, write the word in the space.**

Kidnapped by aliens

I am sure you have heard of Marion Taylor,	..............✓..............
haven't you? Marion was the young girl she	.........*she*.........
kidnapped by aliens in 1993. Not only that was	1) ....
she given a ride to a distant planet, but whether she	2) ....
also managed to take some photos of the aliens	3) ....
who they had taken her prisoner, since she had been	4) ....
carrying herself a camera when they captured her.	5) ....
Whenever I hear stories like this I assume so	6) ....
that they have been made them up. It is hard to believe	7) ....
Marion's story, owing to the fact that she was	8) ....
only ten years old at the time. Besides this, it was	9) ....
turned out that she spent most of her time watching	10) ....
science fiction videos. One cannot really believe in	11) ....
that there are really little green aliens who they fly	12) ....
all the way to our planet just so that they can kidnap	13) ....
people. Nevertheless, although Marion became	14) ....
famous and her photos were bought by a newspaper	15) ....
for a great deal of money.	

1 Complete each sentence with a word from the box.

buffet	coach station	departure lounge	harbour	quay
cabin	~~deck~~	destination	platform	runway

a) Most of the young people on the boat slept on the ....*deck*............. in their sleeping bags.

b) As the train drew in to the station, Terry could see her sister waiting on the ....

c) I was so nervous about flying that I left my bag in the ....

d) By the time I got to the .... , the bus to Scotland had left.

e) As soon as the boat left the .... , the storm began.

f) We hadn't had anything to eat, but luckily there was a .... on the train.

g) I'm afraid there is only one first-class .... free on the boat.

h) Tim reached Paris safely, but his luggage didn't reach its ....

i) There was a queue of cars on the .... , waiting for the car-ferry to the island.

j) Our plane nearly crashed into a fire-engine on the ....

2 <u>Underline</u> the most suitable word or words.

a) David's plane was *cancelled/<u>delayed</u>* by thick fog.

b) The ship's owner agreed to give the *crew/passengers* a pay-rise.

c) The plane from Geneva has just *grounded/landed*.

d) We hope that you will enjoy your *flight/flying*.

e) Because of heavy snow, their plane was *diverted/deviated* to Luton.

f) I won't be long. I'm just packing my last *luggage/suitcase*.

g) You have to *check in/check up* an hour before the plane leaves.

h) All duty free goods must be *declared/surrendered* at customs.

i) The plane *took off/took up* and was soon high over the city.

j) I bought a *simple/single* ticket, as I was going to return by car.

k) A sign above the seats in the plane says 'Fasten your *life belt/seat belt*'.

l) On the plane the *flight attendant/waitress* brought me a newspaper.

3 Use a word or words from exercises 1 or 2 to complete each sentence. The word may be in a different form.

a) I had to .... *cancel* .... my tickets, because I was ill and couldn't travel.

b) The train for London is now arriving at .... three.

c) The plane .... on time but arrived half an hour late.

d) We finally reached our .... after travelling all day.

e) It was hard to find a seat on the train as there were so many
    ....

f) While we were waiting at the station we had a bite to eat in the
    ....

g) I felt seasick so I went to my .... and tried to sleep.

h) Do you want a return ticket, or a .... ?

i) The customs officer asked Bill if he had anything to ....

j) There is a small .... here for fishing boats and yachts.

k) How much .... can I take with me on the plane?

l) The 8.55 from Hull will be 30 minutes late. We apologise for the
    ....

4 Match the words in the box with a suitable definition (a–j).

| an expedition | a flight | a tour | a voyage | a package tour |
| an itinerary | a trip | travel | a~~cruise~~ | a crossing |

a) A journey by ship for pleasure. .... *a cruise* ....

b) A journey by plane. ....

c) The plan of a journey. ....

d) An informal word for *journey*. Sometimes meaning *a short journey*. ....

e) A journey for a scientific or special purpose. ....

f) A holiday which includes organised travel and accommodation. ....

g) Taking journeys, as a general idea. ....

h) A journey by sea. ....

i) An organised journey to see the sights of a place. ....

j) A journey from one side of the sea to the other. ....

5 Use a word from 4 in each sentence.

a) The travel agent will send you the ...*itinerary*... for your trip.

b) My neighbours went on a guided .... of Rome.

c) Last time I went from England to France we had a very rough ....

d) The first prize in the competition is a luxury Mediterranean ....

e) When you go on a/an .... , you pay one price for everything.

f) The college organized a/an .... to search for the ancient ruins.

g) Olympic announces the arrival of .... OA 269 from Athens.

h) The *Titanic* sank on its first .... in 1912.

i) .... is one of my main interests.

j) Mr Dean is away on a business .... at the moment. Can I help you?

6 Replace the words in *italics* in each sentence with a word from the box.

camp-site	book	hostel	accommodation	double room
hitch-hike	~~a fortnight~~	guest-house	vacancy	porter

a) I stayed in France for *two weeks* last year. ...*a fortnight*...

b) It's difficult to find *anywhere to stay* here in the summer. ....

c) We had no money so we had to *get lifts in other people's cars*. ....

d) I'd like a room for the night please. A *room for two people*. ....

e) The place where we stayed wasn't a hotel but *a private house where you pay to stay and have meals*. ....

f) I'd like to *reserve* three single rooms for next week, please. ....

g) It was raining, and we couldn't find *a place to put our tent*. ....

h) I'd like a room for the night, please. Do you have a *free one*? ....

i) The school has its own *place for students to stay*. ....

j) We gave a tip to the *person who carried our bags in the hotel*. ....

7 Use a dictionary to find compound words beginning *sea-*. Complete each sentence with one of these words.

a) Last year we didn't go to the mountains. We went to the ...*seaside*... instead.

b) There's a restaurant near the harbour that serves wonderful ....

c) The beach was covered in piles of smelly green ....

d) This town is very high up. It's a thousand metres above ....

e) We drove along the .... but we couldn't find anywhere to park.

f) Tourists were throwing bread to the .... flying behind the ship.

g) Luckily I had taken some travel pills so I didn't feel ....

h) Children were building sand castles on the ....

8   Choose the most suitable word or phrase to complete each sentence.

a) They .... *C* .... all day swimming and sunbathing at the beach.

A) did   B) used   C) spent   D) occupied

b) The hotel room .... over a beautiful garden.

A) viewed out   B) faced up   C) opened up   D) looked out

c) We didn't .... to the station in time to catch the train.

A) get   B) reach   C) arrive   D) make

d) I was in such a hurry that I left one of my bags ....

A) out   B) aside   C) on   D) behind

e) Mr Hill had his money stolen and couldn't .... his hotel bill.

A) pay up   B) pay   C) pay for   D) pay out

f) Jane lost her case. It did not have a/an .... with her name on.

A) ticket   B) poster   C) label   D) identification

g) Take the bus, and .... at Oxford Circus.

A) get out   B) get off   C) get down   D) get away

h) I was too tired to .... my suitcase.

A) unpack   B) empty   C) put out   D) disorder

i) On the first day of our holiday we just .... by the hotel pool.

A) enjoyed   B) calmed   C) comforted   D) relaxed

j) The wind was blowing so much that we couldn't .... our tent.

A) raise   B) put up   C) make up   D) build

9   Rewrite each sentence, beginning as given, so that it contains an expression with *have*.

a) I sunbathed for a while, and then went swimming.

I sunbathed for a while, and then ...*I had a swim.*.......................................

b) I really enjoyed my holiday last year.

I ....

c) David crashed his car while he was driving to Spain.

David ....

d) When we left, Maria wished us a safe journey.

'Goodbye', said Maria, 'and ....,'

e) Most of the people on the beach were wearing very little.

Most of the people on the beach ....

....

f) We couldn't decide about our holiday but then Sue thought of something.

We couldn't decide about our holiday until Sue ....

....

g) There was a party at Martin's house last night.

Martin ....

h) Brenda couldn't go away for the weekend because she was busy.

Brenda couldn't go away for the weekend because she ....

....

i) Ian didn't know how to water-ski, but he gave it a try.

Ian didn't know how to water-ski but he ....

....

j) Laura suspected that the hotel food was going to be bad.

Laura ....

10 **Decide which answer (A, B, C or D) best fits each space.**

Holidays

Is it better to go on a package (1) ....*B*.......... , or to (2) .... on your
own? I suppose the answer depends on what kind of (3) .... you are. A
complicated tour organized by a travel (4) .... has some advantages.
You have a/an (5) .... , which gives you definite (6) .... and
arrival dates, and a list of all your (7) .... The (8) .... may
be cheaper, as it has been (9) .... in advance, so you spend less time
worrying about where you are going to (10) .... If you book your
own hotel, you might have trouble finding a/an (11) .... , unless you
are going to stay for a (12) .... , for example. On the other hand,
organizing your own (13) .... can be fun. Many students
(14) .... or buy cheap train tickets, and (15) .... the night in
student hostels or guest-houses.

1) A travel	B tour	C journey	D cruise
2) A travel	B trip	C voyage	D tourist
3) A voyager	B passenger	C tourist	D mover
4) A office	B agent	C tour	D operation
5) A timetable	B scheme	C notice	D itinerary
6) A departure	B parting	C leave	D quitting
7) A cancellations	B expeditions	C organisations	D destinations
8) A bedrooms	B staying	C flat	D accommodation
9) A preserved	B booked	C reservation	D hotels
10) A stay	B pass	C live	D cross
11) A empty	B free	C vacancy	D available
12) A fortnight	B daytime	C fifteen days	D passage
13) A voyage	B expedition	C trip	D package
14) A auto-stop	B hitch-hike	C lift	D journey
15) A have	B at	C for	D spend

Work and employment

1 Match each job in box A with a place in box B. More than one answer may be possible.

A ~~cashier~~ farmer mechanic photographer receptionist cook hairdresser miner pilot vicar dentist librarian musician porter waiter

B ~~bank~~ garage studio kitchen coal-mine cockpit hotel office surgery salon field concert hall restaurant church library

cashier/bank ....

....

....

2 Match each job from the box with the sentence which best refers to the job.

accountant   chef   estate agent   plumber   refuse collector
firefighter   carpenter   ~~vet~~

a) Yesterday I had to give an injection to an injured bull.   ....*vet*........

b) I get rather tired of picking up rubbish all day.   ....

c) I can help you sell your house.   ....

d) I can make new doors for the wardrobe if you like.   ....

e) Make sure that the fish is fresh by looking at the eyes.   ....

f) I'll come round and replace all the pipes in the kitchen.   ....

g) Unless you keep the receipts you'll pay more tax.   ....

h) The cause was either an electrical fault or a cigarette.   ....

3 Which person from 1 and 2 above would you need in each situation?

a) One of the radiators has burst and flooded your bedroom.   ..*plumber*..

b) You have to carry a lot of heavy bags at the airport.   ....

c) You think you need three fillings.   ....

d) Your fringe is too long and you want a perm.   ....

e) The floorboards in the living room need replacing.   ....

f) Your pet goat has started sneezing.   ....

g) You have read the menu twice and you are feeling hungry.   ....

h) Your car makes a funny whistling noise.   ....

4   Complete each sentence with a word from the box. Use the words more than once.

business	job	~~living~~	work

a) Jack makes his ......*living*..... working as a journalist.

b) She has just left to go to .... , I'm afraid.

c) They worked very hard and now have their own ....

d) There are still nearly two million people without ....

e) The cost of .... has risen greatly over recent years.

f) Stop interfering! This is none of your ....

g) Lucy has a very good .... in an international company.

h) I can't come out tonight. I've got too much .... to do.

i) Some ....-men came and dug a hole in the road outside.

j) An early .... by Picasso was sold for £3,000,000.

5   Complete each sentence with a word from the box.

call	draw	fall	get	take	come	face	fill	~~go~~	turn

a) I think we should ....*go*......... over our plan again before we tell the managing director.

b) Have you .... up with any ideas for advertising the new products?

c) Our deal with the Chinese company may .... through, but we can sell the machinery to the German firm if necessary.

d) You have to .... in this form, and return it to the manager.

e) She didn't .... on with her boss, so she left the company.

f) If they don't give us a better price, we'll .... down their offer.

g) I'm afraid we have to .... up to the fact that we are losing money.

h) Our lawyers are going to .... up a new contract tomorrow.

i) A multinational company is trying to .... over our firm, but we want to stay independent.

j) We had to .... off the office party because of the economic situation.

6   Complete each sentence (a–h) with a suitable ending (1–8). Use each ending once.

a) If you work hard, the company will give you ....4..........

b) In a different job I could get a higher ....

c) The best way to find new staff is to put a/an ....

d) Because he had stolen the money, we decided that ....

e) She has a pleasant personality but hasn't got the right ....

f) In the meeting we are going to discuss the ....

g) I think it would be a good idea to send in your ....

h) We cannot give you the job without ....

1   qualifications for a job of this kind.

2   advertisement in the local press on Friday.

3   application for the job as soon as possible.

4   promotion to a more responsible position.

5   references from your previous employer.

6   dismissing him was the only possible action we could take.

7   salary and better conditions of employment.

8   appointment of a new sales representative.

7   Use the word given in capitals at the end of each line to form a word that fits in the space in the same line.

Leaving a job

I recently left my job in an ......*advertising*.... agency   ADVERTISEMENT

after a disagreement with my boss. She accepted my

(2) .... but warned me that because of the   RESIGN

(3) .... situation, I might have to get used to the   ECONOMY

idea of being (4) .... for a while. I thought that she   EMPLOY

was trying to make a point, but after I had made over

fifty (5) .... to other companies, I realised that she   APPLY

was right. Although I am a (6) .... designer, I   QUALIFICATIONS

didn't receive any offers of a job. After that I tried

working from home, but it was not very (7) .... Then   PROFIT

I became an (8) .... in a fast-food restaurant,   EMPLOY

even though my (9) .... were extremely low.   EARN

I wish I had accepted early (10) .... from my old job.   RETIRE

That is what I disagreed with my boss about!

8 <u>Underline</u> the most suitable word or phrase.

a) The building workers were paid their *income/salary/<u>wages</u>* every Friday.

b) She's only been here three weeks. It's a/an *overtime/temporary* job.

c) When he retired he received a monthly *bonus/pension/reward*.

d) Apparently she *earns/gains/wins* over £60,000 a year.

e) While the boss is away, Sue will be *in charge/in control/in place* of the office.

f) Could I have two days *away/off/out* next week to visit my mother?

g) Paul was always arriving late, and in the end he was *pushed/sacked/thrown*.

h) When I left the job, I had to hand in my *application/dismissal/notice* three weeks beforehand.

i) How much exactly do you *do/make/take* in your new job?

j) If you have to travel on company business, we will pay your *costs/expenses/needs*.

9 Rewrite each sentence so that it contains the word or words given, and so that the meaning stays the same. Do not change the words given in any way.

a) Terry works in a different place now.   JOB

   Terry has a different job now.

b) A good boss looks after everyone in the company.   EMPLOYER

   ....

c) I am sure you will learn a lot in this job.   EXPERIENCE

   ....

d) This job is a good way to earn money, but that's all.   LIVING

   ....

e) The firm gave me a rise after I had worked there a year.   RAISED

   ....

f) The company was profitable last year.   MADE

   ....

g) I had to be interviewed at head office.   ATTEND

   ....

h) My annual salary is £12,000.   A YEAR

   ....

i) Jill is employed by a firm of accountants.   WORKS

   ....

j) We advertised the job in the paper.   PUT

   ....

10 **Decide which answer (A, B, C or D) best fits each space.**

Choosing a job

One of the most difficult decisions is choosing what to do for a
(1) ....*B*......... . For example, do you want to follow a definite
(2) .... , and (3) .... a low (4) .... at the beginning,
but have good (5) .... in a company that trains its (6) .... ?
Or are you more interested in taking any kind of work, because you need a/an
(7) .... ? You may have to (8) .... the fact that a good
(9) .... can be difficult to find. In that case, why not take a
(10) .... one? You will gain some useful (11) .... Remember
that even if you have the right (12) .... , you may have to
(13) .... lots of application forms before you are asked to
(14) .... an interview. But don't worry if you don't know what you
want to (15) .... exactly. You'll enjoy finding out!

1) A salary	B living	C employee	D work
2) A company	B training	C business	D career
3) A earn	B gain	C win	D take
4) A money	B profit	C cheque	D salary
5) A hopes	B prospects	C futures	D promotions
6) A employers	B crew	C staff	D persons
7) A money	B cash	C account	D income
8) A face up to	B go over	C come up with	D call off
9) A work	B labour	C job	D seat
10) A temporary	B overtime	C profitable	D short
11) A experiences	B experienced	C experience	D experiencing
12) A qualifications	B exams	C letters	D degrees
13) A fall through	B get on	C turn down	D fill in
14) A be	B attend	C make	D advertise
15) A work	B job	C do	D employ

Sport and leisure

1 Complete each sentence with a word from the box.

handlebars	racket	rope	glasses	net	~~costume~~
whistle	saddle	gloves	rod	club	ice

a) When Brenda entered the swimming competition she bought a new
   ......*costume*...... .

b) I learned to ride a horse without using a ....

c) Gemma tried to hit the golf-ball with her .... , but missed it.

d) After the tennis match, one of the players jumped over the ....

e) Diana's bike crashed into a tree, and she was thrown over the ....

f) A mountain-climber's life may depend on their ....

g) Open-air skating can be dangerous if the .... is too thin.

h) Peter put his .... in front of his face to protect himself from his
   opponent's punches.

i) Suddenly the referee blew his .... and pointed to the penalty spot.

j) Skiing can be dangerous if you don't wear dark ....

k) I had to play the doubles match with a borrowed ....

l) Terry went fishing with the new .... his parents gave him.

2 Match the words in the box with a suitable comment (a–h).

billiards	crossword	embroidery	hiking	draughts
gambling	~~cards~~	model-making		

a) Catherine dealt, and gave me the ace, king and queen of hearts.
   ......*cards*......

b) You need a small needle, and threads of different colours. ....

c) I couldn't do ten down, so I used the dictionary. ....

d) Ian glued the parts together wrongly because he didn't read the instructions.

   ....

e) When Ellen is losing, she knocks the pieces off the board. ....

f) The path we want doesn't seem to be on the map. ....

g) Nigel missed the red, and put the pink in the pocket by mistake.

   ....

h) I want to put £20 on 'Ealing Comedy' to win in the 4.30 at York.

   ....

3   Underline the most suitable word.

a) Sue came first in the 5000 metre *competition/game/race*.

b) Jack and Eddie arranged to meet outside the football *ground/field/pitch*.

c) Brenda goes jogging every morning to keep *exercised/fit/trained*.

d) Our team *beat/defeated/won* the match by two goals to nil.

e) The local stadium isn't large enough for so many *audience/viewers/spectators*.

f) I'm afraid I don't find basketball very *interested/interesting*.

g) The final result was a/an *draw/equal/score*.

h) Norman won first *medal/prize/reward* in the cookery competition.

i) All *competitors/rivals/supporters* for the race should make their way to the track.

j) Collecting matchboxes is Rebecca's favourite *leisure/occupation/pastime*.

4   Replace the word or words in *italics* in each sentence with a word from the box.

arranged	outdoors	record	second	captain	postponed	referee
side	champion	~~professionally~~	score	spare		

a) Mary plays tennis *as a way of earning her living.* professionally

b) Tomorrow's hockey match has been *put off for another time.* ....

c) In motor racing last year William Green was the *best driver of all.* ....

d) The player with the lowest *number of points* wins the game. ....

e) A match between the two top teams has been *fixed* for next month.

   ....

f) I like going swimming in my *free* time. ....

g) Jane Briggs was *the runner-up* in the 100 metres hurdles. ....

h) Who is the *player in charge* of your football team? ....

i) She won all her matches this season, which is a *best ever performance*.

   ....

j) Charles was sent off for punching the *person who controls the match.*

   ....

k) We decided to hold this year's dancing competition *in the open air.* ....

l) Everyone agreed that United were the best *team.* ....

5 Use the word given in capitals at the end of each line to form a word that fits in the space in the same line.

How a hobby can make you angry!

Recently I decided to take up (1) .*photography*. as a hobby. PHOTOGRAPH

I like taking snaps, but I am not very (2) .... SKILL

My snaps are either a complete (3) .... for FAIL

technical reasons, or are just not very (4) .... First IMAGINE

I decided that to be (5) .... , I would have to buy new SUCCESS

equipment. Just then I had an (6) .... piece of good EXPECT

luck. A friend who works in a camera shop said she

could sell me a (7) .... camera. A customer had VALUE

left it at the shop to be repaired, but there had been

a (8) .... , and it was actually for sale. UNDERSTAND

I thought this was a rather (9) .... explanation BELIEF

and so I asked her some more questions. She said

she had had a (10) .... with the customer and he AGREE

had thrown the camera at her because she disliked his photos!

6 Choose the most suitable word or phrase to complete each sentence.

a) Mary stopped swimming and just ....*B*........ on the surface.

   A) sank   B) floated   C) dived   D) poured

b) Jack turned the last corner and .... for the finishing line.

   A) approached   B) arrived   C) waited   D) headed

c) David was trying to .... another cyclist when he crashed.

   A) overpass   B) overcome   C) overtake   D) overcharge

d) You have to .... the person with the ball until you catch them.

   A) chase   B) rush   C) jump   D) drop

e) The fans climbed over the fence to .... paying.

   A) avoid   B) prevent   C) abandon   D) refuse

f) I fell over while skiing and my sister had to .... a doctor.

   A) bring   B) take   C) fetch   D) carry

g) It's very easy to .... over when the snow is hard.

   A) slide   B) skid   C) skate   D) slip

h) Don't .... the road until all the runners have gone by.

   A) pass   B) cross   C) across   D) pass by

i) The swimmers .... forward as they waited to begin the race.

   A fell   B) crawled   C) rolled   D) leaned

j) When I was hiking in the mountains, I .... on a snake.

   A) tripped   B) stepped   C) surprised   D) carried

7 Complete each sentence with a word from the box.

| anywhere | dinner | ready | through | back | lost | right |
| together | ~~better~~ | off | stuck | used | | |

a) After Paul's leg was injured, it took him a long time to get ......*better*...... .

b) Unfortunately Sally rode her bike into the mud and got ....

c) Before the race I went to the stadium to get ....

d) Some of the competitors got .... because of the thick fog.

e) I tried learning to do embroidery but I didn't get ....

f) She worked on her stamp collection and he got the ....

g) I didn't get .... from the match till late because of the crowds.

h) David practised hitting the golf ball until he got it ....

i) Kate enjoyed riding the horse but found it hard to get ....

j) I tried to phone the tennis club but I couldn't get ....

k) We have a great time whenever our rugby team gets ....

l) I can't get .... to playing football on plastic grass!

8 Rewrite the sentences in 7 above so that each one contains one of the words in the box, and does not contain a form of *get*.

| answer | dismount | perfected | strange | became | home | prepare |
| succeed | cooked | meets | ~~recover~~ | way | | |

a) *After Paul's leg was injured, it took him a long time to recover.*

b) ....

c) ....

d) ....

e) ....

f) ....

g) ....

h) ....

i) ....

j) ....

k) ....

l) ....

9 **Decide which answer (A, B, C or D) best fits each space.**

Sport

Someone once said that there are three kinds of people who are
(1) ....*C*........ in sport: people who (2) .... part, people who watch,
and people who watch (3) .... television. It's very easy to make fun of
stay-at-home sports (4) .... , but on the other hand, television does
enable us to enjoy all kinds of (5) .... events. We can watch a racing
car (6) .... another, see a cyclist (7) .... the finishing line, or
enjoy the goals of our favourite football (8) .... The first time I
watched a tennis (9) .... was on television, and I found it
(10) .... interesting. It's not always easy to (11) .... long
distances to football (12) .... , and television is a good solution. Of
course, you can (13) .... used to sitting indoors all the time, and this
is dangerous. We should all try to (14) .... fit, and have other interests
and (15) ....

1)	A playing	B really	C interested	D succeed
2)	A take	B have	C make	D get
3)	A on	B with	C by	D from
4)	A people	B centres	C programmes	D fans
5)	A the	B future	C sports	D athlete
6)	A cross	B overtake	C or	D from
7)	A overtake	B and	C cross	D professional
8)	A group	B class	C band	D team
9)	A match	B it	C which	D that
10)	A valuable	B imaginatively	C unexpectedly	D real
11)	A trip	B tour	C pass	D travel
12)	A areas	B grounds	C teams	D fans
13)	A or	B which	C get	D is
14)	A keep	B make	C do	D have
15)	A customs	B habits	C pastimes	D leisure

1 Complete the labels with suitable words from the box. Not all words given are suitable.

> belt   handbag   shoe   suit   blouse   dress   jacket   skirt   suitcase
> boot   earring   socks   tie   briefcase   ~~glasses~~   shirt   waistcoat

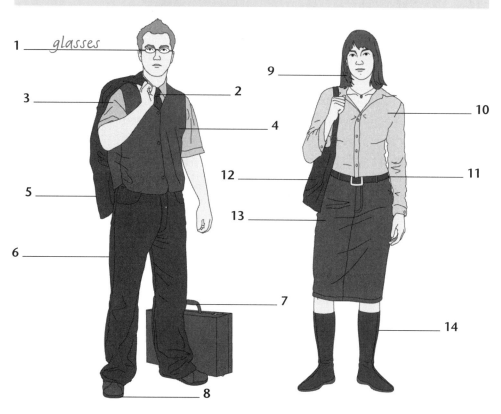

1 _glasses_
3
2
4
5
6
8
9
10
12
11
13
7
14

2 <u>Underline</u> the most suitable word or phrase.

a) At Harry's school, the children have to wear a special *style/<u>uniform</u>*.

b) If we go to the Embassy ball we'll have to wear *fashion/formal/polite* clothes.

c) I really like Jack's new *dress/suit/trouser*.

d) In the summer I always wear shirts with short *collars/cuffs/sleeves*.

e) Paul answered the door wearing his pyjamas and his *dressing gown/nightdress*.

f) You get really dirty repairing a car unless you wear *overalls/underwear*.

g) I didn't get wet in the rain because I put on my plastic *mac/overcoat/tights*.

h) When it snows, Freda always wears a/an *anorak/glove/scarf* around her neck.

i) David had to stop three times to tie up his small daughter's *shoelaces/soles*.

j) My hands were cold so I put them in my *pockets/turn-ups*.

k) The waitresses in this restaurant all wear white *aprons/dungarees/robes*.

l) When Tom goes to a party he always wears a *bow/butterfly/knot* tie.

3 Use the word given in capitals at the end of each line to form a word that fits in the space in the same line.

Father and son

My next-door neighbour has a very unusual (1) *appearance* .	APPEAR
He has long hair with a (2) .... in the middle, and	PART
usually wears an old pair of jeans and a (3) .... shirt.	STRIPE
His clothes are very (4) .... for working in a bank, but	SUIT
that is what he does! Unless he (5) .... when he gets to	DRESS
work and changes his clothes! His clothes are usually filthy	
and I am sure he never washes them or takes them to	
the (6) .... When he wears a coat it is always	CLEAN
old and (7) .... , and even on very cold days it is	WEAR
(8) .... all down the front. The funny thing is that his	BUTTON
son is very (9) .... , always wears the latest styles, and	FASHION
never wears casual clothes, even on an (10) .... occasion.	FORMAL

4 Correct any errors in these sentences. Some sentences contain no errors.

a) This shirt is too small, it's not my ~~number~~ *size*.

b) You have so many clothes. Why did you buy this cloth as well?

c) What costume did you wear to the fancy dress party?

d) Joan was dressed completely in white.

e) I like your new trouser. How much was it?

f) As far as I can see, the man in this photograph wears a suit.

g) What are you wearing to the party this evening?

h) You're soaked! Put out your clothes immediately!

5 Complete the word in each sentence. Each space represents one letter.

a) It's cold today. I'm going to put on a thick s *w e a t e r* .

b) Graham usually wears a leather j _ _ _ _ _ .

c) My trousers are falling down! I must buy a b _ _ _ .

d) It's too hot for trousers. I'm going to wear my s _ _ _ _ _ .

e) Let's roll up our shirt s _ _ _ _ _ _ and start work.

f) I can't wear these jeans! They are too t _ _ _ _ .

g) I bought this lovely s _ _ _ scarf in Japan.

h) Don't forget to put your clothes away in the w _ _ _ _ _ _ _ .

6   **Choose the most suitable word or phrase to complete each sentence.**

a) My hands were so cold that I couldn't ....*D*......... my coat buttons.

A) open   B) remove   C) put out   D) undo

b) Those trousers are far too big. Why don't you have them .... ?

A) taken in   B) let out   C) taken up   D) let in

c) I don't think that purple shirt .... with your yellow skirt.

A) suits   B) fits   C) goes   D) wears

d) This jacket is the kind of thing I want. Can I .... ?

A) wear it   B) dress it   C) take it off   D) try it on

e) You look really silly! Your pullover is on ....

A) upside down   B) inside out   C) round and round   D) side by side

f) I don't want a pattern. I prefer just a/an .... colour.

A) plain   B) simple   C) clear   D) only

g) You look hot in that coat. Why don't you .... ?

A) put it on   B) take if off   C) put it away   D) take it out

h) I went shopping today and bought a new winter ....

A) costume   B) outfit   C) suit   D) clothing

7   **Choose the most suitable word or phrase to complete each sentence.**

a) If I wear a long-sleeved shirt, I usually ....*C*......... the sleeves.

A) put up   B) take up   C) roll up   D) get up

b) That skirt is very short. Why don't you have it .... ?

A) left out   B) set in   C) let down   D) taken round

c) The thief wore gloves so that his fingerprints didn't ....

A) give him in   B) give him away   C) give him out   D) give him up

d) I can't walk in these high-heeled boots. I keep ....

A) falling off   B) falling back   C) falling out   D) falling over

e) Why is my swimming costume too small? What are you ....

A) seeing to   B) getting at   C) making up   D) putting out

f) I'm .... money every week to buy a new sports jacket.

A) making for   B) getting over   C) putting aside   D) turning in

g) Some of the young people in my town .... very strange haircuts!

A) go out with   B) go in for   C) go through with   D) go back on

h) Before we choose a dress for you, let's .... all the shops.

A) look into   B) look through   C) look up   D) look around

8 **Decide which answer (A, B, C or D) best fits each space.**

Choosing clothes

Are you one of the thousands of people who eagerly follow every new
(1) ....*B*........ that appears? Or are you one of those who go to the shops and
just buys whatever they can find in their (2) .... that (3) ....
them? Or perhaps you order from a mail-order catalogue, and then have to send
everything back because nothing (4) ....? Whatever (5) ....
of shopper you are, one thing is certain. Everyone finds (6) ....
important. According to a recent survey, people spend more time either buying
clothes, or thinking about buying them, or looking at them in shop
(7) ...., than they do on most other products, (8) .... from
food. And the reason is obvious. Clothes are an important part of our
(9) .... At work, you may need to impress a customer, or persuade
the boss that you know what you are doing, and clothes certainly help.
(10) .... dressed people, so they say, get on in the world. And as far as
attracting the opposite sex is concerned, clothes also play a vital role. If a friend
who has been (11) .... the same old jacket or the same old dress
suddenly appears in the (12) .... fashion, you can be sure that
romance is in the air. And apart from work and romance, there are the
influences of sport, music and leisure on the way we (13) .... So
excuse me while I (14) .... on my tracksuit and training
(15) .... I'm just dashing off for some fast window-shopping.

1) A appearance	B fashion	C uniform	D dress
2) A place	B price	C size	D self
3) A suits	B makes	C takes	D likes
4) A sizes	B styles	C fits	D measures
5) A means	B typical	C idea	D kind
6) A out	B clothes	C dresses	D vests
7) A centres	B sale	C times	D windows
8) A apart	B or	C according	D taken
9) A nowadays	B appearance	C looking	D events
10) A well	B good	C best	D fancy
11) A dressing	B putting on	C carrying	D wearing
12) A last	B minute	C latest	D complete
13) A clothes	B have	C dress	D go
14) A put	B dress	C wear	D have
15) A fit	B shoes	C tonight	D again

5 Towns and buildings

1 Underline the most suitable word.

a) As you can see, the garden has two ornamental iron *doors/gates* and there is a stone *path*/*pavement* leading to the house.

b) This is the front *entry/entrance*, but there is another door at the *edge/side* of the house.

c) All the rooms have *covered/fitted* carpets.

d) All the *cupboards/wardrobes* in the kitchen and the *bookshelves/library* in the living room are included in the price.

e) There is a beautiful stone *chimney/fireplace* in the living room, and there are *sinks/washbasins* in all the bedrooms.

f) At the top of the *stairs/steps* there is a *coloured/stained* glass window.

g) The bathroom has a *shower/washer* and modern mixer *pipes/taps*.

h) At the top of the house there is a/an *attic/cellar* and the garden contains a *glasshouse/greenhouse* and a garden *hut/shed*.

i) There is a wooden *fence/wall* on one side of the garden, and a *bush/hedge* on the other.

j) This is a fine *single/detached* house in a quiet *neighbourhood/suburb*.

2 Match the words in the box with a suitable explanation (a–l). Not all words given are possible.

curtains	drive	parking	shelf	central heating	dishwasher
furniture	radiator	stool	cook	doormat	landing
rug	door knocker	~~letterbox~~	settee/sofa		

a) Rectangular hole in the front door. .....*letterbox*.....

b) Long narrow rectangular piece of wood or metal fixed to the wall.

....

c) Short road between the street and a house or its garage. ....

d) Use this if you want someone to open the front door. ....

e) Put the dirty dishes in this. ....

f) This system makes the house warm. ....

g) A small carpet. ....

h) More than one person can sit on this. ....

i) An area at the top of some stairs. ....

j) Wipe your feet on this before you enter the house. ....

k) Pull these to cover the windows. ....

l) Small seat without back or arms. ....

3 Complete each sentence (a–j) with a suitable ending (1–10) so that the meaning of the word in *italics* is clear. Use each ending only once.

a) I would prefer to live in a *cottage* ....*6*........

b) The shopping centre has a *multi-storey car park* ....

c) My grandmother bought a *bungalow* ....

d) Jenny lives in a small *flat* ....

e) This street is only for *pedestrians* ....

f) Helen and John live in a *square* ....

g) Peter has moved to a London *suburb* ....

h) This village is surrounded by lovely *countryside* ....

i) Sue's new house is *unfurnished* ....

j) My house is *semi-detached* ....

1 on the third floor of a modern block.

2 and he commutes to work in the centre.

3 with room for over 2000 vehicles.

4 but the rent is so high that she cannot afford much furniture.

5 which has a beautiful garden in the middle.

6 in a small village in the country.

7 and the neighbours often bang on the wall.

8 because she had difficulty climbing stairs.

9 with fields, woods, streams and a small lake.

10 and cars and lorries are not allowed.

4 Complete each sentence with the words *home*, *house* or a word formed from one of these words.

a) The old couple decided to live in an old people's ......*home*...... .

b) Jane can't stand washing and ironing and other ....

c) Graham bought a terraced .... in a quiet city street.

d) Many .... people sleep on the streets of London.

e) Jack was unable to look after his children so he employed a ....

f) I come from Newcastle. It's my .... town, you could say.

g) Paul used to live on the river on a .... boat.

h) When I went to boarding school I felt very .... sick at first.

i) Our first home was on the .... estate on Oakwood Hill.

j) Pour yourself a drink and make yourself at ....

5   Choose the most suitable word or phrase to complete each sentence.

a) The view from the skyscraper ....*D*......... over New York harbour.

A) shows up   B) sees about   C) stands up   D) looks out

b) The old houses opposite are going to be ....

A) broken down   B) knocked down   C) put down   D) taken down

c) ....! You're about to push the wheelbarrow over my foot!

A) hang up   B) stop off   C) get away   D) look out

d) Please .... the rubbish because the dustman is coming tomorrow.

A) take in   B) make up   C) put out   D) tie down

e) Please come and unblock our drains! I'm .... you!

A) doing without   B) counting on   C) seeing to   D) waiting for

f) I can't put these plants in pots. I've .... earth.

A) run out of   B) put up with   C) given up   D) come up with

g) We .... through the window by climbing up a ladder.

A) fell out   B) got in   C) ended up   D) set off

h) I've been planting trees all day and I'm ....

A) worn out   B) taken in   C) run down   D) grown up

6   Use the word given in capitals at the end of each line to form a word that fits in the space in the same line.

A house in the country

When Ann decided to move house, it was mainly because
she was tired of the (1) .....*neighbourhood*..... she lived in. It was   NEIGHBOUR
crowded, there was a (2) .... of parking places, and   SHORT
the view from her (3) .... windows was of distant   STAIRS
factory chimneys. Luckily she arranged the (4) ....   SELL
of her house very easily, and with a small (5) .... from   LEND
the bank, was able to buy a house in the country. It was an
old farm building, which had been (6) .... and turned into   BUILD
a modern house. After loading all her belongings in a van,
Ann managed to get them into the new house (7) ....   DAMAGE
She (8) .... most of the rooms with what she already   FURNITURE
owned. Even her curtains were the right (9) .... for the   LONG
windows and she only had to buy a new (10) .... for   COOK
the kitchen. It seemed too good to be true. Surely something
would go wrong!

7 <u>Underline</u> the most suitable word or phrase.

a) Laura was sitting beside the fire in a comfortable *armchair/sofa*.

b) We drove out of the village along a winding *lane/path*.

c) Steve redecorated his room with flowery *posters/wallpaper*.

d) Put the meat in the *cooker/oven* for two hours.

e) These plums are ripe. They need *picking/picking up*.

f) Peter was in the garden mowing the *flowers/lawn*.

g) We used to keep the coal downstairs in the *cave/cellar*.

h) Why don't you put the car in the *car park/parking*?

i) Kate lives in a flat on the first *floor/storey*.

j) Put your wet socks on the *central heating/radiator* to dry.

k) Let's take the *runway/motorway*, we'll get there faster.

l) Go and get the lawnmower. The grass *is/are* very long.

m) I like the painting but I don't like the *frame/surrounding*.

n) Mary has a lot of small ornaments on her window *shelf/sill*.

o) There's someone *at/on* the door. Can you see who it is?

8 Match the words in the box with a suitable explanation (a–o).

| shutters | ceiling | chimney | pillow | kennel | blind | cushion |
| roof | rubbish | urban | bunk | ~~duvet~~ | kerb | litter | rural |

a) Put this over you if you are cold in bed. ....*duvet*.........

b) Put this behind your back if you are sitting uncomfortably. ....

c) This describes city places. ....

d) These protect your windows outside and can be closed in bad weather.

    ....

e) This is paper dropped in the street. ....

f) This is the top of the room. ....

g) This is a bed with others above it. ....

h) This describes country places. ....

i) This is the top of the house. ....

j) Put this under your head when you go to sleep. ....

k) Close this to keep the sunlight out of your room. ....

l) This is anything you throw away in the dustbin. ....

m) This is home for your pet dog. ....

n) This is the stone edge of the pavement at the side of the road.

    ....

o) The smoke goes up this from the fireplace. ....

9   Decide which answer (A, B, C or D) best fits each space.

Moving in

The entrance to the flat was at the (1) ....*A*......... of the house. Jane had to walk along a (2) .... across the lawn and past a (3) .... full of gardening equipment. Inside the back door there was a flight of (4) .... and then another door on the (5) .... It was a (6) .... flat with a bedroom, living room, kitchen and bathroom. There was not a lot of (7) .... but certainly enough for a student like Jane. There was a/an (8) .... in the living room with an electric fire, and the kitchen had a small (9) .... and a fridge. The bathroom did not have a bath, only a (10) .... and a basin, but Jane didn't mind. She was thinking about other problems. There wasn't a washing (11) .... , and there was no (12) .... heating. It was raining outside, and the flat felt damp and chilly. On the bed there were some (13) .... and a duvet, but no (14) .... It was lucky that Jane had brought a sleeping bag. As she was wondering what to do next, there was a knock (15) .... the door.

1) A side	B inside	C beginning	D garden
2) A road	B way	C path	D stairs
3) A room	B shed	C cellar	D floor
4) A ladder	B upstairs	C rooms	D stairs
5) A roof	B landing	C balcony	D bottom
6) A multi-storey	B semi-detached	C furnished	D cottage
7) A furniture	B rent	C neighbours	D housing
8) A oven	B fireplace	C cooker	D cooking
9) A cook	B cookery	C cooker	D cooking
10) A waterfall	B shower	C splash	D sink
11) A machine	B up	C room	D powder
12) A central	B much	C radiator	D good
13) A wrappings	B rugs	C carpets	D blankets
14) A whites	B sheets	C spreads	D cloths
15) A for	B behind	C to	D at

1 Complete each sentence with a word from the box.

captain	crew	guard	pedestrian	~~chauffeur~~	cyclist	mechanic
flight attendant		conductor	driver	motorist	traffic warden	

a) The company chairman has a Rolls-Royce driven by a ....*chauffeur*.......... .

b) When my car broke down a passing .... towed it to a garage.

c) The police wanted me to describe the .... of the car.

d) The four passengers on the ship had dinner with the ....

e) The train couldn't leave until the .... waved his green flag.

f) Hilary was given a parking ticket by a ....

g) Before take-off, the .... told me to fasten my seat belt.

h) When I got on the ship, one of the .... helped me find my cabin.

i) There isn't a .... on this bus, you pay the driver.

j) Eddie is a keen .... and rides his bike to work every day.

k) The bus mounted the pavement and injured a ....

l) Jim works as a .... in a local garage.

2 Complete the labels with suitable words from the box.

~~roof rack~~	bonnet	bumper	tyre	exhaust	windscreen	wheel
engine	headlight	mirror	steering wheel	aerial	boot	wiper	wing

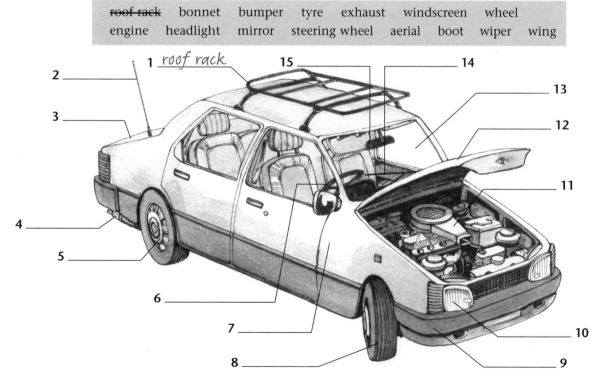

1 *roof rack*

227

3 Choose the most suitable word or phrase to complete each sentence.

a) The ship stopped because two passengers had fallen .... *B* ....

A) upside down   B) overboard   C) underground   D) inside out

b) The .... was crowded with passengers waiting for the train.

A) platform   B) quay   C) runway   D) pavement

c) We had to stop for petrol at a filling ....

A) garage   B) service   C) pump   D) station

d) Mary looked up the fastest train to Glasgow in the ....

A) catalogue   B) timetable   C) dictionary   D) programme

e) The train was very crowded because there were only four ....

A) coaches   B) waggons   C) trucks   D) cars

f) Peter's car .... off the icy road and fell into a ditch.

A) crashed   B) collided   C) hit   D) skidded

g) I dropped my wallet from the boat but luckily it ....

A) drifted   B) floated   C) sank   D) rescued

h) Everything went dark when the train entered a/an ....

A) underground   B) tunnel   C) tube   D) metro

i) David missed his train because of the queue in the ticket ....

A) office   B) agency   C) room   D) lounge

j) To get to our hotel we had to cross the railway ....

A) road   B) route   C) rails   D) line

4 Use the word given in capitals at the end of each line to form a word that fits in the space in the same line.

A letter of apology

I am writing to apologise for the (1) ..*cancellation*.. of your Happy   CANCEL

Holiday Coach Tour to Aberdeen. (2) .... our luxury   FORTUNE

coach was involved in a (3) .... in France a week ago,   COLLIDE

and our driver has been (4) .... obliged to remain there   EXPECT

for the moment. The coach was travelling on a road (5) ....   SUIT

for heavy traffic, and the accident was (6) .... Luckily   AVOID

none of the passengers suffered any (7) .... , and we have   INJURE

complained to the authorities that the road needs (8) ....   WIDE

Our new coach will be fitted with (9) .... seat belts for   ADJUST

the safety and comfort of passengers. We will of course

return the (10) .... you have made for your holiday as   PAY

soon as possible.

5 Complete each sentence with *sail* or *ship*, or a word formed from one of these words.

a) Jack has been working as a ....*sailor*....... for ten years.

b) We're all flying home but our furniture is being ....

c) What time does the ferry set .... ?

d) We are expecting a .... of coffee from Brazil this week.

e) We have decided to go for a .... tomorrow afternoon.

f) When Paul was young, he .... round the world.

g) It's time you were aboard .... We're leaving soon.

h) Do you like .... ? Or do you prefer water-skiing?

i) Graham works in the harbour as a .... clerk.

j) The boats on the lake had brightly coloured ....

6 Match the words in the box with a suitable description (a–j).

chain	gear	parachute	bonnet	cockpit	handlebars
brakes	deck	oars	~~wings~~		

a) An aeroplane has two of these. ....*wings*.........................

b) Change this in a car to change speed. ....

c) Hold these when you ride a bicycle. ....

d) This will save your life if you fall from a plane. ....

e) You need these to row a boat. ....

f) This might be on a bicycle or around your neck. ....

g) Put these on if you want to stop. ....

h) Your car engine is usually under this. ....

i) Walk on this when you are on a ship. ....

j) The pilot of a plane sits in this. ....

7 Complete each sentence with one suitable word.

a) I'm really .....*looking*.... forward to sailing in Jean's new yacht.

b) In cities, cars and other vehicles .... up most of the space.

c) We'll come with the van and .... up the rest of the furniture.

d) When the storm began, the small boat .... for the nearest harbour.

e) How can you .... up with all those exhaust fumes!

f) We can't .... up with that speedboat in this rowing boat!

g) Jane likes .... off by driving her sports car at 100 miles an hour.

h) A fire engine arrived and soon .... out the fire.

i) Little Johnny is in the garden .... out his new tricycle.

j) One way of .... with pollution is to use unleaded petrol.

8   Decide which answer (A, B, C or D) best fits each space.

Past, present and future

A hundred years ago, most people travelled (1) ....*B*......... foot, by train, or on horseback. (2) .... had made it possible to travel rapidly over long distances. Bicycles were also becoming (3) .... , after the invention of the air-filled (4) .... , which made cycling a lot more comfortable. Buses, trams and (5) .... railways had already been invented, and cities all over the world already had traffic (6) .... There were very few private cars, and city (7) .... were still full of horses. What a difference a hundred years have (8) .... ! (9) .... we have got (10) .... to the problem of private cars, and some cities are so noisy and (11) .... that in many places (12) .... have been banned from the city centre. How will we be travelling in a hundred years' time? Perhaps (13) .... then there will be only personal helicopters. There may be no need to (14) .... to work or school in the future, since everyone will have a computer at home. There might even be more people walking and horse-riding, for pleasure and (15) ....

1)	A by	B on	C with	D to
2)	A Tracks	B Lines	C Ways	D Railways
3)	A popular	B invented	C then	D handlebars
4)	A boot	B brake	C tyre	D engine
5)	A metro	B buried	C underground	D submerged
6)	A blocks	B sticks	C knots	D jams
7)	A streets	B pavements	C lawns	D carts
8)	A taken	B done	C made	D got
9)	A Presently	B Nowadays	C Then	D Later
10)	A more	B them	C motorists	D used
11)	A even	B polluted	C so	D poisoned
12)	A vehicles	B traffic	C transport	D trips
13)	A cars	B by	C even	D transport
14)	A have	B transport	C decide	D commute
15)	A exercise	B keep fit	C energy	D healthy

Food, restaurants and cooking

1 <u>Underline</u> the most suitable word or phrase.

a) Waiter, could you bring me the *account/<u>bill</u>/addition*, please?

b) It's a very popular restaurant – we should *apply for/book/keep* a table.

c) If you're hungry, why not ask for a large *dish/plate/portion*?

d) Please *help/serve/wait* yourself to salads from the salad bar.

e) Waiter, can I see the *catalogue/directory/menu*, please?

f) This fish is not what I *called/commanded/ordered*.

g) This *dish/plate/serving* is a speciality of our restaurant.

h) Have you tried the *crude/raw/undercooked* fish at the new Japanese restaurant?

i) Paul never eats meat, he's a *vegetable/vegetarian/vegetation*.

j) Have you decided what to have for your main *course/food/helping*?

2 Complete each sentence (a–j) with a suitable ending (1–10). Use each ending once.

a) Dinner's nearly ready. Can you lay ....6..........

b) There's some meat in the fridge. Just warm ....

c) Keep an eye on the milk or it might boil ....

d) Jack likes his steak rare but I prefer mine well ....

e) When we finish lunch, I'll do the washing ....

f) I always cut roast beef with an electric carving ....

g) Mary bought a lovely set of cups and ....

h) They serve a very cheap three course ....

i) I really enjoyed that freshly ground ....

j) If you have finished eating I'll clear ....

1   up if you dry and put the dishes away.

2   it up in the microwave oven for a few minutes.

3   coffee you made for me this morning.

4   meal at the pub opposite the supermarket.

5   knife as it makes really thin slices.

6   the small table in the dining room?

7   saucers in the sales last week.

8   done, but not burnt if you see what I mean.

9   away the plates and bring the next course.

10   over and make a mess on the cooker.

3 Complete each phrase with the most suitable word from the box.

bacon	butter	forks	pepper	beer	chips	grapes
~~saucers~~	bread	chocolate	instant coffee	wine		

a) cups and ......*saucers*......

b) fish and ....

c) knives and ....

d) bread and ....

e) eggs and ....

f) salt and ....

g) a loaf of ....

h) a bottle of ....

i) a can of ....

j) a bar of ....

k) a jar of ....

l) a bunch of ....

4 Complete the labels with suitable words from the box.

frying pan	saucepan	casserole dish	jar	kettle	jug
bowl	~~tin opener~~	mug	food mixer		

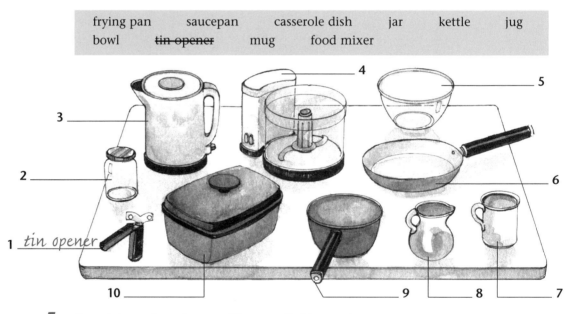

5 Complete each sentence with one suitable word.

a) I'm trying to cut down ......*on*........ fatty food.

b) Don't worry! The smell of garlic wears .... after a while.

c) Let's look .... the market before we buy any vegetables.

d) I can't understand this recipe. Can you work .... what it means?

e) I'm afraid I don't feel up .... eating another cream cake.

f) I visited a farm once, and it put me .... eating meat for a week.

g) I haven't got .... to cleaning the fish yet.

h) Why don't we warm .... last night's leftovers for lunch?

i) Keith usually makes .... his recipes as he goes along.

j) The waiter seemed a bit put .... when we didn't leave a tip.

6 Choose the most suitable word or phrase to complete each sentence.

a) Would you prefer .... *C* .... potatoes or chips?

   A) poached   B) ground   C) mashed   D) powdered

b) I bought this bread four days ago and now it's ....

   A) stale   B) off   C) bad   D) rotten

c) Don't forget to buy a packet of .... peas.

   A) chilled   B) frozen   C) frosted   D) chilly

d) Can you give me the .... for this pie? It's delicious.

   A) prescription   B) instructions   C) ingredients   D) recipe

e) There was a wonderful smell of .... bread in the kitchen.

   A) cooking   B) roasting   C) baking   D) grilling

f) Don't buy those fish, they aren't very ....

   A) fresh   B) new   C) recent   D) young

g) I'd like to eat more of this cake, but it's very ....

   A) fat   B) fatty   C) fattened   D) fattening

h) Waiter, I can't eat this meat. It's under-..................... .

   A) done   B) developed   C) nourished   D) weight

i) Is the hamburger for you to eat here, or to .... ?

   A) go out   B) take away   C) carry on   D) sit down

j) That was fantastic. Could I have a second .... , please?

   A) plate   B) course   C) helping   D) service

7 Make a word or compound word to match the description.

a) A spoon used for putting sugar in tea. .... *teaspoon* ....

b) A cloth put on the table at meal times. ....

c) A metal device for opening bottles. ....

d) A pot in which tea is made. ....

e) An electrical appliance for making toast. ....

f) A cup specially made for coffee. ....

g) An omelette containing mushrooms. ....

h) An electrical appliance for mixing food. ....

i) A napkin made of paper. ....

j) The amount contained in a tablespoon. ....

k) An electrical appliance for washing dishes. ....

8   **Decide which answer (A, B, C or D) best fits each space.**

Chickpea soup

This recipe is both (1) ....*B*......... and cheap. If you use dried chickpeas,
(2) .... them for at least twelve hours in cold water. Drain them and
put them in a large (3) .... with plenty of water. Bring them to the
boil, and then let them simmer gently (4) .... the chickpeas are soft. I
find it easier to use (5) .... chickpeas, which are already cooked. This
(6) .... time, and also guarantees that the chickpeas will be soft, since
it can take hours of boiling before they (7) .... Two small 450 gram
cans are usually (8) .... Strain the chickpeas, but keep some of the
liquid for the soup. (9) .... three tablespoons of olive oil into a
saucepan, and gently heat a chopped (10) .... , two or three cloves of
garlic and some (11) .... carrot. (12) .... half the chickpeas
and turn them in the oil over a low heat. Meanwhile blend the remaining
chickpeas in a food (13) .... until they make a smooth cream. Add
about half a litre of water to the vegetables and bring to the boil. Mix in the
creamed chickpeas and cook slowly. Add salt and (14) .... and a pinch
of mixed herbs. Some (15) .... add lemon juice at the end.

1)	A expensive	B tasty	C worth	D cold
2)	A soak	B bury	C wash	D water
3)	A kettle	B mug	C sink	D saucepan
4)	A when	B until	C if	D enough
5)	A the	B to	C canned	D crude
6)	A makes	B takes	C saves	D gives
7)	A soften	B harden	C widen	D lengthen
8)	A much	B enough	C mine	D few
9)	A Grate	B Peel	C Beat	D Pour
10)	A onion	B up	C one	D water
11)	A melted	B beaten	C poached	D sliced
12)	A One	B Then	C Add	D Serve
13)	A just	B not	C dish	D mixer
14)	A paper	B puppy	C pepper	D poppy
15)	A cookers	B cooks	C cookery	D chiefs

Shops and shopping

1 Underline the most suitable word or phrase.

a) That new clothes shop has a lot of very good *bargains/sales*.

b) On Saturday morning the High Street is full of *customers/shoppers*.

c) It costs £9, so give her £10, and she'll give you £1 *change/rest*.

d) I don't go to that supermarket because it's a bit *priced/pricey*.

e) You cannot return goods without the original *recipe/receipt*.

f) Supasoft Soaps are *for sale/on sale* here.

g) A carrier bag is free with each *buyer/purchase* over £10.

h) If you pay cash, we can give you a 10 per cent *cutting/discount*.

i) How much did you *pay/spend* for your new shoes?

j) This is a good shoe shop, but the *costs/prices* are very high.

2 Rewrite each sentence so that it includes the word given in capitals.

a) I can't manage to see what the price is. Let's ask inside.   MAKE
   I can't make out what the price is. Let's ask inside.

b) Is this coat the right size? Can I check?   TRY
   ....

c) Two masked men robbed the supermarket yesterday.   HELD
   ....

d) You need a new coat. Your old one is too small.   GROWN
   ....

e) I've been shopping all morning. I feel exhausted.   WORN
   ....

f) I'll come and collect the goods on Thursday.   PICK
   ....

g) Sorry, we don't have any bread left.   RUN
   ....

h) Are you going to the chemist's?   CALLING
   ....

i) I don't like supermarkets. I can't bear the queues.   PUT
   ....

j) I don't know whether to buy this car. I'll consider it.   OVER
   ....

3   Complete each sentence with a word from the box. Use each word once only.

change	deliver	find	fit	go	help	order	pay
~~queue~~	serve	try	wrap				

a) You have to ......*queue*..... for ages to pay in this supermarket.

b) In the London area, we .... furniture free of charge in our van.

c) The trousers I bought are the wrong size. I'd like to .... them.

d) Could somebody .... me, please? I've been waiting for ten minutes.

e) Is this a present? Would you like me to .... it for you?

f) I like the colour of this skirt, but it doesn't .... me.

g) Good morning, madam. Can I .... you?

h) We don't have your size at the moment, but we can .... it for you.

i) Can you .... at the other cash desk, please.

j) Would you like to .... on this green pair?

k) I went shopping but couldn't .... exactly what I wanted.

l) Food is so expensive now. Prices seem to .... up all the time.

4   Complete each sentence (a–j) with a suitable ending (1–10). Use each ending once.

a) I bought my new television from a department ....*5*.........

b) Don't forget to write a shopping ....

c) Can you pay over there? This cash ....

d) Most of the tourists went bargain ....

e) Why don't we go to the new shopping ....

f) Quite late at night the little corner ....

g) It would be much better to buy an economy ....

h) Don't forget that we have to stop at the filling ....

i) There's a very nice suit on display in the window ....

j) Mary has just started work as a shop ....

1   centre near the public library?

2   register doesn't work.

3   of that new shop next to the post office.

4   size box of paper tissues.

5   store in the town centre.

6   shop down the road is still open.

7   assistant in a shoe shop.

8   list before we go to the market tomorrow.

9   station to get some petrol.

10   hunting in the old part of the city.

5 Choose the most suitable word or phrase to complete each sentence.

a) I bought these jeans very cheaply in the ....*C*.......... .

A) bargains   B) reductions   C) sales   D) discounts

b) The washing instructions for this shirt are given on the ....

A) label   B) badge   C) notice   D) mark

c) All the small .... closed their shops in protest at the price rises.

A) shop assistants   B) shoppers   C) shopkeepers   D) shop stewards

d) We don't have the CD, I'm afraid. It's out of ....

A) order   B) stock   C) shelf   D) sale

e) The street market was full of .... selling fruit and vegetables.

A) counters   B) boutiques   C) tables   D) stalls

f) The shop opposite my house sells a variety of ....

A) objects   B) purchases   C) goods   D) productions

g) I'm sorry, but the dress you want is not .... in red.

A) possible   B) economical   C) suitable   D) available

h) Every Friday you can buy cheap vegetables in the market ....

A) street   B) place   C) store   D) sales

i) I like street markets, because you shop in the open ....

A) prices   B) sunshine   C) bargains   D) air

j) I like your new car. What .... is it?

A) brand   B) make   C) name   D) label

6 Complete each sentence with a word from the box. Use each word once only.

baked beans	chocolates	jam	orange juice	soap	breakfast cereal
flowers	margarine	paper tissues	~~toothpaste~~		

a) a tube of ......*toothpaste*......

b) a bunch of ....

c) a pot of ....

d) a tin of ....

e) a box of ....

f) a box of ....

g) a packet of ....

h) a bar of ....

i) a carton of ....

j) a tub of ....

7 Match the words in the box with a suitable description (a–j).

| advertisement | bargain | catalogue | deposit | list |
| manager | purse | receipt | ~~trolley~~ | wallet |

a) You push this in the supermarket and fill it with food. ....*trolley*..........

b) You are given this as proof of buying something. ....

c) This tries to persuade you to buy something. ....

d) You put money, especially banknotes, in this. ....

e) This person is in charge of a shop. ....

f) You might make this before you go shopping. ....

g) Leave this if you can't pay now but want to buy later. ....

h) Do this if you want to get a better price. ....

i) Coins are usually carried in this, especially by women. ....

j) Read this to find descriptions of goods. ....

8 Use the word given in capitals at the end of each line to form a word that fits in the space in the same line.

Supermarkets

Nowadays, a great (1) .....*variety*.... of different food is available   VARY

from large supermarkets. There are rarely any (2) ....   SHORT

of fresh food, and there is far less (3) .... of our having   LIKELY

to rely on (4) .... products. Does this mean that   FREEZE

supermarkets have become the most (5) .... shops of   SUCCESS

all time? Certainly they seem to have made some kinds of

food less (6) .... and most people enjoy shopping in   EXPENSE

them. There has been a (7) .... in the number of   REDUCE

(8) .... made against supermarkets in recent years.   COMPLAIN

The assistants are no longer (9) .... , but smile and   POLITE

try to be helpful. Above all, supermarkets have shown a

(10) .... to listen to their customers, and to adapt to   WILLING

customers' needs.

9 Decide which answer (A, B, C or D) best fits each space.

Street markets

Most people enjoy looking for (1) ....*D*......... in street markets. It can be very enjoyable walking around the (2) .... , among the crowds of (3) .... , and trying to spend as (4) .... as possible. Of course it depends (5) .... the market. In fruit and (6) .... markets, there is usually a wide variety of (7) .... produce, but it may not be cheap. There may be goods at (8) .... prices at the end of the day, however. Clothes markets can be a problem, as it is difficult to (9) .... on new clothes in the open (10) .... ! My favourite are antique markets, where although there is not much (11) .... of finding valuable objects which are also cheap, you can enjoy yourself looking at all the things for (12) .... Whatever kind of market you look (13) .... , and whether you buy things or not, you usually (14) .... up feeling completely worn (15) .... Still, it is an interesting way of shopping.

1) A cheap	B sale	C inexpensive	D bargains
2) A tables	B stalls	C boxes	D stores
3) A shoppers	B public	C buys	D goods
4) A little	B soon	C late	D is
5) A from	B with	C on	D to
6) A salads	B green	C farm	D vegetable
7) A new	B fresh	C young	D early
8) A half	B bottom	C reduced	D down
9) A look	B try	C have	D take
10) A time	B shop	C light	D air
11) A likelihood	B instead	C in spite	D luck
12) A that	B all	C sale	D others
13) A round	B for	C up	D out
14) A shut	B bring	C get	D end
15) A clothes	B however	C out	D through

1 Underline the most suitable word or phrase.

a) Sally didn't realise that she had _broken_/countered/denied the law.

b) The police have banned/cancelled/refused parking in this street.

c) I must remember to get a/an agreement/licence/permission for my television.

d) The president admitted that there had been a breakdown of law and crime/government/order.

e) Jim's parents wouldn't agree/allow/let him go to the demonstration.

f) Jake was arrested because he had entered the country falsely/illegally/wrongly.

g) Talking to other students is against the law/orders/rules of the examination.

h) The two men were arrested before they could commit/make/perform any more crimes.

i) I had to take the company to court/justice/law to get the money they owed me.

j) Smoking is compulsory/prohibited/refused near the petrol tanks.

2 Match word in the box with a suitable description (a–l).

blackmailer	forger	hooligan	murderer	shoplifter	vandal
burglar	~~hijacker~~	kidnapper	pickpocket	smuggler	witness

a) This person takes control of a plane or boat by force. ...._hijacker_....

b) This person sees what happens during a crime or accident. ....

c) This person brings goods into the country illegally. ....

d) This person might steal food from a supermarket. ....

e) This person kills someone on purpose. ....

f) This person takes people and demands money for their return.

....

g) This person makes illegal copies of paintings, documents, etc.

....

h) This person damages other people's property. ....

i) This person might steal your wallet in a crowd. ....

j) This person steals from houses. ....

k) This person gets money from others by threatening to tell secrets.

....

l) This person causes trouble at football matches. ....

3 Complete each sentence (a–j) with a suitable ending (1–10). Use each ending once.

a) I decided to buy a burglar alarm after someone broke ....*5*..........

b) When Alan was stopped outside the supermarket he ended ....

c) As it was Sheila's first offence she was let ....

d) After climbing over the prison wall, Peter managed to get ....

e) The old couple who live opposite were taken ....

f) At the end of the trial Hilary was found ....

g) My neighbours admitted denting my car but got away ....

h) The bank at the end of the street was held ....

i) Nobody saw Jack cheating and he got away with ....

j) The hijackers took fifteen people ....

1 in by a salesman who cheated them out of their money.

2 away by stealing a car parked nearby.

3 up at the police station, charged with shoplifting.

4 it, although everyone suspected what had happened.

5 into my house and stole my stereo.

6 off with only a warning.

7 with paying only £100 damages.

8 hostage and demanded £1,000,000 from the authorities.

9 guilty and sentenced to six months in prison.

10 up by two masked men last week.

4 Complete each sentence with a word from the box. Use each word once only.

accused	evidence	guilty	lawyer	statement	~~charged~~
fine	jury	sentence	suspect		

a) The customs officers arrested Bob and ......*charged*...... him with smuggling.

b) The police spent all morning searching the house for ....

c) Jean left her car in a no-parking area and had to pay a/an ....

d) Unfortunately at the end of the trial my brother was found ....

e) The trial took a long time as the .... couldn't reach a verdict.

f) George won his case because he had a very good defence ....

g) The police visited Dawn and asked her to make a/an ....

h) Because of his past criminal record, Brian was the main ....

i) Pauline decided to sue the police because she had been wrongly ....

j) The murderer of the children received a life ....

5 Choose the most suitable word or phrase to complete each sentence.

a) Most schools in my country no longer have ....*D*........ punishment.

   A) physical   B) capital   C) bodily   D) corporal

b) The policemen following the robbers were in .... clothes.

   A) plain   B) ordinary   C) normal   D) simple

c) The two old ladies were .... of their purses.

   A) stolen   B) attacked   C) robbed   D) snatched

d) At the end of the story, the hero manages to arrest the ....

   A) offenders   B) villains   C) wrongs   D) evils

e) I had to answer question A because it was ....

   A) compulsory   B) necessary   C) a must   D) an obligation

f) Charles could not .... having been at the scene of the crime.

   A) refuse   B) object   C) deny   D) alter

g) As there was no evidence, the judge dismissed the ....

   A) trial   B) witness   C) court   D) case

h) If your dog damages your neighbour's property, you could be ....

   A) guilty   B) liable   C) payable   D) illegal

i) After ten years in prison, Stephen was .... and set free.

   A) pardoned   B) released   C) innocent   D) forgiven

j) The detective inspector told the young .... to make some tea.

   A) officer   B) official   C) guardian   D) police

6 Rewrite each sentence, beginning as shown, so that the meaning stays the same.

a) They said that John had stolen the money.

   They accused .....*John of stealing the money.*........................

b) Ian said that he hadn't punched anybody.

   Ian denied ....

c) 'OK, Andy, you can go now,' said the detective.

   The detective gave Andy ....

d) 'James Frogget, you will go to prison for ten years,' said the judge.

   The judge sentenced ....

e) 'I forged the signature,' said Mary.

   Mary admitted ....

f) Harry stole £60,000 and was arrested.

   Harry was arrested ....

g) 'We saw the accused break into the car,' said the witnesses.

   The witnesses stated ....

h) Graham said that he wouldn't go to the police station.

Graham refused ....

i) 'It's true,' said Norman, 'I murdered Alan.'

Norman confessed to ....

j) 'Can you come with me, please,' the detective said to Helen.

The detective asked ....

7 Use the word given in capitals at the end of each line to form a word that fits in the space in the same line.

Arthur's life of crime

At his last trial, nobody believed in Arthur's (1) ...*innocence*.. . He   INNOCENT

had been accused of the (2) .... of a valuable Chinese vase,   THIEF

and was also charged with ten other (3) .... The value of   OFFEND

the (4) .... goods was said to be over £20,000. Arthur said   STEAL

in his own (5) .... that the vase had been put into his car   DEFEND

(6) .... He also pointed out that the Chinese vase was a   ACCIDENT

fake, and was almost (7) .... The judge did not believe   WORTH

Arthur's story. He told Arthur he was a hardened (8) ....   CRIME

and that he deserved a severe (9) .... Then   PUNISH

the judge sentenced Arthur to five years' (10) ....   PRISON

Arthur just smiled. He had spent most of his life in prison and so

he was used to it.

8 Underline the most suitable word or phrase.

a) Harry was told that fishing in the lake was *against*/*by*/*over* the law.

b) Catherine led a secret life *for*/*in*/*of* crime before she was caught.

c) Having trouble with your phone? Send *at*/*for*/*to* Fix-a-phone!

d) I regret to tell you that you are *for*/*in*/*under* arrest.

e) I only attacked the young man *from*/*in*/*with* self-defence.

f) David was often *at*/*in*/*with* trouble with the police when he was young.

g) The robbers' car was hidden *below*/*by*/*from* sight behind the bank.

h) The kidnappers have been caught, and the child is no longer *at*/*in*/*on* danger.

i) Tony was caught by a policeman who was *off*/*out*/*away from* duty and cycling to work.

j) The thieves took the wrong painting *by*/*in*/*under* mistake.

k) The suspicious manager left the safe unlocked *from*/*on*/*with* purpose.

l) The robbers met to plan the bank raid *from*/*in*/*with* secret.

9   **Decide which answer (A, B, C or D) best fits each space.**

Inspector Crumb investigates

'I think I know the identity of the murderer,' said Inspector Crumb, 'and at
(1) ....*B*......... one of the guests in this hotel was a/an (2) .... to the
crime, probably by (3) .... I believe that the same guest is also a
(4) .... , and has been given money by the killer.' 'So whoever
(5) .... this terrible crime is still here,' I said. 'But of course. In
(6) .... he – or she – is in this room, and will soon be (7) ....
arrest.' There was silence for a moment. I noticed that everyone was trying to
look (8) .... , but they all looked guilty instead! 'Do you have any
(9) .... , Inspector,' asked Lady Grimshaw finally, 'or are you simply
(10) .... people for fun? If you intend to (11) .... someone,
you should do it now.' The Inspector smiled. 'I asked you here (12) ....
purpose, Lady Grimshaw. I have been reading your (13) .... , you see,
and it is quite clear that you have told several (14) ....' 'How dare
you!' Lady Grimshaw spluttered. 'Do you (15) .... that you were with
Tim Dawson in the garden on the night of the murder?' the Inspector said. 'You
forgot about the security cameras, you see ...'

1) A last	B least	C the	D school
2) A witness	B offender	C guilty	D verdict
3) A now	B damages	C law	D accident
4) A blackmailer	B hostage	C hooligan	D forger
5) A confessed	B committed	C admitted	D performed
6) A crime	B self-defence	C fact	D danger
7) A to	B having	C under	D my
8) A accused	B suspicious	C ordinary	D innocent
9) A evidence	B witness	C permission	D body
10) A suspecting	B suing	C denying	D accusing
11) A trial	B charge	C sentence	D confess
12) A with	B for	C on	D by
13) A statement	B biography	C evident	D history
14) A people	B errors	C times	D lies
15) A refuse	B deny	C contradict	D suppose

1 <u>Underline</u> the most suitable word or phrase.

a) I like this book, and I've read six *capitals/<u>chapters</u>/prefaces* already.

b) It's not a proper drawing, only a *rough/plan/sketch*.

c) The play is very long but there are three *breaks/intervals/rests*.

d) At the cinema I don't like sitting too near the *film/screen/stage*.

e) We heard a piece by Mozart performed by a German *band/group/orchestra*.

f) Her second book was very popular and became a best *buy/seller/volume*.

g) I like the painting but I can't stand its ugly *border/frame/square*.

h) Robert's new book will be *broadcast/published/typed* in August.

i) I liked the acting, and the *costumes/dressing/outfits* were good too.

j) The best *act/place/scene* in the film is when Jack meets Kate.

2 Complete each sentence with a word from the box. Use each word once only.

announcer	composer	critic	editor	playwright	author
~~conductor~~	director	novelist	sculptor		

a) The orchestra would not be so successful with a different ....*conductor*.... .

b) I want a book on art, but I don't know the name of the ....

c) We must see the new film by that Italian ....

d) The .... said that the sports programme is on after the news.

e) Harry writes for the theatre, but he is not only a ....

f) We saw some interesting metal objects made by a French ....

g) That's a nice piece of music. Who is the .... ?

h) Peter Smith was the only .... who wrote in praise of the film.

i) Charles Dickens is probably the best known British ....

j) The .... of the newspaper usually decides what it contains.

3 Complete each sentence by putting *in, on, at* or *out of* in each space.

a) Harry Smith is hard ....*at*........ work writing his new screenplay.

b) The music was terrible and the singer was .... tune.

c) I can't tell what that is .... the background of the picture.

d) Jane's new book is coming out .... paperback next year.

e) Is there anything good .... Channel 4 this evening?

f) The school put on *Hamlet* .... modern dress.

g) The critics found Joe's kind of writing rather .... date.

h) In the last scene, all the actors are .... stage together.

4 Complete each sentence with a word from the box. Use each word once only.

current	electric	humorous	modern	public	special	dull
gripping	~~live~~	popular	readable	still		

a) No recording can be as good as a ....*live*......... concert in my opinion.

b) It was a very .... story and made me laugh a lot.

c) I couldn't put that book down, it had such a .... plot.

d) Most people find it difficult to understand .... art.

e) My favourite television programmes are about .... affairs.

f) Of course it's possible to like both classical and .... music.

g) Everyone enjoyed the .... effects in the *Star Wars* films.

h) I don't buy books because there's a good .... library nearby.

i) We both found it a very .... film I'm afraid.

j) George doesn't paint people, but mainly does .... life paintings.

k) It was an interesting book, and very ....

l) Unfortunately the boy upstairs is learning the .... guitar.

5 Choose the most suitable word or phrase to complete each sentence.

a) Susan's first painting was a/an ....*A*........ portrait.
   A) self   B) own   C) selfish   D) auto

b) We all enjoyed the play so much that we .... for ten minutes.
   A) booed   B) screamed   C) applauded   D) handed

c) Peter sings every Sunday in the local church ....
   A) concert   B) chorus   C) opera   D) choir

d) I bought this book mainly because it has a very attractive ....
   A) folder   B) cover   C) coat   D) wrapping

e) The play was a success and had very good .... in the papers.
   A) reviews   B) critics   C) advertisements   D) notes

f) If you can't find what you are looking for in the book, use the ....
   A) preface   B) directory   C) list   D) index

g) The average .... watches television for about 15 hours a week.
   A) viewer   B) audience   C) spectator   D) observer

h) First we see their faces from far away, and then we see a ....
   A) side by side   B) foreground   C) replay   D) close up

i) Please note that the next programme is .... for children.
   A) unusual   B) unsuitable   C) unmistakable   D) unreasonable

j) All the members of the .... had a party after the play was over.
   A) scene   B) cast   C) circle   D) drama

6 Use the word given in capitals at the end of each line to form a word that fits in the space in the same line.

The school play

Congratulations to all involved with the school (1) *production* of   PRODUCE

The Woman Next Door. The (2) .... was carried out by the   ADVERTISE

Art Department, and the posters were very (3) .... We   IMAGINE

certainly have some very (4) .... students in our school!   ART

Many people helped with building and painting the (5) ....   SCENE

and the play was written by the English Department, who

managed to create an (6) .... story, with excellent songs.   AMUSE

The music was written by Sue Porter, who also (7) .... the   COMPANY

singers on the piano. Everyone enjoyed a thoroughly (8) ....   ENTERTAIN

evening, and there was a long round of (9) .... at the end.   APPLAUD

Jim Barrett gave a brilliant (10) .... as Sergeant Moss, and   PERFORM

Liz Aitken was a delightful Mrs Jump. Well done everyone!

7 Complete the compound word in each sentence with a word from the box. Use each word once only.

back	book	fair	operas	rehearsal	biography
circle	ground	~~piece~~	scripts		

a) Edward's third book is usually considered his master ....*piece*........ .

b) A lot of people enjoy watching soap .... on television.

c) I found the Prime Minister's auto .... very interesting.

d) Some of the actors still did not know their lines at the dress ....

e) I won't buy the book until it comes out in paper ....

f) We had very good seats in the dress ....

g) There is a black cat painted in the fore .... of the picture.

h) Writing film .... is rather like writing for the theatre.

i) I was fined because I forgot to return my library ....

j) The scene showed them on a roundabout in a children's fun ....

8   Replace the verbs in *italics* with a verb from the box. Do not change the meaning. Change the verb form where necessary.

call off	go over	~~pick up~~	take over	turn up	come out
look up	put on	take up	work out		

a)   My radio doesn't *receive* the BBC World Service very easily.
  My radio doesn't pick up the BBC World Service very easily.

b)   Our school is going to *do* 'The Tempest' next month.
  ....

c)   The management *cancelled* the performance an hour before the opening.
  ....

d)   I *searched* for the reference in the index.
  ....

e)   I can't hear the radio. Can you *make it louder*?
  ....

f)   Colin's new book *is published* next week.
  ....

g)   The conductor *studied* the music carefully before the concert.
  ....

h)   The publishing company was *bought* by a Japanese firm.
  ....

i)   I like detective stories where I can't *think* who committed the murder!
  ....

j)   Jim has *started* painting as a hobby.
  ....

9 Decide which answer (A, B, C or D) best fits each space.

Why read books?

Is it worth reading books, (1) ....*D*......... nowadays there are so many other forms of (2) .... ? Some people say that even (3) .... books are expensive, and not everyone can (4) .... books from a library. They might add that television is more (5) .... and that viewers can relax as they watch their favourite (6) .... All that may be true, but books are still very (7) .... They encourage the reader to use his or her (8) .... for a start. You can read a (9) .... of a book, or just a few pages, and then stop. Of course, it may be so (10) .... that you can't stop! There are many different kinds of books, so you can choose a crime (11) .... or an autobiography, or a book which gives you interesting (12) .... If you find it hard to choose, you can read (13) .... , or ask friends for ideas. Personally, I can't (14) .... without books, but I can (15) .... up television easily enough. You can't watch television at bus stops!

1)	A in	B or	C why	D since
2)	A entertain	B entertainment	C entertained	D entertaining
3)	A paperback	B the	C so	D when
4)	A borrow	B buy	C lend	D take
5)	A excited	B excitable	C exciting	D excitement
6)	A ones	B programmes	C episodes	D cereals
7)	A too	B public	C live	D popular
8)	A imagination	B author	C index	D amusement
9)	A capital	B head	C chapter	D cover
10)	A current	B imagined	C interest	D gripping
11)	A history	B novel	C booklet	D poetry
12)	A advise	B idea	C information	D fact
13)	A announcements	B gossip	C reviews	D prefaces
14)	A do	B make	C have	D take
15)	A pick	B look	C give	D turn

1 <u>Underline</u> the most suitable word or phrase.

a) The fields were flooded after the river burst its <u>*banks*</u>/*edges*/*sides*.

b) After the rain the street was full of *floods/lakes/puddles*.

c) During the storm, the climbers sheltered in a *cave/cliff/valley*.

d) A small *river/stream/torrent* runs across the bottom of our garden.

e) It was difficult to swim because the *waters/waves/tides* were so high.

f) From the *peak/summit/top* of the hill you can see the sea.

g) You must carry a lot of water when you cross the *desert/plain/sand*.

h) In the middle of the square there is an old *fountain/source/tap*.

i) I think it's going to rain. It's very *clouded/clouding/cloudy*.

j) The church caught fire when it was struck by *hurricane/lightning/thunder*.

2 Complete each sentence (a–j) with one of the endings (1–10). Use each ending once.

a) A large green snake ....*5*..........

b) A small brown duck ....

c) A large black and yellow wasp ....

d) A shiny green crab ....

e) An enormous black spider ....

f) A bright green frog ....

g) A black and white puppy ....

h) A herd of cattle ....

i) A dirty black lamb ....

j) A small ginger kitten ....

1 was spinning its web across the window.

2 was plodding across the field, mooing loudly.

3 was buzzing around the jar of honey on the table.

4 was sitting on a branch and miaowing.

5 was slithering across the floor towards me.

6 was sitting on a leaf and croaking.

7 was following the flock, baaing softly.

8 was swimming on the pond and quacking loudly.

9 was barking furiously outside the gate.

10 was pinching Fiona's toe as she stood on the seashore.

3 Complete each sentence with a word from the box. Use each word once only.

> forest   leaves   plant   seeds   trunk   lawn   peel   ~~roots~~   stone   twig

a) We cut down the tree but then we had to dig up its ....*roots*.......... .

b) The road goes through a beautiful pine ....

c) When Tom was eating a cherry, he accidentally swallowed the

....

d) In autumn, these paths are covered in fallen ....

e) Who is going to cut the .... while I am away?

f) We bought Diana a beautiful indoor .... for her birthday.

g) A tree fell, and its massive .... blocked the road.

h) Harry buys .... and grows all his own vegetables.

i) The bird was carrying a .... to build its nest.

j) Some people like eating orange ....

4 Choose the most suitable word or phrase to complete each sentence.

a) The dog ....*B*......... its tail furiously when it saw the children.
    A) shook   B) wagged   C) moved   D) rubbed

b) A large .... of the tree broke off in the storm.
    A) trunk   B) bark   C) twig   D) branch

c) There was field after field of golden .... waving in the wind.
    A) corn   B) bushes   C) grass   D) herbs

d) Before railways were built, many goods were carried on ....
    A) channels   B) water   C) canals   D) river

e) The children enjoyed rolling down the grassy ....
    A) mountain   B) cliff   C) stone   D) slope

f) What kind of .... is your dog?
    A) breed   B) race   C) mark   D) family

g) Some wild animals will become .... if they get used to people.
    A) peaceful   B) tame   C) organised   D) petty

h) There's a .... of blackbirds at the bottom of the garden.
    A) house   B) home   C) cage   D) nest

i) Many people are interested in watching ....
    A) wildlife   B) wilds   C) wilderness   D) wildly

j) You have to sleep under a net to avoid being bitten by ....
    A) lobsters   B) geese   C) cockroaches   D) mosquitoes

5 Use the word given in capitals at the end of each line to form a word that fits in the space in the same line.

A pet parrot

From early (1) ...*childhood*. Jane had always wanted a pet parrot.   CHILD

Her parents told her that a parrot was an (2) .... pet, but Jane   SUIT

insisted. She was worried about the (3) .... of the   DESTROY

rainforests where parrots live, and she felt that parrots needed more

(4) .... Her father argued that a parrot would suffer from   PROTECT

(5) .... if it lived in a house. He also explained that pet   LONELY

parrots are caught by (6) .... , who need money and don't   HUNT

care about protecting species. 'They catch the parrots and send them to

Europe in (7) .... boxes,' he told her. 'And in any case,   WOOD

parrots are very (8) .... and don't make good pets.' Jane soon   OBEY

made an interesting (9) .... , however. She found a pet   DISCOVER

shop which bred parrots instead of importing them. So she took all her

(10) .... and bought a tiny parrot, which she called 'Pixie'.   SAVE

6 Complete the compound word in each sentence with a word from the box. Use each word once only.

forecast   hive   house   side   top   fountain   hole   mower   skin   ~~trap~~

a) There were so many mice we had to buy a mouse.....*trap*............ .

b) Paula was cutting the grass with an electric lawn..................... .

c) There's a drinking..................... on the other side of the park.

d) What's the weather..................... for tomorrow?

e) The hill..................... was covered in beautiful wild flowers.

f) You can see the mountain..................... among the clouds in the distance.

g) At the end of the field was a large stone farm..................... .

h) We collect honey from our own bee..................... .

i) There's a rabbit..................... in the corner of this field.

j) Martin was wearing imitation snake..................... boots.

7 Complete each sentence with one suitable word.

a) I think this fruit juice has gone ....*off*........ . It smells funny.

b) Mind .... ! Our cat has very sharp claws!

c) I keep my dog on a lead, but I let it .... in the park.

d) I like the idea of camping, but I am put .... by the insects.

e) Our dog never got used .... sleeping in its kennel.

f) I don't think I want to find .... whether that bull has sharp horns!

g) My puppy managed to tear .... three of my school books.

h) I've taken .... going for long walks in the countryside.

8 Decide which answer (A, B, C or D) best fits each space.

Pets

If you decide to buy a pet, you should (1) ....*C*........ out as much as possible about the pet you (2) .... Cats are easy to (3) .... after and seem to be (4) .... , but also need the company of people. If your cat finds someone who (5) .... for it more than you do, it will change owners! A small puppy may look like a (6) .... pet, but don't forget that it will (7) .... up. You may not be able to (8) .... up with a very large dog that is too big for its (9) .... and which (10) .... on sleeping on your bed! Unless you (11) .... it, it may attack people, or (12) .... loudly day and night. Nobody loves a (13) .... pet. Perhaps this is why so many people (14) .... in for birds or fish as pets. Whatever you decide in the (15) .... , think carefully before you make a decision.

1) A go	B look	C find	D take
2) A choose	B decide	C take	D do
3) A run	B change	C find	D look
4) A singular	B depended	C independent	D single
5) A feeds	B cares	C looks	D loves
6) A suited	B suiting	C suit	D suitable
7) A grow	B get	C stand	D buy
8) A stay	B live	C put	D feed
9) A lodging	B kennel	C cupboard	D box
10) A relies	B insists	C carries	D concentrates
11) A train	B learn	C lesson	D educate
12) A wag	B quack	C moo	D bark
13) A disobey	B disobeying	C disobedient	D disobeyed
14) A go	B prefer	C decide	D take
15) A house	B fact	C first	D end

People and behaviour

1 Underline the most suitable word or phrase.

a) Please don't push. It's very *bad-tempered/<u>rude</u>/unsympathetic*.

b) Jack hates spending money. He's rather *frank/greedy/mean*.

c) Our teacher is very *proud/strict/tolerant* and won't let us talk in class.

d) Helen never does her homework. She is rather *gentle/lazy/reliable*.

e) I didn't talk to anyone at the party because I felt *ambitious/lonely/shy*.

f) When Harry saw his girlfriend dancing with Paul he felt
    jealous/selfish/sentimental.

g) I don't like people who are noisy and *aggressive/courageous/sociable*.

h) Thanks for bringing us a present. It was very *adorable/grateful/thoughtful* of
    you.

i) Teresa never gets angry with the children. She is very *brave/patient/pleasant*.

j) Tom always pays for everyone when we go out. He's so
    cheerful/generous/honest.

2 Match the words in the box with the descriptions (a–l). Use each word once only.

bad-tempered	determined	lazy	reliable	cheerful	frank	mean
selfish	considerate	honest	~~punctual~~	sympathetic		

a) You always arrive on time. ..*punctual*...

b) You are always happy. ....

c) You do what you say you will do. ....

d) You say exactly what you think. ....

e) You don't think about the needs of others. ....

f) You have a strong wish to get what you want. ....

g) You are unkind, or not willing to spend money. ....

h) You easily become angry with others. ....

i) You think about the needs of others. ....

j) You tell the truth and obey the law. ....

k) You understand the feelings of others. ....

l) You try to avoid work if you can. ....

3 Complete each sentence with a word from the box. Use each word once only.

| ambitious | greedy | polite | ~~sociable~~ | brave | imaginative | proud |
| stubborn | grateful | kind | snobbish | tolerant | | |

a) I think I'll stay here on my own, I'm not feeling very .....*sociable*..... today.

b) Diana wants to get to the top in her company. She is very ....

c) It's not .... to stare at people and say nothing!

d) I think you have to be very .... to write a novel.

e) Thank you for helping me. It was very .... of you.

f) Peter refuses to change his mind, although he is wrong. He's
so ....

g) It was very .... of Sheila to put out the fire on her own.

h) Our neighbours look down on us. They are a bit ....

i) Don't eat all the cakes! You really are becoming .... !

j) If you lend me the money, I'll be very ....

k) I am very .... of my new motorbike.

l) My parents don't mind my crazy hairstyle. They are very ....

4 Use the word given in capitals at the end of each line to form a word that fits in the space in the same line.

Jack's real character

How easy is it to understand another person's character?

My friend Jack, was once a rather (1) ..*annoying*.. person. He was   ANNOY

always getting into trouble at school because he was so (2) ....   OBEY

In class he was very (3) .... and never stopped making   TALK

jokes. The teachers all told him he was (4) .... because   POLITE

he interrupted them. When I met him he was very (5) ....   FRIEND

and didn't want to talk to me at all. People told me that he

stole things, and that he was (6) .... His school work   HONEST

was terrible. He didn't take any (7) .... in his writing, he   PROUD

never spent enough time doing his homework, and he

was not at all (8) .... One day he saw a gang of boys   CONSCIENCE

attacking an old man. Jack hated (9) .... and he fought   VIOLENT

them all until they ran away. He was awarded a medal

for (10) .... After that, people changed their minds   BRAVE

about him.

5 Choose the most suitable word or phrase to complete each sentence.

a) You can't tell what someone is like just from their .... *B* ....

A) character   B) appearance   C) personality   D) looking

b) I was born in Scotland but I .... in Northern Ireland.

A) grew up   B) raised   C) brought up   D) rose

c) Edward was named after one of his father's distant ....

A) family   B) brothers   C) members   D) relations

d) Jane and Brian got married a year after they got ....

A) divorced   B) proposed   C) engaged   D) separated

e) Graham works well in class, but his .... could be better.

A) rudeness   B) behaviour   C) politeness   D) acting

f) Julie had a terrible .... with her parents last night.

A) row   B) discussion   C) argue   D) dispute

g) I got to .... Steve well last year when we worked together.

A) introduce   B) know   C) meet   D) sympathise

h) Is Brenda married or .... ? I don't like to ask her.

A) spinster   B) alone   C) bachelor   D) single

i) Parents have to try hard to understand the younger ....

A) generation   B) people   C) adolescents   D) teenagers

j) My father likes to be called a senior citizen, not an old age ....

A) person   B) relative   C) gentleman   D) pensioner

6 Match the words in the box with a suitable definition (a–l). Use each word once.

| adult   colleague   ~~nephew~~   toddler   best man   fiancé   niece |
| twin   bride   neighbour   sister-in-law   widow |

a) The son of your brother or sister. .... *nephew* ....

b) A woman on the day of her marriage. ....

c) A young child who is learning to walk. ....

d) What a woman calls the man she is engaged to. ....

e) One of two children born at the same time. ....

f) A person who lives near you. ....

g) The daughter of your brother or sister. ....

h) A person who is fully grown. ....

i) A woman whose husband has died. ....

j) At a wedding, the friend of the bridegroom. ....

k) The sister of the person you marry. ....

l) A person you work with. ....

7 Complete each sentence with one suitable word.

a) After a few days they realised they were ....*in*........ love.

b) I went .... with a very interesting girl last week.

c) Andrew acts as .... he was the most important person in the room.

d) After two years, their marriage broke ....

e) John discovered that he was related .... his next-door neighbour.

f) My parents keep treating me .... a child, but I'm not one!

g) I was brought .... by my aunt after my parents died.

h) It was very kind .... you to give me a lift.

i) Teachers should be patient .... small children.

j) James was very disappointed .... his new job.

k) It's very .... of character for Bill to behave like that.

l) Most famous people behave quite normally .... private.

8 Replace the words in *italics* with a verb from the box. Use each verb once only.

call in	fall out	give away	put up with	turn down	count on
get on well with	look up to	take after	~~turn up~~		

a) The wedding was cancelled when the bride failed to *arrive*.
........*turn up*........

b) Susan feels that her boss is someone to *respect*. ....

c) I'm sorry, but I just can't *stand* your behaviour any longer. ....

d) My brother and I really *have a good relationship with* our parents.
....

e) Why don't you *visit my house* on your way home from the shops?
....

f) Tony felt that he could *rely on* his friend Mary. ....

g) The millionaire decided to *make a present* of his money to the poor.
....

h) Paula and Shirley are good friends but sometimes they *quarrel*.
....

i) Jean decided to *refuse* Chris's offer of marriage. ....

j) All three children *behave like* their father and are very sociable.
....

9   **Decide which answer (A, B, C or D) best fits each space.**

Ann Johnson – A confidential report

Ann Johnson has worked at this college for three years. She is a (1) ......*A*........ employee, and (2) .... on well with the other members of the department. We have all found her to be an excellent (3) .... She has always been (4) .... for her lessons, and is an extremely (5) .... member of staff who is able to work independently. I can always (6) .... on her to organize the end of term play, and she has put on some extremely (7) .... productions. Her students often tell me how (8) .... she is, always ready with a smile, and she has been very (9) .... to many of them. In (10) .... she is not very talkative and seems rather (11) .... at first, and might not show her true (12) .... in an interview. Her work is excellent, and she is (13) .... to succeed. She is also quite (14) .... , and has applied for two other positions as Director of Studies. I think that you can count (15) .... Ann to make your school a success, and I recommend her for the post of Director.

1) A conscientious	B conscience	C consciousness	D conscious
2) A goes	B carries	C gets	D likes
3) A colleague	B adult	C employer	D fellow
4) A times	B late	C hourly	D punctual
5) A greedy	B reliable	C stubborn	D lazy
6) A request	B concentrate	C take	D rely
7) A imaginary	B imagination	C imaginative	D imagined
8) A tempered	B cheerful	C frank	D proud
9) A kind	B aggressive	C polite	D mean
10) A first	B times	C usual	D private
11) A but	B shy	C however	D alone
12) A person	B behaviour	C character	D part
13) A used	B determined	C had	D supposed
14) A obedient	B disappointed	C grateful	D ambitious
15) A on	B for	C with	D to

13 | Technology and machines

1 <u>Underline</u> the most suitable word or phrase.

a) This is a small car, but it has a powerful *engine/machine*.

b) Do you use an *electric/electrical* toothbrush?

c) I can't see anything. Where's the light *plug/switch*?

d) I'm going to buy a new *notebook/desktop* PC that I can take to work.

e) You can't use the lift. It's out of *order/work*.

f) If you don't press this button, the washing machine won't *go/move*.

g) Use this torch. The other one doesn't *act/work*.

h) The lights have gone out. It must be a power *break/cut*.

i) A car *factory/industry* has just been built in our town.

j) Who exactly *discovered/invented* the computer?

2 Complete the sentences with a word from the box. Use each word once only.

| icon | website | ~~cursor~~ | pull-down menu | reboot | scroll down |
| download | highlight | paste | engine | | |

a) The text appears at the position of the flashing .... *cursor* ....

b) Hold down the left mouse button and drag the mouse over the text that you want to ....

c) If your computer crashes, you may have to ....

d) To open a document, click on the relevant ....

e) To transfer text to another document you can copy and ....

f) If the text you want is below the part you can see, you can

....

g) Look at the toolbar at the top of the screen and select the option you want from the ....

h) Connect to the Internet and type out the address to go straight to the

....

i) If you can't find the information you want on the website, try typing out a key word into the search ....

j) If you need to get a whole program from the Internet, it can take a long time to ....

3 Complete the labels with the words in the box.

| axe | ~~file~~ | needle | scissors | spade | corkscrew |
| hammer | saw | screwdriver | spanner | | |

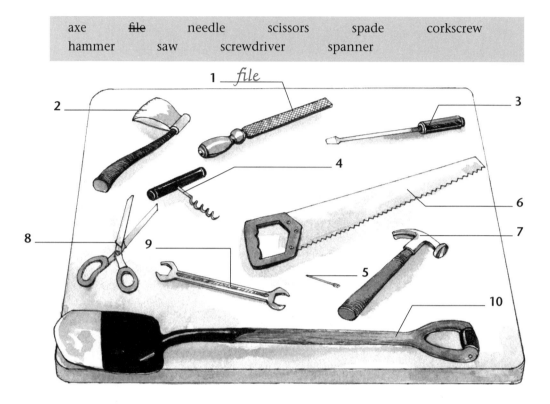

1 _file_
2
3
4
6
7
8
9
5
10

4 Complete each sentence with a suitable word from 3 above. Use each word once only.

a) You can make the edges smooth with a ....*file*........ .

b) You need a .... to open this bottle of wine.

c) I've split my trousers. Do you have a .... and thread?

d) I can't open the back of the television without a special ....

e) You can cut that plank in half with this ....

f) We could chop this tree down if we had a sharp ....

g) I was going to dig the garden but I can't find the ....

h) Oh bother! I've hit my thumb with the .... instead of the nail!

i) You can cut this cardboard if you have some sharp ....

j) This nut is impossible to undo. I need a larger ....

5 Choose the most suitable word or phrase to complete each sentence.

a) James is going to be late. His car has ....*D*.......... .
   A) broken out   B) broken up   C) broken in   D) broken down

b) If your camera is faulty, you should return it to the ....
   A) creator   B) manufacturer   C) inventor   D) builder

c) It is hard to get .... parts for this car if something goes wrong.
   A) extra   B) spare   C) additional   D) emergency

d) I bought this electric drill from a ....-it-yourself shop.
   A) do   B) repair   C) make   D) fix

e) This clock .... on two small batteries.
   A) goes   B) works   C) runs   D) moves

f) Lift the .... and listen for the dialling tone.
   A) microphone   B) dial   C) receiver   D) number

g) Don't touch the wire! You'll get an electric ....
   A) surprise   B) current   C) charge   D) shock

h) It's difficult to repair a car unless you have the right ....
   A) gadgets   B) instruments   C) appliances   D) tools

i) This knife is really .... I'll have to sharpen it.
   A) blunt   B) dull   C) flat   D) frank

j) Don't forget to .... your alarm clock for 6.30.
   A) put   B) set   C) ring   D) go off

6 Use the word given in capitals at the end of each line to form a word that fits in the space in the same line.

How does the DVD work?

When I was young, I always dreamed of becoming a
famous (1) ...*scientist*... . When I was at school I decided to study   SCIENCE
(2) .... , and then become a millionaire by inventing   ENGINE
a wonderful new (3) .... which would make the world   PRODUCE
a better place. Unfortunately, I wasn't very good at technical
subjects. Any time I operate any kind of (4) .... ,   EQUIP
something terrible happens. Machines which use (5) .... ,   ELECTRIC
such as computers or televisions, always seem to give me a
(6) .... shock. The instruction booklets are always   POWER
(7) .... They never help me at all. Nowadays you need   USE
to have (8) .... knowledge just to use the DVD. To   SPECIAL
my great (9) .... it is always a child of six who helps me   EMBARRASS
out of my (10) ....   DIFFICULT

7 Complete each sentence with one suitable word.

a) There's nothing good on the television. Why don't you turn it .... *off* .... ?

b) Can you plug the electric fire .... for me?

c) Hurry up sir. We're just going to lock .... for the night.

d) The machine is quite automatic – it does everything .... itself.

e) We'd better stop for some petrol. We've nearly run ....

f) The parts come from Japan, but we put them .... here in Italy.

g) The workstation consists .... a keyboard, a monitor and a printer.

h) This looks like wood but actually it's made .... plastic.

i) What exactly is a file used .... ?

j) These two metal sections are then bolted .... to make one.

k) Have you saved your accounts file .... my directory by mistake?

8 Replace the words in *italics* with a verb from the box.

break down	go off	~~keep up with~~	pick up	run out	knock down
do without	hang up	look out	put off	stand for	

a) My car isn't as fast as yours. I won't be able to *stay near* you.
   .. *keep up with* ..

b) This torch doesn't work. The batteries must have *been used up*.
   ....

c) This radio doesn't *receive* the BBC World Service very well. ....

d) The car is making a funny noise. I think it's going to *stop working*.
   ....

e) I was going to buy a motorbike, but I was *discouraged* by my parents.
   ....

f) People call me on the phone, but then *put down the receiver*.
   ....

g) *Be careful*! You're going to give yourself an electric shock! ....

h) It's difficult to *manage if you don't have* a washing machine.
   ....

i) The letters DVD *mean* digital versatile disc, actually. ....

j) Without a fridge, fresh food will *become bad* very quickly. ....

k) They used special equipment to *demolish* that block of flats.
   ....

9   Decide which answer (A, B, C or D) best fits each space.

Do it yourself

What do you do when something (1) .... *C* .... down? Are you the kind of person who knows how things (2) .... ? Or do you prefer to have them (3) .... by an expert? Personally, when I use a (4) .... I always hit my finger, and I can never (5) .... anything with my screwdriver because I can never find it. Despite having all the wrong (6) .... , and despite being a useless (7) .... , I recently decided to take my bike to pieces and (8) .... it. I had (9) .... out of money as usual, and as I use my bike (10) .... getting to college, I had no choice. It was making a terrible noise, and the front tyre was (11) .... I had a few (12) .... but I didn't have any (13) .... parts. I managed to (14) .... the wheel and take it off, but then I lost my (15) .... , and couldn't put the wheel back on properly. At least I am taking more exercise, as I now have to walk to college.

1) A falls	B repairs	C breaks	D runs
2) A do	B make	C fix	D work
3) A repaired	B out	C sometimes	D operated
4) A drill	B scissors	C hammer	D spade
5) A drive	B unscrew	C cut	D unwind
6) A equipment	B contents	C instruments	D gadgets
7) A technician	B engineer	C machine	D mechanic
8) A make	B fix	C build	D construct
9) A spent	B paid	C run	D fallen
10) A and	B because	C by	D for
11) A flat	B empty	C over	D bad
12) A chances	B tools	C information	D advice
13) A spare	B emergency	C renew	D repair
14) A remove	B smooth	C fill	D undo
15) A saw	B plug	C spanner	D file

1 <u>Underline</u> the most suitable word or phrase.

a) Many people were injured when the building *demolished/<u>collapsed</u>*.

b) The ship radioed to say that it was in *difficulties/dangers*.

c) The government has announced plans to help the *poor/poverty*.

d) There was a large *demonstration/manifestation* against nuclear power in Manchester yesterday.

e) Everyone agrees that the *environment/nature* must be protected.

f) There has been another *increase/rising* in the level of crime.

g) There are few jobs here and many people are *away from work/unemployed*.

h) The train was in a/an *accident/collision* with a bus on a level crossing.

i) The driver of the bus admitted that he had *done/made* an error.

j) No ships are sailing today because of the *high/storm* winds.

2 Complete each sentence with a word from the box. Use each word once only.

disaster	emergency	hooliganism	living	disease	~~famine~~
injuries	rubbish	earthquake	floods	invasion	slums

a) Food has been sent to areas in Africa suffering from ...... *famine* ....

b) Many people live in overcrowded .... on the edge of the city.

c) The cost of .... has risen steadily this year.

d) Thousands of buildings fell down during a severe ....

e) .... at football matches has been reduced this year.

f) The .... of Ruritania has been condemned by the United Nations.

g) The eruption of the volcano was a terrible ....

h) Hundreds of people drowned during the ....

i) Two of those involved in the crash had serious ....

j) Large cities face the problem of what to do with household ....

k) Doctors announced that there was now a cure for the ....

l) During the storm there were hundreds of .... calls.

3 Choose the most suitable word or phrase to complete each sentence.

a) Most young people want to ....*B*......... more about green issues.

   A) look up   B) find out   C) deal with   D) make out

b) Everyone knows about pollution problems, but not many people have .... any solutions.

   A) thought over   B) got round to   C) looked into   D) come up with

c) Many factories break the anti-pollution laws and ....

   A) put up with it   B) take it over   C) get away with it   D) come round to it

d) Disposing of waste and rubbish is a hard problem to ....

   A) carry out   B) put up   C) get away   D) deal with

e) More people in cities should .... cycling instead of using cars.

   A) rely on   B) take up   C) set up   D) get around to

f) Most governments seem to .... dealing with environmental problems.

   A) put off   B) make up for   C) do without   D) take after

g) In some countries environmental organizations have been .... to inform people and gain their support.

   A) set off   B) make up   C) set out   D) set up

h) Unless we .... the problem, many animals could become extinct.

   A) face up to   B) look up to   C) turn up to   D) get up to

i) Quite soon, the world is going to .... energy resources.

   A) run out of   B) get into   C) keep up with   D) come up against

j) We must believe that problems can be solved, and not just ....

   A) make up   B) look up   C) give up   D) put up

4 Replace the words in *italics* with a word or phrase from the box.

banned	ignored	increased	polluted	solved	flooded
improved	overpopulated	protected	unemployed		

a) Smoking has been *made illegal* in pubic places in some countries. ....*banned*....

b) Famine is a serious problem, and it hasn't been *dealt with* yet. ....

c) Many kinds of wild animals need to be *guarded by the law*. ....

d) Living conditions have been *made better* in some parts of the world. ....

e) Our local lake has been *made dirty* by nearby factories. ....

f) A problem which is *not thought about* does not simply go away. ....

g) A lot of people in industrial areas are *without work*. ....

h) After the recent storms, the town was *filled with water*. ....

i) Some countries are *inhabited by too many people*. ....

j) Recently the number of people riding bicycles has *grown larger*. ....

5 **Choose the most suitable word or phrase to complete each sentence.**

a) I'm glad I .... C .... my plane! I've just heard that it's broken down.

A) lost   B) refused   C) missed   D) altered

b) The cruise ship hit a rock and ....

A) sank   B) drowned   C) flooded   D) crashed

c) I lost the keys to my house and had to climb in .... the window.

A) by   B) to   C) through   D) with

d) The village was completely .... in an earthquake.

A) collapsed   B) destroyed   C) ruined   D) broken

e) The bus driver couldn't .... the accident.

A) protect   B) control   C) provide   D) prevent

f) After police found drugs there, the disco was ....

A) closed down   B) banned   C) ignored   D) abolished

g) During the match, someone .... fire to the stadium.

A) set   B) put   C) opened   D) caught

h) We decided not to go camping because of the .... rain.

A) great   B) amount   C) heavy   D) extra

i) I had to shut the window because the noise outside was ....

A) shouting   B) unbearable   C) in danger   D) enormous

j) When the fire broke out, an electronic alarm ....

A) came in   B) opened up   C) went off   D) put out

6 **Use the word given in capitals at the end of each line to form a word that fits in the space in the same line.**

A modern Robinson Crusoe

After a (1) ...*collision*... between two ships in the Atlantic, Alan	COLLIDE
Connaught from Dundee ended up (2) .... living on a	EXPECT
desert island. 'I fell (3) .... and no-one noticed.	BOARD
A few hours later I found myself lying (4) .... on a	EXHAUST
beach after swimming for miles. It was (5) .... too, not	FREEZE
warm and sunny, like Crusoe's island. The only (6)	SOLVE
I could find was to dig a hole in the sand as a shelter.'	
After an (7) .... in the weather, Alan waited to be rescued.	IMPROVE
'There was little food and no fresh water. It was an (8)	HEALTH
life, and I felt ill most of the time. I suffered from (9)	LONELY
too, but then I found a village on the other side of the island!'	
he said. 'The people had moved there after the (10) .... of	DESTROY
their homes by a volcano. Luckily they had a radio, and a ship	
soon came to rescue me.'	

7 Match the words in the box with the definitions (a–j).

aid	conservation	drought	famine	riot	~~charity~~
demonstration	emergency	pile-up	strike		

a) An organization which collects money to help those in need. ......*charity*......

b) When an area is desperately short of water. ....

c) The act of protecting animals, or parts of the environment. ....

d) When people march through the streets to show their opinions.

....

e) A collision involving several vehicles. ....

f) When an area is desperately short of food. ....

g) Something unexpected which must be dealt with quickly. ....

h) When people stop working through disagreement with their employers.

....

i) Help (money, food, etc.) given by governments or other organizations.

....

j) When a crowd of people is violent and out of control. ....

8 Complete each sentence with one suitable word.

a) The fireman put his life ....*at*........ risk to rescue the child.

b) Teachers have decided to go .... strike next month.

c) Sue has a lot of work to do and is .... stress at the moment.

d) The coach driver went through a red light .... mistake.

e) Many people are dying .... hunger in the desert area.

f) The boat which sank was crowded .... people.

g) The two countries are now .... war with each other.

h) .... an emergency, break the glass.

i) When the fire brigade arrived, the church was no longer .... fire.

j) When the volcano erupted, a party of tourists was .... danger.

9   Decide which answer (A, B, C or D) best fits each space.

A letter to the editor

Dear Sir,

We are writing to suggest that all cars should be (1) ....*B*......... from the centre of the city as soon as possible. The amount of (2) .... from car exhaust fumes is now (3) ...., and we believe that the public must be (4) .... Apart from this, the streets are crowded (5) .... cars, and our lives are at (6) .... when we try to cross the road! There has been a huge (7) .... in the amount of traffic recently, and the government just seems to put (8) .... the problem, instead of (9) .... it. Unless we (10) .... the traffic problem, and seriously consider some of the (11) .... , life in our city will become (12) .... Our organization, Cities for People, has been (13) .... to make the government do something! We are holding a (14) .... next week in the city centre, and hope that many people will (15) .... us.

Yours faithfully,

Mary Kingwood, Secretary, Cities for People

1) A stopped	B banned	C removed	D altered
2) A this	B problem	C driving	D pollution
3) A unbearable	B much	C overcrowded	D exceeded
4) A preserved	B saved	C exhausted	D protected
5) A from	B in	C with	D between
6) A risk	B danger	C urgent	D problem
7) A size	B number	C growing	D increase
8) A out	B away	C up	D off
9) A going through	B dealing with	C closing down	D keeping up with
10) A look for	B make out	C face up to	D come round to
11) A solutions	B errors	C suggestions	D matters
12) A lifeless	B uninhabitable	C impossible	D destruction
13) A taken after	B set up	C carried out	D looked into
14) A pile-up	B riot	C organization	D demonstration
15) A join	B bear	C increase	D agree

1 <u>Underline</u> the most suitable word or phrase.

a) There were ten people waiting in the doctor's *office/surgery/ward*.

b) After I ate the shellfish, I *experienced/fell/happened* ill.

c) George's cut arm took over a week to *cure/heal/look after*.

d) David fell down the steps and twisted his *ankle/heel/toe*.

e) Everyone admired Lucy because she was tall and *skinny/slim/thin*.

f) I've been digging the garden and now my back *aches/pains/injuries*.

g) Whenever I travel by boat I start feeling *hurt/sick/sore*.

h) The doctor can't say what is wrong with you until she *cures/examines/recovers* you.

i) Use this thermometer and take his *fever/heat/temperature*.

j) I seem to have *caught/infected/taken* a cold.

2 Replace the words in *italics* with one of the words from the box. Use each word once only.

agony	body	breath	look	stomachache	beard
brains	heart	~~spine~~	tongue		

a) Janet fell from her horse and injured her *backbone*. ....*spine*........

b) I had a very bad toothache, and was in *great pain* all night. ....

c) The police discovered the *dead person* buried in the garden. ....

d) One thing you can say about Ann, she has certainly got *intelligence*.

....

e) They have a new house right in the *centre* of the countryside.

....

f) Italian is actually Mary's native *language*. ....

g) Before I dived in the water, I took a deep *mouthful of air*. ....

h) After dinner, Jack had a *pain from eating too much*. ....

i) Shirley had a strange *expression* on her face. ....

j) David managed to grow a *lot of hair on his face*. ....

3 Complete each sentence with a word from the box. Use each word once only.

| cheek knees neck ~~throat~~ waist chin lips nose thumb wrist |

a) After speaking for two hours, the lecturer had a sore ....*throat*........ .

b) Terry was on his hands and .... , looking for the fallen coin.

c) Paul gave his aunt an affectionate kiss on the ....

d) There was such a terrible smell that I had to hold my ....

e) Stan is deaf, but he can understand people by reading their ....

f) I never wear a watch because I don't like the weight on my ....

g) One of the boxers punched the other on the .... and knocked him out.

h) When Diane was a baby, she used to suck her ....

i) I've lost a lot of weight, especially around the ....

j) Norma wears a heart on a gold chain around her ....

4 Complete each sentence (a–j) with a suitable ending (1–10). Use each ending once.

a) I think we should send for an ambulance ....*3*........

b) Some people go jogging every morning ....

c) It would be a good idea for you to go to the dentist's ....

d) The doctor gave Andy an injection ....

e) I'm going into hospital tomorrow ....

f) We took the cat to the vet ....

g) Susan took two aspirins ....

h) Nobody could find a stretcher ....

i) The doctor gave Helen a prescription ....

j) I bought some special cream ....

1 to have that bad tooth of yours taken out.

2 to check whether it had recovered from its accident.

3 to take old Mrs Jones to hospital.

4 to put on my sunburnt arms and legs.

5 to get rid of her headache.

6 to reduce the pain and help him sleep.

7 to take to the chemist's.

8 to keep fit, or to lose some weight.

9 to carry the injured man out of the building.

10 to have an operation on my foot.

5 Choose the most suitable word or phrase to complete each sentence.

a) Martin hasn't quite ....*B*......... his illness yet.

  A) recovered B) got over C) looked after D) suffered

b) Pauline .... birth to a baby girl yesterday afternoon.

  A) was B) put C) had D) gave

c) Your leg isn't broken but it is badly ....

  A) fractured B) bruised C) bandaged D) bent

d) Several angry drivers shook their .... at me as I drove away.

  A) fists B) arms C) hands D) elbows

e) That was a bad fall! Have you .... yourself?

  A) harmed B) damaged C) wounded D) hurt

f) Each time I sneezed, everyone said, '.................... you!'

  A) Cough B) Bless C) Cold D) Thank

g) Stop making that noise! You're getting on my .... !

  A) muscles B) brains C) nerves D) blood

h) As the little boy cried, large .... rolled down his cheeks.

  A) drips B) tears C) puddles D) streams

i) I had severe toothache and half my face was badly ....

  A) swollen B) rounded C) exploded D) injured

j) I've got a headache, and I don't feel very ....

  A) healthy B) fit C) sane D) well

6 Use the word given in capitals at the end of each line to form a word that fits in the space in the same line.

A visit to the doctor's

Jim decided to visit the doctor after his trip to the jungle.

He was normally a tall (1) ..*muscular*. person, but over the past	MUSCLE
month he had lost a lot of (2) .... He had also noticed	WEIGH
that his ankles and knees had become rather (3)	PAIN
He thought that he might have eaten or	
drunk something (4) .... or caught	POISON
some kind of (5) .... disease. The doctor	INFECT
took some blood for tests and told Jim to go back a week	
later. This time the doctor had an optimistic (6) .... on her	EXPRESS
face, and Jim felt quite (7) .... 'Don't worry,' said the	HEART
doctor, 'it's nothing serious. You haven't caught an (8)	CURE
disease, or anything terrible like that. It's a simple virus, and	
you will need some (9) .... Take these tablets twice a	TREAT
day for two weeks, and you'll make a full (10) ....'	RECOVER

7   Match each sentence (a–j) with a suitable sentence (1–10) below which has the same meaning.

a)   Henry's heart was in the right place. ....4..........

b)   Paul held his tongue. ....

c)   Richard jawed away for at least an hour. ....

d)   Dave had a lot of cheek to talk like that. ....

e)   Keith couldn't stomach his new boss. ....

f)   Harry backed his boss. ....

g)   William kept poking his nose in. ....

h)   Graham thumbed a lift to work. ....

i)   Charles put his foot in it. ....

j)   Jack's heart ached to be where he belonged. ....

1   He talked.

2   He supported him.

3   He said the wrong thing.

4   He was kind.

5   He was rather rude.

6   He didn't say anything.

7   He interfered in other people's business.

8   He hitchhiked.

9   He missed home.

10   He didn't like him.

8   Complete each sentence with one suitable word.

a)   I am afraid she is suffering ......*from*...... an incurable disease.

b)   I was .... agony all night with earache.

c)   I think you've put .... a lot of weight lately.

d)   The effect of this drug will slowly wear ....

e)   You really get .... my nerves sometimes!

f)   After Jack fainted it was several minutes before he .... round.

g)   Is Carol being operated .... tomorrow?

h)   Harry went .... with flu during his holiday.

i)   Peter was treated .... minor injuries and shock.

j)   Don't worry. I'll take care .... you myself.

9 Decide which answer (A, B, C or D) best fits each space.

A disastrous holiday

The day Gerald arrived at the Almara Beach Hotel, he fell (1) ....A......... the stairs. The manager called a/an (2) .... , but fortunately Gerald's leg was only badly (3) .... , and not broken. The doctor (4) .... swimming as further (5) .... but gave Gerald a/an (6) .... for some tablets in case his leg became (7) .... The next day Gerald sunbathed by the pool, and then took a deep (8) .... and dived into the water. There was not very much water in the pool, and he (9) .... one of his arms when he hit the bottom. This time he complained to the hotel manager, who sent a special meal to Gerald's room. Later that night, Gerald was (10) .... from a (11) .... back, the injuries to his arm and leg, and also had a terrible (12) .... He had a high (13) .... and felt terrible. Luckily he had the tablets the doctor had given him to (14) .... the pain. As he reached for them, he fell out of bed and broke his (15) .... He spent the rest of his holiday in bed.

1) **A** down	**B** to	**C** with	**D** for
2) **A** stretcher	**B** prescription	**C** ambulance	**D** emergency
3) **A** sick	**B** bruised	**C** hurt	**D** infected
4) **A** went	**B** prevented	**C** said	**D** recommended
5) **A** medicine	**B** cure	**C** drugs	**D** treatment
6) **A** recipe	**B** paper	**C** prescription	**D** order
7) **A** painful	**B** pained	**C** painless	**D** pain
8) **A** end	**B** breath	**C** mouthful	**D** water
9) **A** hurt	**B** injury	**C** ached	**D** sore
10) **A** ill	**B** injured	**C** suffering	**D** damaged
11) **A** sunny	**B** sunburnt	**C** sunshine	**D** grilled
12) **A** agony	**B** hurt	**C** heat	**D** stomachache
13) **A** pain	**B** temperature	**C** ache	**D** degree
14) **A** hold	**B** check	**C** rid	**D** reduce
15) **A** waist	**B** lips	**C** wrist	**D** throat

1   Underline the most suitable word or phrase.

a) I haven't got enough money, I'm afraid. Could you *borrow/lend* me some?

b) This car is too expensive. We can't *afford/pay* it.

c) There's a small flat to *hire/let* in Bridge Street.

d) How much do you *earn/gain* in your new job?

e) She's a good dentist, but she doesn't *charge/spend* too much.

f) I bought this coat in the sales. It was *decreased/reduced* a lot.

g) Jack made his *fortune/treasure* buying and selling property.

h) How much do you *reckon/value* that house would cost?

2   Replace each word or phrase in *italics* with a word or phrase from the box which has the opposite meaning.

cash	generous	profit	well off	poverty
purchase	take out	worthless		

a) I was surprised by how *mean* Charles was. ....*generous*....

b) Janet says that she is very *hard up* at the moment. ....

c) Last year their business made a huge *loss*. ....

d) I'd like to *pay in* £100 please. ....

e) Most people in the city live in great *prosperity*. ....

f) The manager insisted that I paid by *cheque*. ....

g) Jean was able to make only one *sale* during the morning. ....

h) The old painting I found in the loft turned out to be *valuable*. ....

3   Complete each sentence with a word from the box. Use each word once only.

safe	wealth	pension	rent	tip	credit card	loan	receipt

a) The old couple had only a small ......*pension*...... to live on.

b) My uncle Sam acquired his considerable .... selling cars.

c) David never carries cash with him and pays for everything by

....

d) I wouldn't have been able to buy my boat without a bank ....

e) The shop won't change any goods without the original ....

f) Keith didn't like the waiter so he didn't leave a ....

g) The house is not in very good condition so the .... is low.

h) We keep all our money and valuables in this .... in the floor.

4 Match each sentence (a–h) with a suitable response (1–8). Use each response once only.

a) Who do I make the cheque out to? ....6..........

b) We seem to be spending a lot of money lately. ....

c) The house has burnt down! What are we going to do? ....

d) How much do you want for this drawing? ....

e) Did you inherit this house? ....

f) Do we still owe the bank any money? ....

g) Can we change money at the hotel to pay the bill? ....

h) Why are you putting so much money in the bank? ....

1 Sorry, but it's not for sale.

2 I'm saving up to buy a new motorbike.

3 Perhaps we should try to economise a bit.

4 Yes, my Aunt Clara left it to me.

5 Well, we've nearly paid it all back.

6 To JB Woolbury PLC.

7 I think they accept travellers cheques anyway.

8 Don't worry, we're insured.

5 Choose the most suitable word or phrase to complete each sentence.

a) I bought these shoes in the sale. They were a real ....C.......... .

   A) cheap   B) economy   C) bargain   D) purchase

b) If you put your money in the bank, it will earn ten per cent ....

   A) interest   B) profit   C) deposit   D) investment

c) John asked his parents if they would pay off his ....

   A) rents   B) debts   C) accounts   D) credits

d) Adults have to pay £8 to get in, but children under fourteen get in

   ....

   A) free   B) nothing   C) penniless   D) open

e) I'm trying to save for my holidays so I'm .... some money each week.

   A) putting in   B) putting aside   C) putting behind   D) putting up

f) Just a minute! You've forgotten to .... your cheque!

   A) mark   B) make   C) place   D) sign

g) The blackmailer asked for the money in used ....

   A) notes   B) cheques   C) paper   D) cash

h) I gave the assistant ten euros and she gave me four euros ....

   A) rest   B) money   C) coins   D) change

6   Use the word given in capitals at the end of each line to form a word that fits in the space in the same line.

Money! Money! Money!

Helen had always dreamed of becoming a (1) ...*wealthy*...	WEALTH
woman, and imagined living in a (2) .... mansion,	LUXURY
and how her friends would praise her (3)	GENEROUS
when she gave them expensive presents. In reality she	
was usually hard up. She had some (4) .... and a	SAVE
small life (5) .... , but her antique shop was not really	INSURE
very (6) .... Every time she took money out of the bank,	PROFIT
the (7) .... checked her account, and told her how little	CASH
there was in it! Helen had taken out a (8) .... a month	LEND
before. How could she repay it? Then one day she noticed	
an old painting in her shop. She had thought it was (9)	WORTH
but as she brushed away the dust, she saw the (10)	SIGN
at the bottom. It said 'Renoir'! She was rich at last!	

7   Complete each sentence with a word or phrase formed from *pay*. Each space represents one word.

a) You can pay the full price now, or make six monthly ..*payments*. .

b) If you lend me the money, I'll .... next week.

c) I haven't got enough money to .... the suit now.

d) We .... a lot of money on decorating this house.

e) I must do something about all these .... bills.

f) Please make the cheque .... to R.D. Smith.

g) Take this money and .... to the bank.

h) I like my job, and it's very ....

8   Match the words in the box with a suitable definition (a–h). Use each word once only.

accountant	cashier	~~heir~~	pensioner	agent
customer	investor	swindler		

a) Someone who inherits money or property. ....*heir*..........

b) Someone who has retired. ....

c) Someone who keeps or checks financial records. ....

d) Someone who buys things in a shop. ....

e) Someone who pays out money in a bank. ....

f) Someone who represents others in business. ....

g) Someone who puts money into a business. ....

h) Someone who cheats people out of money. ....

9 **Decide which answer (A, B, C or D) best fits each space.**

Money matters

Are you always (1) ....*B*......... up? Do you often have to (2) ....
money from your parents whenever you need a little extra (3) .... ? If
you (4) .... too much, and save too little, you will end up with more
(5) .... than friends. You know the solution, of course: just save a
small (6) .... every month. Most banks will pay (7) .... on
your savings, and you will soon be able to (8) .... all those things
which seemed to cost too much before. The trouble is, you're a university
student, and many banks treat you like a child. But not us. If you open a/an
(9) .... with Smith Fulton Bank before October 31st, we'll not only
send you your own (10) .... book and credit (11) .... , but
you'll also receive a copy of our booklet 'Putting Money (12) .... for
Your Future'. Smith Fulton can pay your (13) .... , help you with
special student (14) .... , and your friendly branch (15) ....
can give you advice for the future. We believe in you. Why not believe in us
and open an account?

1)	**A** shut	**B** hard	**C** debt	**D** money
2)	**A** borrow	**B** lend	**C** save	**D** pay
3)	**A** cheque	**B** pension	**C** wealth	**D** cash
4)	**A** sign	**B** spend	**C** cost	**D** cheat
5)	**A** owe	**B** loans	**C** debts	**D** profits
6)	**A** amount	**B** number	**C** note	**D** rest
7)	**A** receipts	**B** credits	**C** rents	**D** interest
8)	**A** lend	**B** economise	**C** afford	**D** spend
9)	**A** cheque	**B** customer	**C** bill	**D** account
10)	**A** loan	**B** cheque	**C** cash	**D** money
11)	**A** plastic	**B** tip	**C** card	**D** cheque
12)	**A** aside	**B** up	**C** inside	**D** work
13)	**A** sales	**B** bets	**C** bargains	**D** bills
14)	**A** coins	**B** loans	**C** fortunes	**D** pensions
15)	**A** miser	**B** swindler	**C** manager	**D** cashier

Feelings and opinions

1 <u>Underline</u> the most suitable word or phrase.

a) When Dick saw his neighbour kick his dog he became *angry/nervous*.
b) Sue wasn't really *interested/interesting* in the film.
c) We were both *afraid/anxious* that we would miss the plane.
d) I wish you wouldn't snap your fingers. It's very *annoying/worrying*.
e) You're not *scared/thrilled* of spiders, are you?
f) If we forget to do our homework, our teacher gets *cross/terrifying*.
g) Tim completely lost his temper! He was absolutely *furious/upset*.
h) Your written work is full of *careless/naughty* mistakes.

2 Replace the word(s) in *italics* with a suitable word from the box. Use each word once.

| confused | fascinating | scared | depressed | dull | glad | ~~naughty~~ | upset |

a) I'm afraid the children have been very *badly-behaved* today. ....*naughty*........
b) I felt a bit *frightened* when I went into the dark room. ....
c) Jean was very *unhappy* when her kitten was run over. ....
d) This film we saw last night was rather *boring*. ....
e) This is a *really interesting* book. You must read it. ....
f) I'm so *happy* that Helen has got the job she wanted. ....
g) Sometimes when I hear the news I feel very *miserable*. ....
h) Sorry I gave you the wrong tickets. I got a bit *mixed up*. ....

3 Complete each sentence with a word or phrase from the box. Use each word or phrase once only.

| ~~blush~~ | grin | shake your head | scream | cry | nod your head |
| wave | yawn | | | | |

a) When you feel embarrassed you might ....*blush*........ .
b) When you feel tired or bored you might ....
c) When you want to show agreement you might ....
d) When you want to show amusement you might ....
e) When you feel upset you might ....
f) When you want to show disagreement you might ....
g) When you are scared or in pain you might ....
h) When you want to attract someone's attention you might ....

4 Match each sentence (a–j) with a suitable response (1–10). Use each response once only.

a) How do you feel about folk music? .... *6* ....

b) Do you have any comment on the Prime Minister's decision? ....

c) I feel really miserable today. ....

d) Is it all right if I invite some friends round? ....

e) Shall I do the washing-up? ....

f) I like this vase. Is it an antique? ....

g) Don't you think you should treat your mother better? ....

h) Is my homework all right? ....

i) Do you think I should order the tickets in advance? ....

j) Did you enjoy the concert? ....

   1 You can do whatever you like, as far as I'm concerned.
   2 In my opinion, the most important matter has been forgotten.
   3 Mind out, you might drop it!
   4 I didn't think much of it, actually.
   5 I'm sorry, but it just won't do.
   6 I'm not very keen on that kind of thing, to be honest.
   7 No, don't bother, I'll do it.
   8 Why don't you mind your own business!
   9 Never mind, cheer up!
   10 No, it's not worth it.

5 Match each word or phrase from the box with a suitable description (a–j).

| co-operative | determined | helpful | obedient | ~~realistic~~ | dependable |
| embarrassed | imaginative | quarrelsome | tolerant | | |

a) If you this, you face up to facts. ...... *realistic* ....

b) If you are this, you might make up stories. ....

c) If you are this, you carry out instructions. ....

d) If you are this, you don't give up easily. ....

e) If you are this, you put up with other people's differences. ....

f) If you are this, people can count on you. ....

g) If you are this, you keep falling out with other people. ....

h) If you are this, you might put yourself out for someone else. ....

i) If you are this, you can't put up with people looking at you. ....

j) If you are this, you get on well working with others. ....

6   Use the word given in capitals at the end of each line to form a word that fits in the space in the same line.

Film review

Battle for your heart is the new film starring Hugh

Grade. I'm afraid that my first (1) ...*impression*.. was not   IMPRESS

very favourable. The scenes of violence are (2) ....   OFFEND

and the main character, Tony, is simply (3) ....   IRRITATE

The audience is supposed to feel great (4) .... for   ADMIRE

Tony, an army officer, who is accused of (5) ....   COWARD

because he fails to attack the village where the (6) ....   ADORE

Miranda lives with her old father. Tony saves

their lives, and although the idea of marrying Tony

has little (7) .... for her, Miranda agrees to it out   ATTRACT

of (8) .... However, she is still in love with Alex,   GRATEFUL

one of the enemy army, and wants to remain (9) ....   FAITH

to him. The dialogue and acting are just as bad

as the plot. At the end, I breathed a sign of (10) ....   RELIEVE

7   Complete each sentence with one suitable word.

a)   You should be ashamed ....*of*......... your behaviour!

b)   Do you like chocolate cake? I am very fond .... it.

c)   Young David has got .... trouble as usual.

d)   Are you laughing .... me? Do I look funny?

e)   That was a terrible thing to do! I'm extremely cross .... you!

f)   I don't believe .... spending a lot of money on clothes.

g)   You look a bit fed .... Is anything the matter?

h)   I'm very keen .... classical music, actually.

i)   In reply to Jack's questions, Sue shook .... head.

j)   Cheer .... ! Try laughing for a change.

8   Decide which answer (A, B, C or D) best fits each space.

Noisy neighbours

Julie always thought of herself as an easy going and (1) ....D......... person, who put up with people's differences. She hardly ever became (2) .... about anything, and believed that if you treated people well, they would (3) .... with you. That is, until Alex and Harry moved in next door. At first, when their music woke her in the night, she was just a bit (4) .... , but did not feel (5) .... She shrugged her (6) .... and said to herself, 'Never mind, I make a lot of noise sometimes. I'll go round and (7) .... , in as nice a way as possible.' When she knocked at Alex and Harry's door she said, 'I'm not very (8) .... on loud music, to be (9) .... Do you think you could turn it down a bit?' They just (10) .... , and then Alex said, 'You can think whatever you like, as far as we're (11) ....' Then they shut the door in Julie's face. By the end of the week, Julie felt angry, but was determined not to (12) .... her temper. She had hardly slept, and kept (13) .... all the time, but she kept busy. The next time she called next door, she gave Harry and Alex a present. 'It's just a cake I made for you. Please (14) .... my apologies for last time!' And that day the noise stopped. 'What a (15) .... ,' thought Julie. 'Now there's some peace and quiet and I can read my favourite book *The History of Poison* ...'

1) A dull	B glad	C quarrelsome	D tolerant
2) A upset	B helpful	C fascinating	D careless
3) A scream	B like	C co-operate	D mind
4) A furious	B irritated	C annoying	D thrilled
5) A realistic	B guilty	C conscience	D offended
6) A shoulders	B arms	C hands	D head
7) A cry	B quarrel	C complain	D fall out
8) A interested	B like	C happy	D keen
9) A loud	B honest	C upset	D nervous
10) A whispered	B cried	C waved	D grinned
11) A concerned	B determined	C decided	D embarrassed
12) A have	B lose	C shout	D break
13) A blushing	B snoring	C yawning	D growling
14) A accept	B take	C attempt	D invite
15) A believe	B naughty	C shame	D relief

18 Education and learning

1 <u>Underline</u> the most suitable word or phrase.

a) Jack decided to take a <u>*course*</u>/*lesson* in hotel management.
b) Sheila always got good *marks/points* in algebra.
c) After leaving school, Ann *studied/trained* as a teacher.
d) Peter decided not to *go in/enter* for the examination.
e) My sister *learned/taught* me how to draw.
f) I can't come to the cinema. I have to *read/study* for a test.
g) In history we had to learn a lot of dates by *hand/heart*.
h) I hope your work will improve by the end of *course/term*.
i) Martin *failed/missed* his maths exam and had to sit it again.
j) If you have any questions, *raise/rise* your hand.

2 Complete each sentence with a word from the box. Use each word once only.

cheat	copy	memorise	pay	revise	concentrate
divide	pass	~~punish~~	underline		

a) Our teachers used to ......*punish*...... us by making us stay behind after school.
b) If you .... twenty-seven by nine, the answer is three.
c) Try to .... the most important rules.
d) It is difficult to .... attention in a noisy classroom.
e) Pauline tried her best to .... the end of year examinations.
f) Your work is the same as Harry's. Did you .... his work?
g) Your mind is wandering! You must .... more!
h) Helen decided to .... all her work at the end of every week.
i) It's a good idea to .... important parts of the book in red.
j) The teacher saw Jerry trying to .... in the exam.

3 Match the words in the box with a suitable definition (a–j). Use each word once only.

classmate	examiner	learner	principal	pupil	coach
graduate	~~lecturer~~	professor	tutor		

a) Someone who teaches at a university. ......*lecturer*.........

b) Someone who has a college degree. ....

c) The head of a school. ....

d) Someone who studies at primary or secondary school. ....

e) The most important teacher in a university department. ....

f) Someone who teaches one student or a very small class. ....

g) Someone in the same class as yourself. ....

h) Someone who trains a sports team. ....

i) Someone who writes the question papers of an examination. ....

j) Someone who drives but has not yet passed a driving test. ....

4 Complete each sentence (a–j) with a suitable ending (1–10). Use each ending once.

a) Joe was absent most of the time ....*4*.........

b) Sue wanted to do the experiment for herself ....

c) James was a very gifted pupil ....

d) Lucy couldn't find a duster to clean the board ....

e) Dave could pick up languages very easily ....

f) Brenda wanted to leave space for corrections ....

g) Tony didn't pay attention in class ....

h) Helen was educated at home by her parents ....

i) Brian attended evening classes in photography ....

j) Cathy wanted to get into university ....

1   so he didn't have any problems passing his exams.

2   so he started talking in French after only a few days.

3   so she had to study for the entrance examinations.

4   so his name was removed from the register.

5   so he didn't go out with his friends much during the week.

6   so she wrote her answers in the corner.

7   so she didn't have many friends of her own age.

8   so she wrote everything on alternate lines.

9   so she went to the science laboratory.

10   so he could never remember what the teacher had said.

5   **Choose the most suitable word or phrase to complete each sentence.**

a) Helen's parents were very pleased when they read her school ....*A*........ .

A) report   B) papers   C) diploma   D) account

b) Martin has quite a good .... of physics.

A) result   B) pass   C) understanding   D) head

c) In Britain, children start .... school at the age of five.

A) kindergarten   B) secondary   C) nursery   D) primary

d) Edward has a .... in French from Leeds University.

A) certificate   B) degree   C) mark   D) paper

e) My favourite .... at school was history.

A) topic   B) class   C) theme   D) subject

f) It's time for a break. The bell has ....

A) gone off   B) struck   C) rung   D) sounded

g) Our English teacher .... us some difficult exercises for homework.

A) set   B) put   C) obliged   D) made

h) Before you begin the exam paper, always read the .... carefully.

A) orders   B) instructions   C) rules   D) answers

i) If you want to pass the examination, you must study ....

A) hard   B) enough   C) thoroughly   D) rather

j) Most students have quite a good sense of their own ....

A) grasp   B) ability   C) idea   D) information

6   **Use the word given in capitals at the end of each line to form a word that fits in the space in the same line.**

School report

Margaret started English Literature this term, and I

am afraid that her (1) *introduction* to the subject has not been   INTRODUCE

entirely (2) .... She has not shown much enthusiasm,   SUCCESS

and does not always pay (3) .... in class. Her assignments   ATTEND

are often (4) .... , because she is so untidy, and because   READ

of her (5) .... to check her work thoroughly. She failed   FAIL

to do any (6) .... before the end of term test, and had   REVISE

poor results. She seems to have the (7) .... idea that   MISTAKE

she can succeed without studying. She has also had many

(8) .... and has frequently arrived late for class. This   ABSENT

has resulted in several (9) .... Although   PUNISH

Margaret is a (10) .... student in some respects, she   GIFT

has not had a satisfactory term.

7 Complete each sentence with a form of *do, make* or *take.*

a) Have you ...... *done* ...... exercise 3 yet?

b) I can't come this afternoon. I'm .... an English exam.

c) Jack has .... very well this term.

d) I'm afraid that you haven't .... any progress.

e) Sue didn't know the answer, so she .... a guess.

f) You all look tired. Let's .... a break.

g) This is a good composition, but you have .... a lot of errors.

h) I think you should .... yourself more seriously.

i) The teacher gave a lecture, and the class .... notes.

j) Paul finds maths difficult, but he .... his best.

8 Complete each sentence with a word beginning as shown. Each space represents one letter.

a) Charles has a good kn_o_w_l_e_d_g_e of the subject.

b) These children are badly behaved! They need more d_ _ _ _ _ _ _ _.

c) Everyone agrees that a good e_ _ _ _ _ _ _ _ is important.

d) If you don't know a word, look it up in your d_ _ _ _ _ _ _ _.

e) Maths is easy if you are allowed to use a c_ _ _ _ _ _ _ _ _.

f) Keith spent four years studying at u_ _ _ _ _ _ _ _ _.

g) Some apes seem to have as much i_ _ _ _ _ _ _ _ _ _ as humans!

h) I find listening c_ _ _ _ _ _ _ _ _ _ _ _ tests rather difficult.

i) At the age of eleven I went to s_ _ _ _ _ _ _ _ school.

j) I enjoyed doing e_ _ _ _ _ _ _ _ _ in the laboratory.

9 Complete each sentence with one suitable word.

a) If you have a problem, put .... *up* .... your hand.

b) Please pay attention .... what your teacher says.

c) Mary has a degree .... civil engineering.

d) David was punished .... throwing chalk at the teacher.

e) I was very good .... maths when I was at school.

f) What's the answer if you multiply 18 .... 16?

g) We had to write a composition .... 'Our Ideal School'.

h) Please write this .... your exercise books.

i) You might not understand things even if you learn them .... heart.

j) When Sue visited Italy, she soon picked .... the language.

10   Decide which answer (A, B, C or D) best fits each space.

Learning how to learn

There is usually one important (1) .... *C* .... missing from most school
(2) .... Very few students are (3) .... how to organize their
learning, and how to (4) .... the best use of their time. Let's take some
simple (5) .... Do you know how to (6) .... up words in a
dictionary, and do you understand all the (7) .... the dictionary
contains? Can you (8) .... notes quickly, and can you understand
them (9) .... ? For some reason, many schools give learners no
(10) .... with these matters. Teachers ask students to (11) ....
pages from books, or tell them to write ten pages, but don't explain
(12) .... to do it. Learning by (13) .... can be useful, but it is
important to have a genuine (14) .... of a subject. You can
(15) .... a lot of time memorizing books, without understanding
anything about the subject!

1)	A theme	B book	C subject	D mark
2)	A agendas	B timetables	C terms	D organizations
3)	A taught	B learnt	C educated	D graduated
4)	A take	B give	C get	D make
5)	A sentences	B results	C rules	D examples
6)	A find	B look	C research	D get
7)	A information	B advise	C subjects	D themes
8)	A do	B send	C make	D revise
9)	A after	B afterwards	C lastly	D at last
10)	A teaching	B ability	C instruction	D help
11)	A concentrate	B remind	C forget	D memorize
12)	A how	B what	C why	D it
13)	A the way	B heart	C now	D law
14)	A information	B success	C understanding	D attention
15)	A pass	B waste	C tell	D use

1 **Use your dictionary to complete the word in each sentence.**

a) The children never do what I tell them to! They are very dis *obedient* .

b) It won't rain in August, surely! That seems extremely un...................... .

c) No, I told you not to sell the shares! You must have mis...................... .

d) Jack gets very good marks, and is an out.................... student.

e) If you co.................... with the police you will receive a light sentence.

f) Dave was in the first sub.................... that sailed to the North Pole.

g) Just heat up the rice, it's been pre.................... .

h) Mr Jones is incredibly rich. In fact he's a multi.................... .

2 **Complete each sentence with a word formed from the word in *italics*, beginning as shown. Begin the word with a prefix from the box.**

| ~~dis-~~ | in- | non- | over- | re- | un- | vice- | trans- |

a) I'm not *satisfied* with your work. I am ...... *dissatisfied* ...... with it.

b) She doesn't have the *usual* kind of haircut. It's very ....

c) Mary is sailing across the *Atlantic*. She is on a .... voyage.

d) Dan is the *President's* assistant. He is the ....

e) Terry is no longer a *smoker*. Now he is a ....

f) Don't wear a *formal* suit. The dinner is quite ....

g) You haven't *written* this clearly. It'll have to be ....

h) This steak is *cooked* too much. It's ....

3 **Complete each sentence with a word formed from a word in the box, ending as shown.**

| astonish | fool | music | thought | back | ~~free~~ | lead | short |

a) I don't want to be a slave! I demand my .... *free* ....dom.

b) How kind of you to bring flowers! That was very ....ful.

c) Martin plays the guitar, but he isn't a very good ....ian.

d) Our school has closed because there is a ....age of teachers.

e) Brian is one of the world's ....ing architects.

f) Imagine my ....ment when the cat started to speak!

g) Don't be ....ish! There is no such thing as a ghost!

h) I prefer to begin at the end and go ....wards.

4   Complete each sentence with a word formed from a word in box A. Use one of the prefixes or suffixes in box B.

A

care	employ	home	postpone	satisfied	charge
friend	~~night~~	pronounce	skirts		

B

dis-   mis-   out-   ~~over~~   -less   -ment   -ship   -ee

a) I travelled to Scotland on the ......*overnight*...... train and slept all the way.

b) You're always breaking things! Why are you so .... ?

c) Jane knows a lot of French words, but she tends to .... them.

d) We all believe in .... between the people of different nations.

e) Bad weather caused the .... of nearly all the football programme.

f) George was very .... with the service at the hotel.

g) We live in a flat on the .... of London.

h) Patsy thought the shop assistant had .... her.

i) David was tired of being a/an .... so he started his own company.

j) The government is providing more money to help .... people.

5   Complete the compound word in each sentence with a word from the box.

bow	cut	helmet	powder	storm	case	~~fire~~	place	steps	writing

a) I could hear the sound of gun.........*fire*......... coming from the main square.

b) We had to take shelter during a severe thunder......................... .

c) Nobody can read the doctor's hand......................... .

d) You look awful. Why don't you have a hair......................... ?

e) I wanted to do some washing but I've run out of soap......................... .

f) If you ride a motorbike you have to wear a crash......................... .

g) There isn't room in here for another book......................... .

h) After the shower, the sun came out and there was a rain......................... .

i) I could hear the sound of foot......................... . Someone was coming!

j) At one end of the room is a lovely old stone fire......................... .

6 Use the word given in capitals at the end of each line to form a word that fits in the space in the same line.

Evening classes

Recently I decided to go to evening classes twice a
week. During the day I work in a (1) ...*secretarial*... agency   SECRETARY
as a telephonist. It is not a very interesting (2) ....   OCCUPY
and I get bored. I also got tired of coming home
every evening, putting a (3) .... meal in the oven   FREEZE
and then watching TV. So I decided to take up (4) ....   CARPENTER
as a hobby. Perhaps I should give you an (5) .... for   EXPLAIN
my choice. Learning a skill is a good (6) .... to the   SOLVE
problem of boring work. Also, I felt I was a (7) ....   FAIL
because any time I tried to put up a shelf, for example,
it always fell down! Now I am quite a (8) .... wood-   SUCCESS
worker! I am working on the (9) .... of some   CONSTRUCT
furniture at the moment. And although there are only
two other girls in the class, I don't feel any (10) ....   EMBARRASS
I've turned out to be the best student in the class!

7 <u>Underline</u> the most suitable word or phrase.

a) Helen doesn't look well. She is extremely *slim/<u>thin</u>*.
b) It's really hot today, but it's nice and *chilly/cool* in here.
c) Peter *nodded/shook* his head in agreement.
d) I can't pay you anything for this old coin. It's *priceless/worthless*.
e) The house was surrounded by a *high/tall* fence.
f) The sun is shining, and it's a/an *attractive/lovely* day.
g) This chicken is good. It's very *tasteful/tasty*.
h) Be careful of the next corner. It's rather *dangerous/harmful*.
i) Graham left the film before the end because he was *bored/lazy*.
j) When I saw him scratch my car I got very *angry/nervous*.

8   Complete each sentence with a word formed from a word in the box.

| do | fall | get | ~~make~~ | set | draw | feel | give | put | take |

a) Those children next door are ......*making*...... a lot of noise.

b) I don't really .... like going out this evening.

c) You don't have to hurry. You can .... your time.

d) Armstrong was the first person to .... foot on the Moon.

e) The director .... us permission to park our motorbikes here.

f) Can you .... me a favour? I need some help with the garden.

g) I can't talk now. I'm just .... lunch.

h) When something goes wrong, people always .... the blame on me!

i) Tom has just .... in love yet again!

j) I would like to .... your attention to these instructions.

9   Rewrite each sentence so that it has the same meaning, and contains the word given in capitals. Do not change the word in any way.

a) The forest outside the town started burning last night.   CAUGHT

...*The forest outside the town caught fire last night.*...................

b) Suddenly Janet started crying.   TEARS

....

c) What's your occupation?   DO

....

d) We'll have to decide soon.   DECISION

....

e) Can you look after my plants while I'm away?   TAKE

....

f) You will write or phone, won't you?   TOUCH

....

g) Diane had a baby boy last week.   GAVE

....

h) Peter always remains calm in an emergency.   HEAD

....

i) Stop holding the steering wheel!   LET

....

j) He can't possibly win the race.   STANDS

....

20 Word formation 2

1 Add one of the prefixes in the box to each incomplete word so that it makes sense. Use each prefix once only.

auto-	dis-	ex-	in-	mis-	non-	~~over~~	semi-	sub-	un-

a) Dick was very tired and suffering from ....*over*..........work.

b) We couldn't see the magician! He had become ....visible.

c) I could only cross the road by going down a ....way.

d) Nobody believed what Mary wrote in her ....biography.

e) Let me introduce you to Janet, my ....-wife.

f) What he said was not clear. In fact it was rather ....leading.

g) Unfortunately our football team lost in the ....-final.

h) Mr Smith regrets that he is ....able to accept your invitation.

i) This is a good train, it goes to Manchester ....-stop.

j) Oh bother, my pencil sharpener has ....appeared again.

2 Complete each sentence with a word formed from a word in the box, ending as shown.

drink	equal	hand	hope	partner	employ	green
harm	~~neighbour~~	wide				

a) Carol and Andy have just moved into a new .....*neighbour*...hood.

b) My new ....er is paying me a much higher salary.

c) The local council have decided to ....en the main road.

d) Jerry picked up a ....ful of the money and smiled.

e) I'm a terrible card player. I'm really ....less.

f) It's a kind of blue colour, but a bit ....ish too.

g) Bill now works in ....ship with two other architects.

h) Don't drink from the stream. You don't know if the water is ....able.

i) Most people say that they believe in the ....ity of men and women.

j) Doctors have proved that smoking is ....ful.

3   Complete each sentence with a word formed from a word in box A. Use one of the prefixes or suffixes in box B.

A
| art | cycle | friend | hope | national | circle | ~~edible~~ | ground |
| mountain | young | | | | | | |

B
| fore- | ~~in-~~ | inter- | semi- | tri- | -eer | -ful | -ist | -ly | -ster |

a) I can't eat this! It's completely ......*inedible*...... .

b) John has been interested in sailing ever since he was a/an ....

c) The teacher arranged the desks in a/an ....

d) I like it here. The people are really ....

e) There are two figures in the .... of the picture.

f) You have to have a good head for heights if you are a ....

g) It's much safer for a young child to ride a/an ....

h) Scientists are .... that a cure for the disease will be found.

i) Most countries have signed a/an .... agreement banning whaling.

j) Paintings by this .... have been sold for millions of pounds.

4   Use the word given in capitals at the end of each line to form a word that fits in the space in the same line.

How to become Prime Minister

Jack had never wanted to be a (1) ..*politician*.. . First of all, he   POLITICS
suffered from terrible (2) .... and blushed violently   SHY
when he had to make a speech. He also (3) .... with   SYMPATHY
people who refused to vote. After all, what difference did
it make? As a speaker, he was slow and (4) .... and   ORGANIZE
never knew what to say. He began his career as a last-minute
(5) .... for a speaker who failed to turn up. Later he   PLACE
learned to (6) .... his tie, give a big smile, and read the   STRAIGHT
speech which had been prepared by his (7) .... speech-   PERSON
writer. People liked him. 'He has a kind of (8) .... ,'   INNOCENT
they said. They did not mind that he had no (9) .... ,   IMAGINE
and seemed quite (10) .... in what he was saying.   INTEREST
They applauded him and then made him Prime Minister.

5 <u>Underline</u> the most suitable compound word.

a) The bus from Glasgow arrives at the central <u>bus station</u>/bus stop.

b) Bob only works *half-time/part-time* at the moment.

c) Joan has lovely clothes and is always *well-dressed/well-worn*.

d) Some of Bill's ideas are rather *old-aged/old-fashioned*.

e) We left our car in the multi-storey *car park/car parking*.

f) Martin is now a *well-known/well-written* novelist.

g) Thank you. You gave me a good *haircut/haircutting*.

h) Excellent. That was a *first class/first course* lunch!

i) I prefer *self-made/homemade* jam to the jam you buy in shops.

6 Complete the compound word in each sentence with a word from the box.

clothed	handed	~~hearted~~	looking	mouthed	eared
legged	minded	tempered			

a) Thank you for helping me, and being so kind-........*hearted*........ .

b) We searched all day, but had to return home empty-........................... .

c) Paul didn't have time to think, but jumped into the river fully-........................... .

d) It seems that long-.................... people can run faster.

e) Try to concentrate and remember! You are so absent-........................... .

f) Mary is very attractive, and her husband is good-........................... too.

g) Stop shouting! I'm tired of your loud-........................... comments!

h) Mike gets angry easily. He's a bit short-........................... .

i) Steve's book was dirty and dog-........................... .

7 Complete each sentence with one suitable word which is the opposite of the word in *italics*.

a) The team expected an easy *victory*, but suffered a crushing ....*defeat*........ .

b) The bridge is *dangerous*! It's not .... to cross it.

c) I'm sorry, I can't *accept* your invitation. I have to .... it.

d) David thought he would *fail* the exam, but he managed to ....

e) We had a good *take-off*, but the .... was a bit bumpy.

f) This loaf isn't *fresh*! Do you always sell .... bread?

g) The pirates *dug up* the treasure, and then .... it somewhere else.

h) These books are supposed to be *different*, but they are very ....

i) I enjoyed the *opening* of the film, but not the ....

8   Complete each sentence with one of the words in the box. Use each word once only.

> bear   catch   gain   ~~make~~   think   break   drop   lose   take   waste

a) Don't ....*make*........ such a fuss! I'll only be gone a week!

b) I try not to .... touch with my old friends.

c) What this paper says doesn't .... much relation to the truth.

d) Please .... me a line and tell me all your news.

e) Come on, hurry up, don't .... time.

f) I managed to .... sight of the prince through the crowd.

g) He says he's going to walk, but he'll probably .... better of it.

h) Ann was able to .... a lot of experience in her first job.

i) Please .... a seat. I'll be with you in just a moment.

j) I will .... the news to Dave of his sister's accident.

9   Rewrite each sentence so that it has the same meaning, and contains the word given in capitals. Do not change the word in any way.

a) Nothing you do will alter anything.   DIFFERENCE
  ...*Nothing you do will make any difference.*...

b) I hope I'm not inconveniencing you.   TROUBLE
  ....

c) Let's measure the room.   TAKE
  ....

d) Mark looked disappointed when I told him my name.   FELL
  ....

e) The old car suddenly started burning.   FLAMES
  ....

f) Susan didn't know where she was.   WAY
  ....

g) I can't bear to look at that boy!   SIGHT
  ....

h) Helen became responsible for the business.   CHARGE
  ....

i) What did you do while you were waiting for the train?   TIME
  ....

j) I now think differently about this matter.   MIND
  ....

10   Complete each sentence with one suitable word.

a) Go away. I want to be ....*by*........ myself.

b) I met Jack at the airport completely .... chance.

c) This wasn't an accident! You did it .... purpose.

d) We have similar tastes, and a lot of other things .... common.

e) Don't worry! Everything is .... control.

f) I'm going to study much harder .... now on.

g) Our birthday presents took him completely .... surprise.

h) This painting is now .... loan to the National Gallery.

i) Let's go to Brighton this year .... a change.

j) The little boy who had lost his parents was .... tears.

1 Complete each sentence with a word from the box. Each word is used three times.

do	make	have	~~take~~	give

a) ....*Take*.... one of these pills three times a day before meals.

b) All the dishes on the menu look good, but I think I'll .... the fish.

c) Can I .... a suggestion? Why don't we have the party on a different day?

d) He said he would .... me a lift to the airport.

e) I can't stand those rap singers! They .... me such a headache!

f) I don't usually .... well in mathematics, but I'm quite good at English.

g) I like babysitting, although the children always .... such a mess.

h) I wonder if they have that dress in my size? I .... a size 10.

i) I'll .... everything I can to help.

j) I'm sorry, I .... absolutely no idea.

k) In your revision you should .... priority to tenses.

l) It doesn't matter if you don't win. Just .... your best.

m) People say that the English .... a good sense of humour.

n) We don't normally give refunds, but in this case we'll .... an exception.

o) We live near the station. You can walk or .... the bus.

2 Match each group of adjectives (a–j) with a suitable noun.

a) a close/a long-distance/a tough — challenge
b) a difficult/an exciting/a huge   support
c) complete/firm/wide   trend
d) lasting/wide-spread/minor   race
e) first/everyday/body   language
f) wonderful/wasted/ideal   opportunity
g) effective/interview/traditional   love
h) latest/pirate/live   technique
i) deep/true/platonic   damage
j) growing/clear/disturbing   recording

3 Complete each sentence with a verb from box A and a noun from box B.

A | enrol   lose   reach   ~~shake~~   suit   tackle   waste   withdraw

B | chance   course   ~~head~~   money   mood   patience   problem   target

a) I knew he disagreed with my idea when I saw him ..... *shake* ..... his ..... *head* ..... .

b) This music doesn't really .... my .... Can we listen to something more lively?

c) Stay calm, don't .... your .... It's nearly finished.

d) The situation is serious, but I'm not sure what's the best way to .... the ....

e) Jorge works as a salesman now. He gets an extra bonus every month if he can .... his ....

f) I need to find a cash machine to .... some ....

g) If you want to do First Certificate you can .... on the .... in the middle of September.

h) It's a great opportunity for you. You shouldn't .... the .... to go to London.

4 <u>Underline</u> the adverb that does not make a common collocation with the verb in **bold**.

a) He **talked** <u>*dominantly*</u>/*openly*/*vaguely* about the political situation in his country.

b) It **means** *exactly*/*precisely*/*evidently* what it says.

c) Patricia **danced** *wildly*/*gracefully*/*severely* around the room.

d) The coffee bar inside the shop is **run** *quickly*/*efficiently*/*independently*.

e) Sara *greatly*/*instantly*/*hardly* **recognized** her brother.

f) He **searched** *clearly*/*frantically*/*thoroughly* for the missing book.

g) My project **focuses** *mainly*/*specifically*/*carefully* on young people's attitudes to smoking and drinking.

h) It was **raining** *enormously*/*heavily*/*non-stop* all day.

i) She **feels** *deeply*/*exactly*/*strongly* about the rights of people in poor countries.

j) Her flight has been *slightly*/*unavoidably*/*inevitably* **delayed**.

5 Complete each sentence with a noun from box A and a noun from box B.

A | crash   holiday   market   rice   rubbish   ~~sales~~   skills   visitor |

B | centre   collection   landing   leader   production   shortage   ~~staff~~   weekend |

a) I like shopping there. The .... *sales staff* .... are usually very helpful.

b) Coke sells more than Pepsi in my country. It's the ....

c) You can get a free map of the town from the ....

d) The plane was out of control and had to make a ....

e) .... is rising in China because the farmers are using more modern machinery.

f) We only have a .... twice a week and so it can be a bit smelly at the back of the flats.

g) We're facing a serious .... in our hospitals and so we have to recruit nurses from other countries.

h) The roads will be very busy on Friday evening as it's a

....

6 Complete each sentence with a verb phrase from the box.

| allowed to   asked to   dare to   due to   happy to   hard to |
| manage to   slow to   tend to   ~~try to~~ |

a) Close your eyes and .... *try to* .... relax completely.

b) Unfortunately, the doctors say his condition is .... respond to treatment.

c) Work on our new kitchen is .... start this weekend.

d) It is .... believe that the holiday is nearly over.

e) I'd be .... show you around Lisbon.

f) Everyone is .... give generously to the charity.

g) I wondered how old she was but I didn't .... ask.

h) Candidates are not .... use dictionaries in the exam.

i) The window is stuck. See if you can .... open it a little bit.

j) Newspapers .... stress bad news rather than good news.

7 Complete these common idioms with a word from the box.

| cons | nerves | ~~blue~~ | cheese | cards | first | race | red | nutshell | cake |

a) I just didn't see the other car. It came out of the ....*blue*........ .

b) I'm going to move to the country. I've had enough of the rat ....

c) I'm completely different to my sister. We're like chalk and ....

d) I receive my salary next Friday. At the moment I'm in the ....

e) It's a difficult decision. There are many pros and ....

f) She rushed into her second marriage head ....

g) I know how to programme the DVD. It's a piece of ....

h) I'm not sure if we're going to move house, but it's on the ....

i) I can't stand him. He really gets on my ....

j) I could have explained in more detail, but that's the problem in a ....

8 Complete each sentence with an adverb from box A and an adjective from box B.

A

| absolutely | blissfully | eternally | seriously | ~~largely~~ |
| radically | ridiculously | virtually | | |

B

| changed | ~~created~~ | destroyed | grateful | happy |
| overpriced | overweight | superb | | |

a) The problems in Africa were ....*largely created*........ by the colonial powers.

b) This chocolate mousse is .... ! I'm going to have some more.

c) In his early films he looked OK, but now he's ....

d) There's almost nothing left of the town. It was .... by the earthquake.

e) I'm .... that I left the country before the war started.

f) Our performance in the World Cup was a disaster. The tactics of the team must be .... if we want to win next time.

g) Look at those designer shoes! They're .... ! I'm going to wait until the January sales.

h) For the first few months after her marriage she was ....

Formation rules

1 Tenses

Present simple

I/you/we/they like.   She/he/it likes.

Do you like?   Does she like?

You don't like.   He doesn't like.

Present continuous

I am going.   You/we/they are going.

She/he/it is going.   Am I going?

Are you going?   Is she going?

I am not going.   You aren't going.

She isn't going.

Present perfect

I/you/we/they have left.   She/he/it has left.

Have they left?   Has she left?

They haven't left.   He hasn't left.

Present perfect continuous

I/you/we/they have been waiting.   She/he/it has been waiting.

Have you been waiting?   Has she been waiting?

We haven't been waiting.   He hasn't been waiting.

Past simple

1 I/you/she/he/it/we/they started.   (Regular)

    Did you start?

    You didn't start.

2 I/you/she/he/it/we/they went.   (Irregular)

    Did you go?

    You didn't go.

Past continuous

I/she/he/it was going.   You/we/they were going.

Was he going?   Were you going?

She wasn't going.   You weren't going.

Past perfect

I/you/she/he/it/we/they had left.

Had he left?

They hadn't left.

Past perfect continuous

I/you/she/he/it/we/they had been waiting.

Had they been waiting?

He hadn't been waiting.

Future perfect

I/you/she/he/it/we/they will have finished.

Will they have finished?

They won't have finished.
Future perfect continuous
I/you/she/he/it/we/they will have been waiting.
Will they have been waiting?
They won't have been waiting.
Will
See Grammar 3 and 19.

2 Indirect speech

'I always drink milk.'	He said that he always drank milk.
'I'm leaving.'	She said she was leaving.
'I'll be back soon.'	He said he would be back soon.
'I've forgotten it.'	She said she had forgotten it.
'I took it.'	He said he had taken it.
'I was reading.'	She said she had been reading.
'I had left by then.'	She said she had left by then.
'I must go.'	She said she had to go/must go.
'I can help.'	He said he could help.
'I would like to help.'	She said she would like to help.
'If I had a car, I'd go.'	He said that if he had a car he would go.

3 The passive

He helps.	He is helped.
He is helping.	He is being helped.
He has helped.	He has been helped.
He helped.	He was helped.
He was helping.	He was being helped.
He will help.	He will be helped.
He will have helped.	He will have been helped.

4 Infinitives

Present:	to like
Passive:	to be liked
Past:	to have liked
Past passive:	to have been liked

5 Participles (*-ing* forms)

Present:	liking
Present passive:	being liked
Past:	having liked
Past passive:	having been liked

Word list

broadcast (v) 10
bruised 15
buffet 1
bumper 6
bungalow 5
bunk 5
burglar 9
bush 5
button 4
buzz 11

cabin 1
call in 12
call off 10
camp-site 1
canal 11
cancel 6
cancelled 1, 9
capital punishment 9
carpenter 2
carpet 5
case 2, 9
cash 16
cashier 16
cast (n) 10
catalogue 4, 7, 8
catch a cold 15
catch fire 11
cattle 11
cashier 2
casserole 7
casual 4
cause trouble 9
cave 5, 11
ceiling 5
cellar 5
central heating 5
certificate 18
chain 6
champion 3
change (n) 8, 16
channel 11
chapter 10
character 12

(in) charge 2
charge (v) 9, 16
charity 14
chauffeur 6
cheap 16
cheat (v) 9, 18
check in 1
cheek 15
cheer up 17
cheerful 12
chef 2
chemist 8
cheque 16
chimney 5
chin 15
choir 10
chop (v) 7, 13
chorus 10
cliff 11
close down 14
close up 10
clothing 4
cloudy 11
club (golf) 3
coach (n) 6
coach (v) 18
cockpit 2, 6
cockroach 11
coin 16
collapse (v) 14
collar 4
colleague 12
collect 14
collection 3
collide 6
collision 14
come out 10
commit 9
commute 5
competition 1
competitor 3
complain 8
composer 10
compulsory 9

computer 13
concentrate 18
concert 10
condemn 14
condition 14
conductor (bus) 6
conductor (music) 10
confess 9
confused 17
congratulations 10
conscience 12
conservation 14
considerable 16
considerate 12
control 14
cooker 2, 5
corn 11
corporal punishment 9
costume 3, 4, 10
cottage 5
cough (v) 15
count on 12
countryside 5
courageous 12
course 7, 18
court 9
covered 1
coward 17
crab 11
credit card 16
crew 1, 6
crime 9
criminal 9
critic 10
croak 11
cross (adj) 17
crossing 1
crossword 3
cruise 1
cry (v) 17
cuff 4
cupboard 5
cure (v) 14, 15
current (adj) 10

nightdress 4
nil 3
nod 17
note (n) 10
notice (n) 2
novelist 10
nursery 18
nut 13

oar 6
obey 11
object 9
off (adj) 7
offence 9
offend 17
offender 9
open-air 3
opera 10
operation 15
opponent 3
optician 2
orchestra 10
order (n) 9
order (v) 7, 8
out of order 13
outdoors 3
outfit 4
oven 5
overall 4
overboard 6
overcoat 4
overcrowded 14
overpopulated 14
overtake 3
overtime 2

pack (v) 1
package (tour) 1
pain 15
parachute 6
pardon 9
parking ticket 6
pass 18
pastime 3

path 5
patient (n) 12
pavement 5
pay attention 18
pay back 16
pay in 16
peak 11
pedestrian 5
peel (n) 11
peel (v) 7
pension 2, 16
pensioner 12
perform 10
performance 3, 10
permission 9
personality 2, 12
personnel manager 2
petrol 13
photographer 2
pick 5
pick up (receive) 10, 13
pick up (learn) 18
pickpocket 9
pile-up 14
pill 1
pillow 5
pin 13
pinch 11
pitch 3
plain 4, 11
plant (n) 11
plate 7
platform 1, 6
playwright 10
pleasant 12
plod 1
plug 13
plumber 2
poached 7
point (n) 18
poison (n) 15
police station 9
polite 4, 8, 12

polluted 14
porter 1, 2
portion 7
position (job) 2
poster 1, 5
pour 3, 7
poverty 14, 16
powdered 7
power cut 13
preface 10
prescription 7, 15
prevent 3
priced 8
pricey 8
primary 18
principal 18
prize 3
produce (v) 10
professionally 3
professor 18
profit 2, 16
progress (n) 18
prohibited 9
promotion 2
propose 12
prospects 2
prosperity 16
protect 14
proud 12
publish 10
puddle 11
pump 6
punch (n) 3
punch (v) 3
punctual 12
punish 18
punishment 9
puppy 11
purchase (n) 8, 16
(on) purpose 9
purse 8
put (money) aside 16
put away 4

put off 13
put on 4, 10
put up with 12

quack 11
qualifications 2
quarrel 12
quay 1, 6
queue (n) 6
queue (v) 8

race 3
racket 3
radiator 5
rail 6
raise (v) 2, 12, 18
raw 7
razor 13
receipt 2, 8, 16
receiver 13
recipe 7
reckon 16
recommend 15
recording 10
recover 15
reduce 8, 14, 16
reduction 8
referee 3
references 2
refuse 9
refuse collector 2
register 18
registered 2
rehearsal 10
related 12
relation 12
relationship 12
relax (v) 1
release 9
reliable 12
relieve 17
rely on 12
rent (n) 5, 16
report (n) 18

rescue 6
respect (v) 12
resign 2
result 3
retire 2
return (ticket) 1
review 10
revise 18
reward 3
riot 14
rise 2, 18
risk 14
rival 3
roast 7
robe 4
rod 3
roll 3
roof rack 6
root 11
rope 3
rotten 7
round and round 4
row (n) 12
row (v) 6
rub 11
rubbish 2, 5
rude 12
rug 5
run out 13
runway 1, 6
rural 5

sack (b) 2
saddle 3
safe (n) 16
salary 2
(for) sale 8, 16
(on) sale 8
sales representative 2
sandal 4
sane 15
saucepan 7
save 6
save up 16

saw 13
scared 17
scarf 4
scene 10
science 13
scissors 13
score (n) 3
scream 17
screen 10
screwdriver 13
script 10
sculptor 10
seasick 1
seat belt 1, 6
secondary 18
seed 11
self-defence 9
selfish 12
semi-detached 5
sentence 9
sentimental 12
separated 12
serve 2, 7, 8
service 7
set 13, 18
set fire 14
settee 5
shake 17
shed 5
shock 13
shoelace 4
shoplifter 9
shopper 4, 8
shopping centre 5
shower 5
shrug 17
shutter 5
shy 12
side by side 4
sign (v) 16
sill 5
single (ticket) 1
single 12

sink (n) 5
sink (v) 3, 6, 14
skate (v) 3
sketch 10
skid 3, 6
skill 3
skin 11
skinny 15
skyscraper 5
sleeve 4
slice 7
slide (v) 3
slim 15
slip 3
slither 11
slope 11
slum 14
smooth 13
smuggler 9
snake 11
snobbish 12
sociable 12
sofa 5
sole 4
solve 14
sore 15
source 11
spade 13
spanner 13
spare 13
special 13
spectator 3
spend 8, 16
spider 11
spin 11
spine 15
spinster 12
split 13
square 5
stage 10
stained 5
stair 5
stale 7

stall 8
stand for 13
statement 9
steadily 14
steak 7
steering wheel 6
stock 8
stocking 4
stomachache 15
stool 5
storey 5
stream 11
stretcher 6
strict 12
strike (n) 14
stubborn 12
style 4
subject 18
suburb 5
succeed 3
suck 15
sue 9
suffer 15
suit (n) 4
suit (v) 4
suitable 8
summit 11
supporter 3
surgery 2, 15
suspect (v) 9
swindler 16
switch 13
swollen 15
sympathetic 12

take after 12
take away 7
take in (deceive) 9
take in
(make tighter) 4
take off 1
take out 15, 16
take over 10
take up (adopt) 3, 10

take up
(make shorter) 4
tame 11
tap 5
temporary 2
tear (n) 15
temperature 15
tent 1
term 18
terraced 5
terrifying 17
thermometer 15
thin 15
thoughtful 12
thread 3
threaten 9
thrilled 17
throat 15
thumb 13, 15
thunder 11
tide 11
tie 4
tights 4
tip 16
toddler 12
toe 15
tolerant 12
tongue 15
tool 13
toothache 15
toothpaste 8
top 11
tour 1
track 3
tracksuit 4
traffic warden 6
train (v) 18
transport 6
trap 11
treasure 16
treat (v) 12, 15
trial 9
trolley 8

Grammar index

Grammar answers

Grammar 1

1 1) *c* 2) d 3) b 4) a

2 a) *had forgotten*
b) was watching
c) used to live
d) was driving
e) had gone
f) had eaten
g) was doing
h) used to like
i) were you doing
j) had told
k) used to

3 a) *was trying*, stopped, offered
b) paid, had phoned
c) was not wearing, didn't notice, was driving
d) lay, were feeding
e) admitted, had hit, hadn't damaged
f) wasn't listening, was thinking
g) felt/was feeling, finished/had finished, fell
h) got, had disappeared
i) phoned, didn't answer, were you doing
j) didn't go, was raining

4 a) *unsuitable*
b) unsuitable
c) suitable
d) suitable
e) unsuitable
f) suitable
g) suitable
h) unsuitable
i) suitable
j) unsuitable

5 1) *invited*
2) did not hesitate
3) had discovered
4) had ever been
5) believed
6) never existed/had never existed
7) felt
8) vanished/had vanished
9) become/had become
10) had hidden
11) believed
12) were still keeping/still kept
13) set off

14) was looking forward
15) climbed
16) studied
17) were resting
18) noticed
19) was waving
20) shone/were shining

6 a) After *collecting the parcel, Norman realised it was the wrong one.*
b) Before leaving the house, Sue checked that she had her keys.
c) While parking his car, Mark noticed the wing-mirror was broken.
d) After cleaning the house, Julia fell asleep on the sofa.
e) Before buying a new television, Brian checked all the prices.
f) While skiing in Switzerland, Alan met his old friend, Ken.
g) After taking two aspirins, Kate felt a lot better.
h) Before going out for the evening, Sheila washed her hair.

Grammar 2

1 a) *1* b) 1 c) 1 d) 2 e) 2
f) 1

2 a) *Have you seen*
b) has been writing
c) has been asking
d) Did you give, saw
e) haven't been listening
f) have found
g) Have you two met
h) Did you meet

3 a) *had*, stayed
b) have/have had, saw
c) have come
d) saw, Have you sold
e) have you been doing
f) have found, went
g) has been killing, have made
h) promised, haven't finished

4 a) *for*
b) since
c) recently

d) today
e) before
f) since
g) last night
h) for ages
i) since
j) how long

5 a) *has been learning*
b) since I went to
c) Mary has become
d) been here since
e) time I have been
f) did Helen and Robert get
g) been wearing those trousers for
h) haven't spoken for a
i) already had something to
j) haven't played water-polo/have never played water-polo

6 a) *has eaten*
b) have you bought
c) have been singing
d) has been learning
e) have you invited
f) have been sitting
g) has been raining
h) has worn
i) have done
j) have been trying

7 1) *has discovered*
2) has been drilling
3) found
4) has discovered
5) lent
6) gave
7) has been
8) have already welcomed
9) has asked
10) happened
11) found
12) got
13) hasn't told
14) refused
15) have asked

8 1) already
2) so
3) have
4) ✓
5) have
6) ✓
7) work
8) been

9) ✓
10) have
11) visiting
12) ✓
13) have
14) ✓
15) have

Grammar 3

1 a) *are you going to buy*
b) I'll be studying
c) is going to
d) gets
e) are coming
f) arrives
g) I'm leaving
h) will have gone

2 a) *am visiting*
b) won't be
c) are you going to buy
d) will have
e) Are you taking/Are you going to take
f) are we going to spend
g) will be staying/is staying
h) does your plane leave

3 a) *will have stopped*
b) will be lying
c) will be working
d) will have left
e) will have been married
f) will be living/will live
g) will be waiting
h) will/is going to land/will be landing
i) will have finished
j) will be watching

4 1) *you will be doing*
2) will soon be able
3) is holding
4) will be
5) will live/will be living
6) will be
7) will have replaced
8) will also be doing/do
9) will be directing
10) (will be) teaching

5 a) *see*, will tell
b) get, will phone
c) will go, do
d) will wait, stops/has stopped
e) will get, opens
f) take/have taken, will feel
g) finish/have finished
h) will let, hear
i) paint, will have
j) will climb, gets/has got

6 1) will
2) have
3) ✓
4) will
5) ✓
6) be
7) not
8) will
9) ✓
10) will
11) ✓
12) be
13) ✓
14) been
15) have

Grammar 4

1 a) *do you do*
b) I'm cooking
c) Do you like
d) are you using
e) do the people here do
f) turn
g) goes
h) are you reading
i) Are you waiting
j) is building

2 a) *do we do*
b) are you looking, Am I wearing
c) am looking after, Do you want
d) drives
e) still have, is getting
f) is Sue dancing
g) looks, wears
h) am writing
i) is not growing, water
j) do you stay, come

3 a) *future*
b) future
c) future
d) present
e) future
f) future
g) present
h) present
i) future
j) future

4 writing, swimming, getting, admitting, annoying, beginning, studying, liking, trying, deciding
a) drop the *e* and add *-ing*: writing
b) double the consonant and add *-ing*: swimming
c) add *-ing*: trying, annoying

5 a) *This flower smells wonderful.*
b) I think you are being very silly.
c) She is having a baby in the summer.
d) Nancy is thinking of moving to Scotland.
e) They are having a meeting.
f) I am seeing Janet this evening actually.
g) Good clothes cost more and more.
h) I am tasting the soup to see if it needs more salt.
i) Helen is having a bath at the moment.
j) I feel that you would be happier in another job.

6 1) *am just writing*
2) appreciate
3) am getting on
4) am really enjoying
5) am studying
6) am spending/spend
7) am still staying
8) am looking for
9) live
10) seem
11) go
12) study
13) am writing
14) think
15) costs
16) am saving
17) gets
18) know
19) have
20) am also learning

Grammar 5

1 a) *Mary's having a*
b) I was having
c) been working here for
d) are having a meeting
e) ages since I have had
f) arrived, David had gone
g) arrives at
h) will have
i) have lost my
j) started wearing glasses

2 1) *decided*
2) had spent
3) are going to move/are moving
4) announced
5) am selling/have sold
6) are going to live
7) loaded
8) have been trying

9) started
10) was mixing
11) opened
12) had told
13) would be/were going to be/were
14) spent
15) have happened
16) woke up
17) was dripping
18) have spent
19) closed down
20) haven't found

3 a) *Jack had already*
b) you ever driven
c) I have been to
d) I was having/eating dinner the
e) are you doing on
f) been doing this job for
g) you own this
h) going to
i) will have been married for
j) last time I went to

4 a) *sat*
2) read
3) was wondering
4) noticed
5) began
6) went
7) Do you go
8) have you been putting off
9) was saying
10) will hurt/is going to hurt
11) suddenly realised
12) had stopped
13) was opening
14) opened
15) called
16) pushed
17) was waiting
18) shouted
19) Have you ever done
20) hates

5 1) been
2) by
3) ✓
4) is
5) about
6) have
7) ✓
8) are
9) ✓
10) have
11) ✓
12) I
13) will
14) at
15) ✓

6 1) *B*
2) D
3) A
4) A
5) C
6) B
7) D
8) C
9) A
10) C
11) B
12) D
13) C
14) A
15) C

Grammar 6

1 a) *Do you like*
b) Did you do
c) Does
d) Have you seen
e) will you get
f) did you go
g) did you get
h) Is

2 a) *'I'll see you tomorrow, Ian,' said Graham.*
b) 'Your swimming things aren't here,' said Pauline.
c) 'Your letter arrived yesterday,' said David.
d) 'I'll see you this evening, Larry,' said Shirley.
e) 'I haven't been at home this morning, Stephen,' said Bill.
f) 'Phone me tomorrow, John,' said Margaret.
g) 'I'm leaving this afternoon, Ron,' said Tim.
h) 'I lost my lighter last night, Michael,' said Christine.

3 a) The police officer told Jack *that he couldn't park there.*
b) Peter told Helen that he would see her in the/the next morning.
c) Janet said that she was taking the 5.30 train the next/following evening.
d) Paul told the dry-cleaners that the trousers had to be ready that afternoon.
e) Susan told them that she had left her umbrella there two days earlier/before.
f) Brian said that the parcel ought to be there by the end of the following week.

g) Diana told me that she liked the/that hotel very much.
h) William said that he thought it was going to rain that night.

4 a) I asked *Peter what time the film started.*
b) The interviewer asked Chris if he watched television every evening.
c) The sales manager asked me why I had applied for the/that job.
d) My bank manager wanted to know if I was taking much money with me to France.
e) Maria asked the examiner when she would know the results of the examination.
f) The flight attendant asked me if I was enjoying my flight.
g) I asked the salesman how the photocopier worked.
h) Sue asked Paul if he had ever been to Japan.

5 a) *to tell him the time*
b) to open the window
c) to get to the cinema
d) much the bike cost
e) would help me
f) have the car for £500
g) was being a bit silly
h) wouldn't arrive until after eight

6 a) Do you think you could tell me *what time the next boat leaves?*
b) Can you tell me where I can change some money?
c) Could you possibly tell me where the toilet is?
d) I'd like to know how much this pullover costs.
e) Can you explain how I get to/to get to Victoria station?
f) Could you tell me if this train goes to Gatwick Airport?
g) Would you mind telling me where you come from?
h) Do you think you could tell me what you think of London?

7 a) *told*
   b) asked, say
   c) told
   d) asked, told
   e) said
   f) said
   g) tell
   h) told

8 a) *denied*
   b) suggested
   c) apologised
   d) reminded
   e) offered
   f) admitted/confessed
   g) doubted
   h) advised
   i) accused
   j) confessed
   k) decided

9 a) Paul reminded *Sue to buy some bread.*
   b) I doubt if/whether it will snow tomorrow.
   c) Jill apologised for not phoning me earlier.
   d) Brenda agreed to share the bill with Dave.
   e) Catherine refused to work on Saturday.
   f) Wendy suggested going out to the café for lunch.
   g) Larry denied ever having been arrested.
   h) Ann offered to help Bob do the decorating.
   i) Tom promised the children that he would take them to the park on Sunday.
   j) William advised Chris to see a doctor.

10 1) it
    2) to
    3) had
    4) ✓
    5) were
    6) had
    7) me
    8) ✓
    9) them
    10) ✓
    11) were
    12) ✓
    13) was
    14) that
    15) ✓

Grammar 7

1 a) *stops, press*
   b) treated, would be
   c) help, will
   d) leaves, will
   e) is, will go
   f) find, will get
   g) take, will lose
   h) I'd be, lived
   i) did, would play
   j) phone, will you be

2 a) *had told, would have helped*
   b) hadn't stolen, wouldn't be
   c) hadn't driven, wouldn't have crashed
   d) smoked, wouldn't feel
   e) hadn't fallen, would have won
   f) had invited, would have been able
   g) had come, would have noticed
   h) would you feel, offered
   i) lent, would pay
   j) caught, would throw

3 a) *had known,* would have met
   b) had come, would have met
   c) had, would be able
   d) hadn't helped, wouldn't have passed
   e) would buy, had
   f) would do, won
   g) trained, would be
   h) had listened, wouldn't have married

4 a) I wouldn't *have got wet if I'd had an umbrella with me.*
   b) Unless you leave me alone, I'll call the police.
   c) If it's snowing, we don't go to school.
   d) If Jack hadn't helped me, I wouldn't have been able to move the table.
   e) If you make me some coffee, I'll give you one of my biscuits.
   f) Unless you'd told me about Sue's hair, I wouldn't have noticed.
   g) Should you see Peter, tell him to be here at 8.00.
   h) If you were to ask me to marry you, I wouldn't accept!

5 a) *1*
   b) 3
   c) 2
   d) 2

6 a) *If I'd known, I'd have told you.*
   b) Tony wouldn't have crashed if he'd been more careful.
   c) If I'd had my credit card with me, I'd have bought the coat.
   d) You wouldn't have got lost if you'd taken the map.
   e) If Graham hadn't lost his watch he wouldn't have missed the plane.
   f) If you hadn't told me her name, I would've found out from someone else.
   g) If I were you, I'd try getting up earlier.

Grammar 8

1 a) *didn't live*
   b) had brought
   c) didn't have to
   d) had told
   e) wouldn't make
   f) could be
   g) had come
   h) would give
   i) were
   j) hadn't bought

2 a) *had gone*
   b) had
   c) would do
   d) hadn't forgotten
   e) wouldn't do
   f) hadn't eaten
   g) had studied
   h) wouldn't leave
   i) knew
   j) went/could go

3 a) *paid*
   b) lived
   c) had
   d) left
   e) didn't
   f) hadn't drunk
   g) practised
   h) learned
   i) knew
   j) stayed

4
1) have
2) have
3) ✓
4) the
5) have
6) to
7) ✓
8) would
9) prefer
10) ✓
11) it
12) have
13) ✓
14) been
15) ✓

5
a) *knew*
b) were
c) didn't smoke
d) saw
e) had been
f) started
g) didn't put
h) had
i) had
j) went

6
a) *could fly*
b) you didn't eat in the
c) time we
d) only we hadn't eaten
e) wish we had
f) wish you wouldn't
g) sooner you didn't
h) wish I wasn't/weren't
i) time we started
j) wish I had gone

Grammar 9

1
a) *has being*
b) was borned
e) will been sent
i) is writing
j) are request

2
a) *hasn't been finished*
b) were arrested
c) had been born
d) will be cancelled
e) had stopped
f) were you told
g) were swimming
h) was ridden
i) had vanished
j) will be asked

3
a) *has already been sold*
b) was knocked down
c) was John given/will John be given

d) was not discovered
e) are dealt with/will be dealt with
f) has since been discovered
g) was announced
h) have been asked
i) was written
j) being invited

4
a) *not possible*
b) *The poetry competition was won by Jane.*
c) not possible
d) not possible
e) This cigarette lighter was lost by one of our visitors.
f) The exact time of the match hasn't been decided yet.
g) not possible
h) Some children are read to by their parents every night.
i) not possible
j) Most of the food at the party was eaten.

5
a) *marketing manager was appointed*
b) is being supplied with furniture
c) was built by
d) has been decided
e) is believed that Jenkins was
f) to get your hair
g) were being followed by the
h) has not been seen since
i) about the trip was put
j) is thought to be good

6
a) *We had our house painted last month.*
b) I am having my hair cut this afternoon.
c) I have had my motorbike stolen.
d) Ricky has had all his teeth taken out.
e) I haven't had my car washed for a long time.
f) We are having the new central heating put in on Saturday.
g) Harry had his nose broken in a fight.
h) Isn't it time you had your television fixed?

7
a) *Freddie is said to have a wife in Scotland.*
b) Nothing is known about Brenda's family.
c) The fire is thought to have been started deliberately./It is thought that the fire was started deliberately.

d) You should have that cut seen to by a doctor.
e) Chris is said to have been in the army.
f) I must have my trousers pressed before I leave.
g) This letter has not been signed.
h) Mary hasn't had her hair cut yet.

8
1) it
2) to
3) it
4) were
5) ✓
6) when
7) was
8) ✓
9) and
10) to
11) ✓
12) ✓
13) is
14) ✓
15) was

Grammar 10

1
a) *rather you didn't*
b) what the time/what time it
c) won't go out unless
d) wish you were
e) said (that) I couldn't
f) advise you
g) wish we had seen
h) told us his
i) me what time the next
j) accused me of

2
1) *B*
2) D
3) A
4) D
5) C
6) B
7) B
8) C
9) A
10) B
11) A
12) C
13) A
14) B
15) C

3
a) *are you being served*
b) time we went
c) had our house painted
d) wish Charles wouldn't complain
e) will be met
f) is thought to have
g) reminded her Mum to
h) you been paid
i) get the letters finished
j) was made to study

4
1) *was walking*
2) started
3) will get
4) reach
5) had remembered
6) had left
7) am always forgetting/always forget
8) Are you going
9) do you want
10) took
11) don't change
12) will fall
13) won't be able
14) have been practising
15) will wait
16) like
17) relaxed
18) have been worrying
19) worry
20) fall

5
1) *is extracted*
2) are mixed
3) dissolves
4) is also found
5) contain
6) be called
7) is made up
8) is used
9) lasts
10) eat
11) also eat/are also eating
12) believe
13) is eaten
14) is said
15) has been definitely proved
16) is known
17) causes
18) damaged
19) damages
20) would be banned

6
1) ✓
2) so
3) ✓
4) up
5) like
6) that

7) ✓
8) was
9) to
10) ✓
11) been
12) me
13) us
14) ✓
15) they

Grammar 11

1
a) *who*
b) none
c) none
d) that
e) which
f) none
g) which
h) none
i) who
j) that

2
a) *that I told you about*
b) not possible
c) not possible
d) that arrested her
e) that knows you
f) that have been damaged
g) not possible
h) not possible
i) that serves very good meals
j) that park outside

3
a) *whose*
b) that
c) that
d) which
e) which
f) which
g) who
h) whose
i) which
j) that

4
a) *which*
b) blank, blank
c) which
d) blank
e) who
f) blank
g) whose
h) blank

5
a) Brenda is *the friend who I went on holiday with*.
b) This is Mr Smith whose son Bill plays in our team.
c) Her book, which was published last year, became a best seller.

d) This is the bank from which we borrowed the money.
e) The person who I told you about is at the door.
f) Jack, whose car had broken down, had to take a bus.

6
a) The hotel, which *was miles from anywhere, was full of guests who had gone there to admire the scenery*.
b) The book I lent you was written by a friend of mine who lives in France.
c) The woman whose jewels were stolen was interviewed by a police officer who was staying in the same hotel.
d) The goal which won the match was scored by a teenager who had come on as a substitute.
e) The boy I was sitting next to in the exam told me the answers.
f) My wallet, which contained over £100, was found in the street by a schoolboy who returned it/was returned by a schoolboy who found it in the street.
g) My friend Albert, whose car was stolen last week, has decided to buy a motorbike.
h) Carol, who is a vegetarian, enjoyed the meal I cooked for her last week.

7
1) *who*
2) who
3) whom
4) blank
5) who
6) which
7) whose
8) which
9) who
10) which
11) which
12) which
13) blank
14) whose
15) who

8
a) *Margaret is the girl I went on holiday with*.
b) The golf club is the only club I am a member of.
c) That's the girl we were talking about.
d) It was a wonderful present, which I was extremely grateful for.

e) This is the school I used to go to.

f) Is this the case we should put the wine glasses in?

g) Can you move the chair you are sitting on?

h) That's the shop I got my shoes from.

i) Is that the person you usually sit next to?

j) This is Bill, who you've heard so much about.

9 a) The train I *got on didn't stop at the station I wanted to go to.*

b) The book I read was the book/one you recommended to me.

c) The ship, which had ignored the warning messages sent to it, hit an iceberg and sank.

d) The postman, who realised I was on holiday, left the parcel you (had) sent me next door.

e) The dog I used to own never barked at people who came to the door.

f) The woman I bought my car from lives in the house you can see over there.

g) The beach we went to on the first day of our holiday was covered in seaweed which smelled a lot.

h) My neighbours, whose three small children make a lot of noise, never apologise.

i) The new computer I bought cost me a lot of money.

Grammar 12

1 a) *to*, off
b) between, opposite
c) in, in
d) on, near
e) in, on
f) against, in
g) on, over
h) in, at
i) at, in
j) into, onto

2 a) *instead of*
b) Regardless of
c) In case of
d) in favour of
e) on behalf of

f) Apart from
g) As for
h) by means of
i) Because of
j) According to

3 a) *possible*
b) not possible
c) possible
d) possible
e) possible
f) possible
g) possible
h) possible

4 a) *off*
b) At
c) in
d) out of
e) under
f) by
g) without
h) on
i) to
j) for

5 a) *in bed*
b) on time
c) in all
d) out of reach
e) by chance
f) out of doors
g) at present
h) in common
i) on the way
j) on business

6 a) *costs*
b) impression
c) fail
d) strike
e) secret
f) stock
g) return
h) breath

7 a) *profit*
b) himself
c) public
d) practice
e) average
f) sight
g) whole
h) detail

8 a) *in two*
b) without a doubt
c) out of work
d) by sight
e) in difficulties
f) by heart
g) in pain

h) on sale

9 a) *under orders*
b) From now on
c) out of danger
d) in person
e) out of tune
f) at any rate
g) in private
h) out of order

10 1) the
2) by
3) ✓
4) to
5) an
6) ✓
7) as
8) with
9) ✓
10) the
11) this
12) ✓
13) the
14) in
15) ✓

Grammar 13

1 a) *to buy*
b) to eat
c) Though
d) Although
e) so as to be
f) though
g) so windy
h) too small
i) the weather
j) so much

2 a) *went shopping to buy herself*
b) is (used) for opening
c) so (that) it would get
d) left early so as not
e) so (that) I could buy
f) in order to save
g) came here to see

3 a) Sam was *so lazy that he lost his job.*
b) The house was too expensive for me to buy.
c) It was such an interesting book that I couldn't put it down.
d) There was so much noise that we couldn't hear the speech.
e) The house wasn't large/big enough to live in comfortably.

f) There is too little time for us to eat now.
g) I'm too busy to come to your party.
h) There were so few students that the class was cancelled.

4 a) *enough*
b) such
c) so
d) not
e) such
f) so
g) too
h) enough
i) such
j) so

5 a) Although *it was cold, we all went for a walk.*
b) While John has done well in French, he has not done so well in Maths.
c) Although I tried to persuade her, I didn't succeed.
d) In spite of the rain, I went swimming.
e) Despite feeling ill, Ann insisted on going to work.
f) Although he had an early lead, Hudson lost the race.
g) While I know that I should pay, I'm not going to.
h) Even though Larry was expected to accept the job, he didn't.

6 a) *It's for painting things.*
b) It's for sticking things.
c) It's for keeping things cold.
d) It's for washing dishes in.
e) It's for putting rubbish in.
f) It's for cleaning your teeth with.
g) It's for opening wine bottles with.
j) It's for locking doors with.

7 1) to
2) ✓
3) even
4) the
5) so
6) ✓
7) in
8) ✓
9) so
10) ✓
11) however
12) so
13) ✓
14) too
15) so

Grammar 14

1 a) *since*
b) later
c) yesterday evening
d) in
e) yet
f) in the afternoon
g) recently
h) on Thursday night
i) since
j) one day

2 a) *last*
b) in
c) already
d) soon
e) next
f) past
g) once
h) ago
i) early
j) just

3 a) *nowadays*
b) eventually
c) lately
d) yet
e) afterwards
f) soon
g) in the end
h) once
i) immediately

4 a) *B*
b) D
c) A
d) B
e) B
f) C
g) D
h) C
i) A
j) B

5 a) *one at a time*
b) over and over again
c) once and for all
d) in the nick of time
e) in a few moments
f) all the time
g) for hours on end
h) This time next week
i) all the year round
j) the other day
k) from time to time
l) all night long

6 a) *at*
b) tonight
c) this
d) then
e) now

f) yet
g) on
h) by
i) after
j) Once

7 a) *B*
b) A
c) A
d) C
e) A
f) B
g) A
h) C
i) A
j) C

Grammar 15

1 1) *which/that*
2) in
3) at
4) so
5) through
6) to
7) who
8) on
9) which/that
10) Of
11) Although
12) until
13) later
14) by
15) who

2 a) *By*
b) later
c) lately/recently
d) at
e) until
f) for
g) in
h) Once
i) other
j) now

3 a) *about*
b) whose
c) despite
d) to
e) whom
f) in
g) although
h) by
i) whom
j) on

4 a) *That is the man from whom I bought my car.*
b) That's the boy whose sister sits behind me at school.
c) Bill, whose computer had broken, had to use a pencil.

d) The girls, who were hungry, decided to have a meal.
e) I live in Croydon, which is near London.
f) Is this the book that I lent you?/Is this the book (that) you borrowed?
g) This is Brenda, who lives upstairs.
h) The present which you gave me is very useful.
i) The car, which was in good condition, wasn't expensive.
j) The person who found the money was given a reward.

5
a) *at, by/near/beside*
b) in, on/over
c) in, case
d) under, on
e) by, for
f) in, in
g) in, by
h) out, by

6
a) *this time last*
b) despite having/despite his
c) was too hot to
d) so tired that she
e) so as not
f) even though I knew
g) so many people that
h) in spite of the fine

7
1) *B*
2) C
3) A
4) A
5) B
6) D
7) C
8) D
9) A
10) C
11) B
12) D
13) B
14) A
15) C

8
1) although
2) in
3) before
4) ✓
5) so
6) ✓
7) they
8) an
9) and
10) so
11) ✓
12) in

13) ✓
14) ✓
15) of

Grammar 16

1
a) *must*
b) don't have to
c) had better
d) could
e) have to
f) can't
g) have to
h) should
i) might
j) should

2
a) *had better give up*
b) should be/get there by
c) I have to bring
d) must be
e) have to have/use
f) you are unable to
g) can't be
h) is bound to be
i) are to report
j) ought to know

3
a) *I don't believe it.*
b) She always is.
c) It's the rule.
d) if you don't want to.
e) It's only natural.
f) It isn't allowed.
g) It's the rule.
h) It's not a good idea.
i) I expect so.
j) That's my advice.

4
a) *might*
b) might
c) must
d) can
e) can't
f) might not
g) can't
h) might
i) must
j) mustn't

5
a) *Helen must feel really lonely.*
b) You can't/mustn't park here.
c) Harry should take a holiday.
d) Brenda can't be over thirty.
e) Do I have to have a different driving licence for a motorbike?
f) What do you think I should do?

g) Mary can stand on her head.
h) You don't have to come with me if you don't want to.
i) Anybody can/could break into this house!
j) The dentist will see you soon. He shouldn't be long.

6
a) *2*
b) 2
c) 1
d) 1
e) 1
f) 2

Grammar 17

1
a) *1*
b) 2
c) 2
d) 2
e) 1
f) 2
g) 1
h) 2
i) 2
j) 2

2
a) *needn't have gone out*
b) was to have become
c) shouldn't have bought
d) can't have enjoyed
e) may have seen
f) must have been
g) might not have meant
h) could have left
i) shouldn't have sold your
j) had to

3
a) *We've missed the turning.*
b) That's why I liked it.
c) There is no other explanation.
d) Why didn't you?
e) There is plenty.
f) I suppose it's possible.
g) I'm sure you haven't.
h) It's the wrong kind.

4
a) *David must have taken your books by mistake.*
b) You shouldn't have parked outside the police station.
c) You needn't have cleaned the floor.
d) Liz can't have met Harry before.
e) Ann might not have left yet.
f) They can't have eaten all the food.

g) Jack should have arrived half an hour ago.
h) Pam and Tim might have decided not to come.
i) The cat must have taken the fish from the table.
j) You needn't have worried after all.

5 a) *2*
b) 2
c) 1
d) 2
e) 1
f) 1

6 1) ✓
2) to
3) gone
4) ✓
5) have
6) be
7) be
8) been
9) ✓
10) didn't
11) had
12) ✓
13) have
14) have
15) ✓

Grammar 18

1 a) *4*
b) 10
c) 6
d) 1
e) 8
f) 5
g) 9
h) 2
i) 7
j) 3

2 a) *6*
b) 10
c) 1
d) 2
e) 8
f) 4
g) 5
h) 3
i) 7
j) 9

3 a) *1*
b) 2
c) 2
d) 2

e) 2
f) 1
g) 1
h) 2

4 a) *you like a lift*
b) you tell me what time
c) were you I'd sell
d) you like me to
e) this is the right way for
f) wish you wouldn't make
g) you think I should
h) about going for

Grammar 19

1 a) *5*
b) 8
c) 1
d) 10
e) 2
f) 6
g) 4
h) 3
i) 7
j) 9

2 a) *4*
b) 8
c) 2
d) 7
e) 1
f) 5
g) 9
h) 10
i) 3
j) 6

3 a) *1*
b) 2
c) 2
d) 1
e) 1
f) 2
g) 2
h) 1
i) 1
j) 2

4 a) *you think of*
b) am grateful
c) all right if I
d) don't we go
e) rather go sailing than
f) you think you could open
g) you mind taking
h) should go
i) are in my
j) Ron on passing his

5 1) a
2) are

3) ✓
4) an
5) ✓
6) with
7) ✓
8) to
9) to
10) it
11) ✓
12) ever
13) to
14) ✓
15) it

Grammar 20

1 1) *had*
2) should
3) miss
4) on
5) must
6) Can/Could
7) is
8) ought
9) should
10) should
11) have
12) could
13) could
14) gave
15) able

2 a) *apologise for breaking*
b) me how to get to
c) would you like some
d) think you should buy a
e) can't have left
f) must be
g) might/could have been
h) needn't have

3 1) ✓
2) have
3) be
4) ✓
5) ✓
6) if
7) am
8) can
9) ✓
10) not
11) ✓
12) or
13) been
14) done
15) be

4 a) *2*
b) 1
c) 3
d) 1
e) 2

f) 3
g) 1
h) 3
i) 1
j) 2

5
1) C
2) D
3) B
4) A
5) C
6) C
7) B
8) A
9) D
10) C
11) D
12) A
13) A
14) C
15) B

Grammar 21

1
a) *weather*
b) hairs
c) chicken
d) businesses
e) works
f) baggage
g) papers
h) accommodation

2
a) blank
b) some/blank
c) an
d) a
e) a
f) some
g) some
h) an

3
a) *journey*
b) paper
c) luggage
d) loaf
e) car park
f) cold
g) licence
h) beach

4
a) *accommodation*
b) advice
c) education
d) paper
e) information/advice
f) job
g) fruit
h) hair
i) help
j) scissors

5
a) *B*
b) A
c) C
d) D
e) A
f) B
g) A
h) C
i) D
j) B

6
a) *2*
b) 1
c) 2
d) 2
e) 1
f) 2
g) 1
h) 2
i) 1
j) 2

7
a) *are a lot of people*
b) these your
c) had good weather
d) was a lot of/lots of traffic
e) has great strength
f) is litter
g) parking allowed
h) this machinery is

8
a) *piece*
b) item
c) flight
d) sheet
e) head
f) slice
g) set
h) clap

9
a) *bread*
b) spelling
c) parking
d) cash
e) information
f) lightning
g) advice
h) luggage
i) cookery
j) accommodation

10
1) *B*
2) A
3) C
4) C
5) A
6) D
7) A
8) C
9) D
10) A
11) B

12) D
13) B
14) A
15) D

Grammar 22

1
a) *blank, the*
b) the, the, the
c) the, blank, blank
d) blank, the, the
e) the/blank, the, blank
f) the, blank
g) blank, blank
h) the, blank
i) the, the, a
j) the, blank

2
a) *the person*
b) the only cinema
c) a Thames barge
d) the British Museum
e) church
f) a milk jug
g) The Prime Minister
h) The computer
i) an open-air theatre
j) the thousand pounds

3
a) *C*
b) B
c) A
d) B
e) D
f) C
g) C
h) A

4 (Suggested answers)
a) *8*
b) 1
c) 4
d) 3
e) 7
f) 6
g) 2
h) 9
i) 5

5
a) *the, the*
b) an, the, the
c) blank, the
d) the, blank, blank
e) blank, blank, blank
f) the, blank, the
g) the, blank, blank
h) blank, a, blank
i) the, blank, the, a
j) a, a

6
a) *only problem here is*
b) good on at the cinema
c) that the fastest you

d) the first time I have
e) French drink
f) faster you drive the more
g) truth is difficult to
h) play the piano

7 a) *under the impression*
b) in a hurry
c) at a profit
d) on the whole
e) on average
f) in pain
g) out of danger
h) in the way
i) the cross-channel ferry
j) the back of my neck

8 a) *blank, a*
b) the, the, the, the
c) a, blank, the, blank
d) blank, blank, a
e) blank, blank
f) a, blank
g) a, blank
h) blank, a, blank
i) the, a/the, blank, the
j) a, the, the

Grammar 23

1 a) *This is all the money I have left.*
b) There were no people at the meeting.
c) Neither singer/of the singers had a good voice.
d) None of the cups is/are clean.
e) All the people were cheering loudly.
f) Each of you deserves promotion/You each deserve promotion.
g) I read both books but I didn't like either of them.
h) Every time I cross the Channel by boat I feel seasick.

2 a) Each *person in the office was given a personal parking space.*
b) There are no good hotels in this town.
c) All you need is love.
d) Neither of these pens writes properly.
e) Each of us is responsible for our own actions.
f) We all feel lonely sometimes.

g) None of the shops is/are open.
h) Neither job was suitable for Helen.

3 a) C
b) D
c) A
d) A
e) D
f) B
g) A
h) B
i) C
j) B

4 a) *either*
b) no
c) each
d) Every
e) no
f) All
g) either
h) each
i) none
j) every

5 a) *every Thursday*
b) none of your
c) all (of) the seats
d) no lorries are allowed
e) day it gets
f) couldn't understand either
g) want to do is listen
h) fewer than 20,000 people
i) children were given
j) is no time to

6 1) the
2) the
3) ✓
4) one
5) a
6) ✓
7) any
8) of
9) ✓
10) a
11) ✓
12) ✓
13) the
14) ✓
15) the

Grammar 24

1 a) *than*
b) as
c) much
d) less

e) little
f) harder
g) does
h) did

2 a) Peter *can't run as fast as Jill (can).*
b) This journey didn't last as long as I thought it would.
c) I arrived later than I expected.
d) You'll have to work harder/faster.
e) I have an elder/older brother.
f) Martin didn't think the first part of the film was as interesting.
g) Paul has been working less carefully than before.
h) This is the earliest train.
i) This café is the nearest.
j) Can't you offer a better price?

3 a) C
b) B
c) A
d) D
e) D
f) C
g) B
h) A
i) C
j) B

4 a) *better*
b) most
c) latest
d) happier
e) deeper
f) hottest
g) better
h) further
i) best
j) worst

5 a) I've never eaten a *better meal.*
b) Fish costs just as much as meat in some countries.
c) I've never had such a good time.
d) The more you run, the fitter you will get.
e) Wednesday is the earliest the doctor can see you, I'm afraid.
f) I must have a rest, I can't go (on) any further.
g) Home computers aren't as expensive as they used to be.
h) Sue knows more Italian than I do.

i) Learning to drive isn't as difficult as/is easier than I thought it would be.
j) John isn't a better skater than Barbara.

6 a) *cost less than mine*
b) are better at maths than
c) is a little taller than
d) was growing angrier and
e) did her
f) isn't/wasn't as good as
g) driven along such a bumpy
h) more you eat, the fatter
i) was the best he could
j) was just as difficult as

7 1) ✓
2) so
3) more
4) the
5) the
6) ✓
7) than
8) of
9) ✓
10) it
11) and
12) the
13) ✓
14) ✓
15) that

Grammar 25

1 1) *Every*
2) the
3) come
4) the
5) that
6) the
7) neither
8) which
9) most
10) the
11) the
12) some
13) none
14) a
15) more

2 a) *never seen a worse*
b) all the sandwiches have been
c) latest novel is not as
d) talk to either of
e) can't swim as well
f) slowly you walk, the longer
g) no good calling
h) was the last person I
i) never been to such a
j) cost less than I (had)

3 a) *slice*
b) flight
c) head
d) sheet
e) item
f) lumps
g) glass
h) helping
i) clap
j) pair

4 a) *Parking is not allowed here./There is no parking here.*
b) There is no/There isn't any furniture in the house.
c) There seem to be a lot of people in this room.
d) Can you give me any information about guided tours of the city?
e) The audience was enthusiastic.
f) Maths is my favourite subject.
g) There is a lot of traffic on this road today.

5 a) *works as a French*
b) that the best you can
c) first lobster I have ever
d) play the violin
e) all you need is
f) of the lifts was

6 a) *them*
b) some
c) some
d) it
e) some
f) a
g) the
h) the

7 1) here
2) more
3) ✓
4) the
5) were
6) ✓
7) one
8) of
9) both
10) ✓
11) ✓
12) than
13) a
14) ✓
15) such

Grammar 26

1 a) *Sorry, but I haven't got round to fixing your bike yet.*
b) Oh bother, we have run out of milk.
c) It took me a long time to get over my illness.
d) Julie must have grown out of biting her nails.
e) I think we've come up with an answer to the problem.
f) I don't think I feel up to playing football today.
g) Ann is someone I really look up to.
h) I must see about having the kitchen painted.
i) Please help me. I'm counting on you.
j) Peter takes after his father.

2 a) *ran into Philip*
b) have to face up to
c) put up with so much
d) got away with
e) called on a few friends
f) are you getting
g) and get my teeth seen

3 a) *for*
b) up
c) against
d) on
e) in
f) across
g) round
h) with
i) into
j) to

4 a) *B*
b) D
c) C
d) A
e) C
f) D
g) A
h) B
i) D
j) C

5 a) *B*
b) B
c) C
d) B
e) A
f) C
g) C
h) A
i) C
j) C

Grammar 27

1 a) *Jack always turns up late for work.*
b) Look up their number in the phone directory.
c) I'm putting money aside to buy a new bike.
d) After a few days the pain in Dave's leg wore off.
e) I'm afraid the match has been called off.
f) The government refused to give in to the demands of the terrorists.
g) We offered them £250,000 for the house but they turned our offer/turned it down.
h) We can put you up if you come to Cambridge.
i) I can't work out how much the whole trip will cost.
j) A large silver limousine drew up outside the house.

2 a) *(a)round*
b) up
c) out
d) off
e) up
f) out
g) up
h) out
i) off
j) out

3 a) *rain has set in for*
b) how to fill in
c) took over this job
d) have made up this
e) you held up
f) broke down
g) to give up (drinking)
h) has been put off until

4 a) *carried*
b) take
c) give
d) try
e) clear
f) falls
g) went
h) fill

5 a) *C*
b) D
c) C
d) C
e) A
f) B
g) D
h) C

6 a) *made up*
b) come out
c) clearing up
d) work out
e) look out
f) give up
g) take off
h) fallen out

7 a) *B*
b) C
c) B
d) A
e) B
f) C
g) A
h) C

Grammar 28

1 a) *playing*
b) to write
c) to pay
d) buying
e) working
f) to feed
g) to meet
h) taking

2 a) *denied cheating*
b) couldn't help laughing
c) regret to tell you that
d) to drink some/to get a drink of
e) suggest taking
f) to turn off the lights
g) appears to have forgotten

3 a) *to eat*
b) not to sell
c) seeing/having seen
d) not to notice/not to have noticed
e) to buy
f) moving/having moved
g) waiting
h) to finish/to have finished

4 a) *demanded*
b) fancy
c) bear
d) refused
e) risk
f) expect
g) intend

Grammar 29

1 a) *in*
b) of
c) of/like
d) at/by
e) on
f) with
g) at
h) to
i) about
j) to

2 a) The old lady was *robbed of her handbag.*
b) John is interested in photography.
c) Helen knows a lot about car engines.
d) France is famous for its food.
e) I am very grateful to your brother for his help.
f) Can you share this book with Stephen?
g) I'm not used to studying all night.
h) Harry is afraid of snakes.
i) Please forgive me for breaking your camera.
j) Peter is good at drawing.

3 a) *ashamed*
b) keen
c) talking/boasting
d) late
e) full
f) trust
g) accused
h) succeeded
i) pleased
j) begins/began

4 a) *is capable of*
b) belongs to
c) applied for
d) died of
e) congratulated Tony on passing
f) lent Jean her
g) was bored by
h) felt sorry for

5 a) *angry*
b) agree
c) approve
d) argued
e) look
f) reminds
g) jealous
h) surprised
i) add
j) ask

6 a) *B*
b) A
c) D
d) C
e) A
f) B
g) A
h) C
i) D
j) B

7 1) with
2) to
3) about
4) ✓
5) and
6) for
7) ✓
8) up
9) them
10) ✓
11) us
12) ✓
13) and
14) ✓
15) last

Grammar 30

1 1) *grew*
2) put
3) join
4) wore
5) getting
6) deal
7) take
8) spent
9) showing
10) getting
11) got
12) grown
13) taken
14) talking/thinking
15) face

2 a) *get round*
b) get on
c) getting at
d) got over
e) got away

3 a) *come out*
b) come up with
c) came across
d) came into
d) come up against

4 a) *miss working*
b) will mean moving to
c) regrets having sold his
d) forget to post

e) to learn how to
f) denied stealing
g) you like to go to
h) mind looking after the
i) promised (that) she would be there
j) our first meeting in

5 a) *B*
2) D
3) C
4) C
5) A
6) D
7) B
8) A
9) B
10) D
11) A
12) C
13) B
14) C
15) A

6 a) *keep*
b) Stand
c) relying/counting/depending
d) looking
e) seen

7 a) *capable of*
b) fond of
c) ashamed of
d) good of
e) jealous of

8 a) *certain about*
b) unhappy about
c) right about
d) anxious about
e) upset about

9 a) *washing*
b) looking
c) bringing
d) taking
e) doing/going

10 a) *taking*
b) got
c) put
d) made
e) getting
f) takes
g) turned
h) think
i) clear/clean

11 a) *to look into*
b) we have run out of
c) fill in
d) broke out

e) getting at
f) won't stand for
g) leave out
h) come across
i) take over
j) got round to it

Grammar 31

1 a) *shall we*
b) should you
c) has he
d) will you
e) are you
f) will you
g) can he
h) haven't you
i) didn't they
j) is he

2 a) *will you*
b) isn't he
c) won't you
d) wasn't he
e) do they
f) do you
g) does it
h) shall we
i) are you
j) doesn't he

3 a) Not only *was Tony late, but he had left all his books behind.*
b) No sooner had I gone to bed than someone rang my doorbell.
c) Seldom have I stayed in a worse hotel.
d) Never have I heard such nonsense.
e) Only then did I realise that I had lost my keys.
f) Rarely has the economic situation been worse.
g) Not once did the manager offer us an apology.
h) Under no circumstances should you send money to us by post.
i) Only after seeing *Hamlet* on the stage did I understand it.
j) Little did the embassy staff realise that Ted was a secret agent.

327

4 a) *Now is the best time to buy a house.*
b) Round the corner came the bus.
c) Up went the price of petrol.
d) On the top of the Acropolis stands the Parthenon.
e) Round and round went the wheels of the engine.
f) In this house lived Winston Churchill.
g) Down went the flag.
h) Now comes the best part of the story.

5 1) C
2) A
3) D
4) A
5) B
6) C
7) D
8) B
9) C
10) A
11) A
12) B
13) C
14) D
15) D

Grammar 32

1 a) *However*
b) as
c) First of all, In addition to this, As a result
d) moreover, In contrast, Personally
e) Owing to, Consequently

2 a) *In*
b) As/Since
c) as
d) on
e) of
f) well
g) For
h) view/opinion

3 1) *A*
2) D
3) C
4) A
5) B
6) C
7) D
8) B
9) D
10) B

Grammar 33

1 a) Whoever *stole the painting must have been tall.*
b) Whatever you do, don't tell Jane I was here.
c) Whatever is the time?
d) Why ever did you tell me a lie?
e) Whenever I go on holiday, the weather gets worse.
f) Wherever have you been?
g) However did you know I was going to be here?
h) Whatever you say, I won't believe you.

2 a) *gave me a pat on*
b) pick a rabbit up by
c) Tanya in the face
d) grabbed the thief by the
e) took the baby by the
f) stung me on the
g) punched me in the
h) patted the dog on the
i) wounded in the arm
j) pat me on the

3 a) There *is a good film on at the local cinema* at the moment.
b) It's impossible for me to drink coffee so late at night.
c) It doesn't matter if you can't answer all the questions.
d) There is nothing in the fridge.
e) It has been a tiring journey.
f) It is a long way to the station.
g) It's time for a break now.
h) It was good to see you.

4 a) Did you *enjoy yourself at the beach, Joe?*
b) What we really need is a new fridge.
c) It's very foggy today.
d) Anyone who believes in ghosts is a bit crazy!
e) Whenever you need me, just call me.
f) It was interesting to talk to you.
g) John has hurt himself.
h) Whatever did you do that for?

5 a) *C*
b) D
c) B
d) A

e) C
f) A
g) D
h) D
i) A
j) B

Grammar 34

1 a) *studying*
b) destroying
c) donkeys
d) flies
e) niece
f) hurried
g) furniture
h) enough
i) welcome
j) hotter
k) receipt
l) wonderful
m) swimming
n) regretted
o) hopefully
p) applying
q) heard
r) insurance
s) happily
t) advertisement

2 a) *search*
b) wait
c) stuff
d) go
e) home
f) come
g) cow
h) white
i) plumber
j) store

3 a) *supplying*
b) destroyed
c) applied
d) loneliness
e) employs
f) cries
g) silliness
h) annoys
i) beautiful
j) prettiness

4 a) *cold*
b) treat
c) blouse
d) ought
e) lost
f) iced
g) gone
h) heart
i) two
j) refer

5 a) *sincerely*, dictionary
b) different, interesting
c) lovely, necessary
d) writing, uninteresting
e) pullover, definitely
f) friend, responsible
g) holiday, quantity
h) likelihood, luggage
i) impatient, student
j) finally, pavement

Grammar 35

1 1) *all*
2) Whoever
3) are
4) there
5) myself
6) which
7) Not
8) no-one
9) There
10) what
11) As
12) After
13) Someone
14) whoever
15) result

2 a) You *should never press both buttons at once under any circumstances.*
b) As it was cold, I decided to wear two pullovers.
c) Did you enjoy yourself at the party?
d) Outside the cinema I was grabbed by the arm.
e) The army was defeated owing to/because of poor organization.
f) Not once did Jean offer her boss a word of apology.
g) There's nothing to eat in the house, I'm afraid.
h) There's no point (in) going on any further tonight.
i) What Sally saw is difficult to describe.
j) Seldom have I had a more relaxing holiday.

3 a) *D*
b) B
c) A
d) C
e) D
f) B
g) C
h) C
i) D
j) B

4 1) that
2) whether
3) ✓
4) they
5) herself
6) so
7) them
8) ✓
9) was
10) ✓
11) in
12) they
13) ✓
14) although
15) ✓

Vocabulary answers

Vocabulary 1

1
a) *deck*
b) platform
c) departure lounge
d) coach station
e) harbour
f) buffet
g) cabin
h) destination
i) quay
j) runway

2
a) *delayed*
b) crew
c) landed
d) flight
e) diverted
f) suitcase
g) check in
h) declared
i) took off
j) single
k) seat belt
l) flight attendant

3
a) *cancel*
b) platform
c) took off
d) destination
e) passengers
f) buffet
g) cabin
h) single
i) declare
j) harbour
k) luggage
l) delay

4
a) *a cruise*
b) a flight
c) an itinerary
d) a trip
e) an expedition
f) a package tour
g) travel
h) a voyage
i) a tour
j) a crossing

5
a) *itinerary*
b) tour
c) crossing
d) cruise
e) package tour
f) expedition
g) flight
h) voyage

i) Travel
j) trip

6
a) *a fortnight*
b) accommodation
c) hitch-hike
d) double room
e) guest-house
f) book
g) camp-site
h) vacancy
i) hostel
j) porter

7
a) *seaside*
b) seafood
c) seaweed
d) sea level
e) sea front
f) seagulls
g) seasick
h) seashore

8
a) *C*
b) D
c) A
d) D
e) B
f) C
g) B
h) A
i) D
j) B

9 (*Suggested*)
a) I sunbathed for a while and then *I had a swim.*
b) I had a good time on my holiday last year.
c) David had a car-crash while he was driving to Spain.
d) 'Goodbye', said Maria, 'and have a safe journey.'
e) Most of the people on the beach had very little on.
f) We couldn't decide about our holiday, until Sue had an idea.
g) Martin had a party at his house last night.
h) Brenda couldn't go away for the weekend because she had work to do.
i) Ian didn't know how to water-ski but he had a go.
j) Laura had a suspicion that the hotel food was going to be bad.

10
1) *B*
2) A
3) C
4) B
5) D
6) A
7) D
8) D
9) B
10) A
11) C
12) A
13) C
14) B
15) D

Vocabulary 2

1 *cashier-bank* cook-restaurant/kitchen, dentist-surgery, farmer-field, hairdresser-salon, librarian-library, mechanic-garage, miner-coal-mine, musician-concert hall/studio, photographer-studio, pilot-cockpit, porter-hotel, receptionist-office, vicar-church, waiter-restaurant

2
a) *vet*
b) refuse collector
c) estate agent
d) carpenter
e) chef
f) plumber
g) accountant
h) firefighter

3
a) *plumber*
b) porter
c) dentist
d) hairdresser
e) carpenter
f) vet
g) waiter
h) mechanic

4
a) *living*
b) work
c) business
d) work
e) living
f) business
g) job
h) work
i) work
j) work

5
a) *go*
b) come
c) fall
d) fill
e) get
f) turn
g) face
h) draw
i) take
j) call

6
a) *4*
b) 7
c) 2
d) 6
e) 1
f) 8
g) 3
h) 5

7
1) *advertising*
2) resignation
3) economic
4) unemployed
5) applications
6) qualified
7) profitable
8) employee
9) earnings
10) retirement

8
a) *wages*
b) temporary
c) pension
d) earns
e) in charge
f) off
g) sacked
h) notice
i) make
j) expenses

9 (Suggested)
a) *Terry has a different job now.*
b) A good employer looks after everyone in the company.
c) I am sure you will gain/get a lot of experience in this job.
d) This job is a living, but that's all.
e) The firm raised my salary after I had worked there for a year.
f) The company made a profit last year.
g) I had to attend an interview at head office.
h) I earn/make £12,000 a year.
i) Jill works for a firm of accountants.
j) We put an advertisement for the job in the paper.

10
1) *B*
2) D
3) A
4) D
5) B
6) C
7) D
8) A
9) C
10) A
11) C
12) A
13) D
14) B
15) C

Vocabulary 3

1
a) *costume*
b) saddle
c) club
d) net
e) handlebars
f) rope
g) ice
h) gloves
i) whistle
j) glasses
k) racket
l) rod

2
a) *cards*
b) embroidery
c) crossword
d) model-making
e) draughts
f) hiking
g) billiards
h) gambling

3
a) *race*
b) ground
c) fit
d) won
e) spectators
f) interesting
g) draw
h) prize
i) competitors
j) pastime

4
a) *professionally*
b) postponed
c) champion
d) score
e) arranged
f) spare
g) second
h) captain
i) record
j) referee
k) outdoors
l) side

5
1) *photography*
2) skilful
3) failure
4) imaginative
5) successful
6) unexpected
7) valuable
8) misunderstanding
9) unbelievable
10) disagreement

6
a) *B*
b) D
c) C
d) A
e) A
f) C
g) D
h) B
i) D
j) B

7
a) *better*
b) stuck
c) ready
d) lost
e) anywhere
f) dinner
g) back
h) right
i) off
j) through
k) together
l) used

8
a) *After Paul's leg was injured, it took him a long time to recover.*
b) Unfortunately Sally rode her bike into the mud and became stuck.
c) Before the race I went to the stadium to prepare.
d) Some of the competitors lost their way because of the thick fog.
e) I tried learning to do embroidery but I didn't succeed.
f) She worked on her stamp collection and he cooked.
g) I didn't arrive home from the match till late because of the crowds.
h) David practised hitting the golf ball until he perfected it.
i) Kate enjoyed riding the horse but found it hard to dismount.
j) I tried to phone the tennis club but there was no answer.

331

k) We have a great time whenever our rugby team meets.

l) I find playing football on plastic grass strange.

9
1) C
2) A
3) A
4) D
5) C
6) B
7) C
8) D
9) A
10) C
11) D
12) B
13) C
14) A
15) C

Vocabulary 4

1
1) *glasses*
2) tie
3) shirt
4) waistcoat
5) jacket
6) trousers
7) briefcase
8) shoe
9) earring
10) blouse
11) belt
12) handbag
13) skirt
14) boot

2
a) *uniform*
b) formal
c) suit
d) sleeves
e) dressing gown
f) overalls
g) mac
h) scarf
i) shoelaces
j) pockets
k) aprons
l) bow

3
1) *appearance*
2) parting
3) striped
4) unsuitable
5) undresses
6) cleaner's
7) worn
8) unbuttoned
9) fashionable
10) informal

4
a) This shirt is too small, it's not my *size*.
b) You have so many clothes. Why did you buy these clothes as well?
c) correct
d) correct
e) I like your new trousers. How much were they?
f) As far as I can see, the man in this photograph is wearing a suit.
g) correct
h) You're soaked! Take off your clothes immediately!

5
a) *sweater*
b) jacket
c) belt
d) shorts
e) sleeves
f) tight
g) silk
h) wardrobe

6
a) D
b) A
c) C
d) D
e) B
f) A
g) B
h) B

7
a) C
b) C
c) B
d) D
e) B
f) C
g) B
h) D

8
1) B
2) C
3) A
4) C
5) D
6) B
7) D
8) A
9) B
10) A
11) D
12) C
13) C
14) A
15) B

Vocabulary 5

1
a) *gates, path*
b) entrance, side
c) fitted
d) cupboards, bookshelves
e) fireplace, washbasins
f) stairs, stained
g) shower, taps
h) attic, greenhouse, shed
i) fence, hedge
j) detached, neighbourhood

2
a) *letterbox*
b) shelf
c) drive
d) door knocker
e) dishwasher
f) central heating
g) rug
h) settee/sofa
i) landing
j) doormat
k) curtains
l) stool

3
a) 6
b) 3
c) 8
d) 1
e) 10
f) 5
g) 2
h) 9
i) 4
j) 7

4
a) *home*
b) housework
c) house
d) homeless
e) housekeeper
f) home
g) house
h) home
i) housing
j) home

5
a) D
b) B
c) D
d) C
e) B
f) A
g) B
h) A

6
1) *neighbourhood*
2) shortage
3) upstairs
4) sale
5) loan

6) rebuilt
7) undamaged
8) furnished
9) length
10) cooker

7 a) *armchair*
b) lane
c) wallpaper
d) oven
e) picking
f) lawn
g) cellar
h) car park
i) floor
j) radiator
k) motorway
l) is
m) frame
n) sill
o) at

8 a) *duvet*
b) cushion
c) urban
d) shutters
e) litter
f) ceiling
g) bunk
h) rural
i) roof
j) pillow
k) blind
l) rubbish
m) kennel
n) kerb
o) chimney

9 1) *A*
2) C
3) B
4) D
5) B
6) C
7) A
8) B
9) C
10) B
11) A
12) A
13) D
14) B
15) D

Vocabulary 6

1 a) *chauffeur*
b) motorist
c) driver
d) captain
e) guard
f) traffic warden
g) steward
h) crew
i) conductor
j) cyclist
k) pedestrian
l) mechanic

2 1) *roof rack*
2) aerial
3) boot
4) exhaust
5) wheel
6) steering wheel
7) wing
8) tyre
9) bumper
10) headlight
11) engine
12) bonnet
13) windscreen
14) wiper
15) mirror

3 a) *B*
b) A
c) D
d) B
e) A
f) D
g) B
h) B
i) A
j) D

4 1) *cancellation*
2) Unfortunately
3) collision
4) unexpectedly
5) unsuitable
6) unavoidable
7) injuries
8) widening
9) adjustable
10) payment

5 a) *sailor*
b) shipped
c) sail
d) shipment
e) sail
f) sailed
g) ship
h) sailing
i) shipping

j) sails

6 a) *wings*
b) gear
c) handlebars
d) parachute
e) oars
f) chain
g) brakes
h) bonnet
i) deck
j) cockpit

7 a) *looking*
b) take/use
c) pick
d) made/headed
e) put
f) keep/catch
g) showing
h) put
i) trying
j) dealing

8 1) *B*
2) D
3) A
4) C
5) C
6) D
7) A
8) C
9) B
10) D
11) B
12) A
13) B
14) D
15) A

Vocabulary 7

1 a) *bill*
b) book
c) portion
d) help
e) menu
f) ordered
g) dish
h) raw
i) vegetarian
j) course

2 a) *6*
b) 2
c) 10
d) 8
e) 1
f) 5
g) 7
h) 4
i) 3
j) 9

3
a) *saucers*
b) chips
c) forks
d) butter
e) bacon
f) pepper
g) bread
h) wine
i) beer
j) chocolate
k) instant coffee
l) grapes

4
1) *tin opener*
2) jar
3) kettle
4) food mixer
5) bowl
6) frying pan
7) mug
8) jug
9) saucepan
10) casserole dish

5
a) *on*
b) off
c) around/round
d) out
e) to
f) off
g) round
h) up
i) up
j) out

6
a) *C*
b) A
c) B
d) D
e) C
f) A
g) D
h) A
i) B
j) C

7
a) *teaspoon*
b) tablecloth
c) bottle-opener/corkscrew
d) teapot
e) toaster
f) coffee cup
g) mushroom omelette
h) food mixer
i) paper napkin
j) tablespoonful
k) dishwasher

8
1) *B*
2) A
3) D
4) B
5) C
6) C
7) A
8) B
9) D
10) A
11) D
12) C
13) D
14) C
15) B

Vocabulary 8

1
a) *bargains*
b) shoppers
c) change
d) pricey
e) receipt
f) on sale
g) purchase
h) discount
i) pay
j) prices

2
(*Suggested*)
a) *I can't make out (what) the price (is). Let's ask inside.*
b) Can I try it on?
c) Two masked men held up the supermarket yesterday.
d) You have grown out of your old one.
e) I feel worn out.
f) I'll come and pick up the goods on Thursday.
g) Sorry, we have run out of bread.
h) Are you calling (in) at the chemist's?
i) I can't put up with the queues.
j) I'll think it over.

3
a) *queue*
b) deliver
c) change
d) serve
e) wrap
f) fit
g) help
h) order
i) pay
j) try
k) find
l) go

4
a) *5*
b) 8
c) 2
d) 10
e) 1
f) 6
g) 4
h) 9
i) 3
j) 7

5
a) *C*
b) A
c) C
d) B
e) D
f) C
g) D
h) B
i) D
j) B

6
a) *toothpaste*
b) flowers
c) jam
d) baked beans
e) chocolates/paper tissues
f) chocolates/paper tissues
g) breakfast cereal
h) soap
i) orange juice
j) margarine

7
a) *trolley*
b) receipt
c) advertisement
d) wallet
e) manager
f) list
g) deposit
h) bargain
i) purse
j) catalogue

8
1) *variety*
2) shortages
3) likelihood
4) frozen
5) successful
6) expensive
7) reduction
8) complaints
9) impolite
10) willingness

9
1) *D*
2) B
3) A
4) A
5) C
6) D
7) B
8) C
9) B
10) D
11) A
12) C
13) A
14) D
15) C

Vocabulary 9

1
a) *broken*
b) banned
c) licence
d) order
e) let
f) illegally
g) rules
h) commit
i) court
j) prohibited

2
a) *hijacker*
b) witness
c) smuggler
d) shoplifter
e) murderer
f) kidnapper
g) forger
h) vandal
i) pickpocket
j) burglar
k) blackmailer
l) hooligan

3
a) *5*
b) 3
c) 6
d) 2
e) 1
f) 9
g) 7
h) 10
i) 4
j) 8

4
a) *charged*
b) evidence
c) fine
d) guilty
e) jury
f) lawyer
g) statement
h) suspect
i) accused
j) sentence

5
a) *D*
b) A
c) C
d) B
e) A
f) C
g) D
h) B
i) A
j) A

6
a) They accused *John of stealing the money*.
b) Ian denied punching/having punched anybody.
c) The detective gave Andy permission to go.
d) The judge sentenced James Frogget to ten years in prison.
e) Mary admitted forging/having forged the signature.
f) Harry was arrested for stealing £60,000.
g) The witnesses stated that they had seen the accused break into the car.
h) Graham refused to go to the police station.
i) Norman confessed to murdering Alan/having murdered Alan/Alan's murder.
j) The detective asked Helen to go with him/her.

7
1) *innocence*
2) theft
3) offences
4) stolen
5) defence
6) accidentally
7) worthless
8) criminal
9) punishment
10) imprisonment

8
a) *against*
b) of
c) for
d) under
e) in
f) in
g) from
h) in
i) off
j) by
k) on
l) in

9
1) *B*
2) A
3) D
4) A
5) B
6) C
7) C
8) D
9) A
10) D
11) B
12) C
13) A
14) D
15) B

Vocabulary 10

1
a) *chapters*
b) sketch
c) intervals
d) screen
e) orchestra
f) seller
g) frame
h) published
i) costumes
j) scene

2
a) *conductor*
b) author
c) director
d) announcer
e) playwright
f) sculptor
g) composer
h) critic
i) novelist
j) editor

3
a) *at*
b) out of
c) in
d) in
e) on
f) in
g) out of
h) on

4
a) *live*
b) humorous
c) gripping
d) modern
e) current
f) popular
g) special
h) public
i) dull
j) still
k) readable
l) electric

5
a) *A*
b) C
c) D
d) B
e) A
f) D
g) A
h) D
i) B
j) B

6
1) *production*
2) advertising
3) imaginative
4) artistic
5) scenery
6) amusing

7) accompanied
8) entertaining
9) applause
10) performance

7 a) *piece*
b) operas
c) biography
d) rehearsal
e) back
f) circle
g) ground
h) scripts
i) book
j) fair

8 a) *My radio doesn't pick up the BBC World Service very easily.*
b) Our school is going to put on *The Tempest* next month.
c) The management called off the performance an hour before the opening.
d) I looked up the reference in the index.
e) I can't hear the radio. Can you turn it up?
f) Colin's new book comes out/is coming out next week.
g) The conductor went over the music carefully before the concert.
h) The publishing company was taken over by a Japanese firm.
i) I like detective stories where I can't work out who committed the murder.
j) Jim has taken up painting as a hobby.

9 1) *D*
2) B
3) A
4) A
5) C
6) B
7) D
8) A
9) C
10) D
11) B
12) C
13) C
14) A
15) C

Vocabulary 11

1 a) *banks*
b) puddles
c) cave
d) stream
e) waves
f) top
g) desert
h) fountain
i) cloudy
j) lightning

2 a) *5*
b) 8
c) 3
d) 10
e) 1
f) 6
g) 9
h) 2
i) 7
j) 4

3 a) *roots*
b) forest
c) stone
d) leaves
e) lawn
f) plant
g) trunk
h) seeds
i) twig
j) peel

4 a) *B*
b) D
c) A
d) C
e) D
f) A
g) B
h) D
i) A
j) D

5 1) *childhood*
2) unsuitable
3) destruction
4) protection
5) loneliness
6) hunters
7) wooden
8) disobedient
9) discovery
10) savings

6 a) *trap*
b) mower
c) fountain
d) forecast
e) side
f) top

g) house
h) hive
i) hole
j) skin

7 a) *off*
b) out
c) off
d) off
e) to
f) out
g) up
h) to

8 1) *C*
2) A
3) D
4) C
5) B
6) D
7) A
8) C
9) B
10) B
11) A
12) D
13) C
14) A
15) D

Vocabulary 12

1 a) *rude*
b) mean
c) strict
d) lazy
e) shy
f) jealous
g) aggressive
h) thoughtful
i) patient
j) generous

2 a) *punctual*
b) cheerful
c) reliable
d) frank
e) selfish
f) determined
g) mean
h) bad-tempered
i) considerate
j) honest
k) sympathetic
l) lazy

3 a) *sociable*
b) ambitious
c) polite
d) imaginative
e) kind

f) stubborn
g) brave
h) snobbish
i) greedy
j) grateful
k) proud
l) tolerant

4 1) *annoying*
2) disobedient
3) talkative
4) impolite
5) unfriendly
6) dishonest
7) pride
8) conscientious
9) violence
10) bravery

5 a) *B*
b) A
c) D
d) C
e) B
f) A
g) B
h) D
i) A
j) D

6 a) *nephew*
b) bride
c) toddler
d) fiancé
e) twin
f) neighbour
g) niece
h) adult
i) widow
j) best man
k) sister-in-law
l) colleague

7 a) *in*
b) out
c) if
d) up
e) to
f) like/as
g) up
h) of
i) with
j) with
k) out
l) in

8 a) *turn up*
b) look up to
c) put up with
d) get on well with
e) call in
f) count on
g) give away

h) fall out
i) turn down
j) take after

9 1) *A*
2) C
3) A
4) D
5) B
6) D
7) C
8) B
9) A
10) D
11) B
12) C
13) B
14) D
15) A

Vocabulary 13

1 a) *engine*
b) electric
c) switch
d) notebook
e) order
f) go
g) work
h) cut
i) factory
j) invented

2 a) *cursor*
b) highlight
c) reboot
d) icon
e) paste
f) scroll down
g) pull-down menu
h) website
i) engine
j) download

3 1) *file*
2) axe
3) screwdriver
4) corkscrew
5) needle
6) saw
7) hammer
8) scissors
9) spanner
10) spade

4 a) *file*
b) corkscrew
c) needle
d) screwdriver
e) saw
f) axe
g) spade

h) hammer
i) scissors
j) spanner

5 a) *D*
b) B
c) B
d) A
e) C
f) C
g) D
h) D
i) A
j) B

6 1) *scientist*
2) engineering
3) product
4) equipment
5) electricity
6) powerful
7) useless
8) specialised
9) embarrassment
10) difficulty/difficulties

7 a) *off*
b) in
c) up
d) by
e) out
f) together
g) of
h) of
i) for
j) together
k) in

8 a) *keep up with*
b) run out
c) pick up
d) break down
e) put off
f) hang up
g) look out
h) do without
i) stand for
j) go off
k) knock down

9 1) *C*
2) D
3) A
4) C
5) B
6) A
7) D
8) B
9) C
10) D
11) A
12) B
13) A
14) D
15) C

Vocabulary 14

1
a) *collapsed*
b) difficulties
c) poor
d) demonstration
e) environment
f) increase
g) unemployed
h) collision
i) made
j) high

2
a) *famine*
b) slums
c) living
d) earthquake
e) Hooliganism
f) invasion
g) disaster
h) floods
i) injuries
j) rubbish
k) disease
l) emergency

3
a) *B*
b) D
c) C
d) D
e) B
f) A
g) D
h) A
i) A
j) C

4
a) *banned*
b) solved
c) protected
d) improved
e) polluted
f) ignored
g) unemployed
h) flooded
i) overpopulated
j) increased

5
a) *C*
b) A
c) C
d) B
e) D
f) A
g) A
h) C
i) B
j) C

6
1) *collision*
2) unexpectedly
3) overboard
4) exhausted

5) freezing
6) solution
7) improvement
8) unhealthy
9) loneliness
10) destruction

7
a) *charity*
b) drought
c) conservation
d) demonstration
e) pile-up
f) famine
g) emergency
h) strike
i) aid
j) riot

8
a) *at*
b) on
c) under
d) by
e) of/from
f) with
g) at
h) In
i) on
j) in

9
1) *B*
2) D
3) A
4) D
5) C
6) A
7) D
8) D
9) B
10) C
11) A
12) C
13) B
14) D
15) A

Vocabulary 15

1
a) *surgery*
b) fell
c) heal
d) ankle
e) slim
f) aches
g) sick
h) examines
i) temperature
j) caught

2
a) *spine*
b) agony
c) body
d) brains

e) heart
f) tongue
g) breath
h) stomachache
i) look
j) beard

3
a) *throat*
b) knees
c) cheek
d) nose
e) lips
f) wrist
g) chin
h) thumb
i) waist
j) neck

4
a) *3*
b) 8
c) 1
d) 6
e) 10
f) 2
g) 5
h) 9
i) 7
j) 4

5
a) *B*
b) D
c) B
d) A
e) D
f) B
g) C
h) B
i) A
j) D

6
1) *muscular*
2) weight
3) painful
4) poisonous
5) infectious
6) expression
7) heartened
8) incurable
9) treatment
10) recovery

7
a) *4*
b) 6
c) 1
d) 5
e) 10
f) 2
g) 7
h) 8
i) 3
j) 9

8 a) *from*
     b) in
     c) on
     d) off
     e) on
     f) came
     g) on
     h) down
     i) for
     j) of

9 1) *A*
     2) C
     3) B
     4) D
     5) D
     6) C
     7) A
     8) B
     9) A
     10) C
     11) B
     12) D
     13) B
     14) D
     15) C

Vocabulary 16

1 a) *lend*
     b) afford
     c) let
     d) earn
     e) charge
     f) reduced
     g) fortune
     h) reckon

2 a) *generous*
     b) well off
     c) profit
     d) take out
     e) poverty
     f) cash
     g) purchase
     h) worthless

3 a) *pension*
     b) wealth
     c) credit card
     d) loan
     e) receipt
     f) tip
     g) rent
     h) safe

4 a) *6*
     b) 3
     c) 8
     d) 1
     e) 4
     f) 5
     g) 7
     h) 2

5 a) *C*
     b) A
     c) B
     d) A
     e) B
     f) D
     g) A
     h) D

6 1) *wealthy*
     2) luxurious
     3) generosity
     4) savings
     5) insurance
     6) profitable
     7) cashier
     8) loan
     9) worthless
     10) signature

7 a) *payments*
     b) pay you/it back
     c) pay for
     d) paid out
     e) unpaid
     f) payable
     g) pay it into
     h) well paid

8 a) *heir*
     b) pensioner
     c) accountant
     d) customer
     e) cashier
     f) agent
     g) investor
     h) swindler

9 1) *B*
     2) A
     3) D
     4) B
     5) C
     6) A
     7) D
     8) C
     9) D
     10) B
     11) C
     12) A
     13) D
     14) B
     15) C

Vocabulary 17

1 a) *angry*
     b) interested
     c) afraid
     d) annoying
     e) scared
     f) cross
     g) furious
     h) careless

2 a) *naughty*
     b) scared
     c) upset
     d) dull
     e) fascinating
     f) glad
     g) depressed
     h) confused

3 a) *blush*
     b) yawn
     c) nod your head
     d) grin
     e) cry
     f) shake your head
     g) scream
     h) wave

4 a) *6*
     b) 2
     c) 9
     d) 1
     e) 7
     f) 3
     g) 8
     h) 5
     i) 10
     j) 4

5 a) *realistic*
     b) imaginative
     c) obedient
     d) determined
     e) tolerant
     f) dependable
     g) quarrelsome
     h) helpful
     i) embarrased
     j) co-operative

6 1) *impression*
     2) offensive
     3) irritating
     4) admiration
     5) cowardice
     6) adorable
     7) attraction
     8) gratitude
     9) faithful
     10) relief

7
a) *of*
b) of
c) into
d) at
e) with
f) in
g) up
h) on
i) her
j) up

8
1) *D*
2) A
3) C
4) B
5) D
6) A
7) C
8) D
9) B
10) D
11) A
12) B
13) C
14) A
15) D

Vocabulary 18

1
a) *course*
b) marks
c) trained
d) go in
e) taught
f) study
g) heart
h) term
i) failed
j) raise

2
a) *punish*
b) divide
c) memorise
d) pay
e) pass
f) copy
g) concentrate
h) revise
i) underline
j) cheat

3
a) *lecturer*
b) graduate
c) principal
d) pupil
e) professor
f) tutor
g) classmate
h) coach
i) examiner
j) learner

4
a) *4*
b) 9
c) 1
d) 6
e) 2
f) 8
g) 10
h) 7
i) 5
j) 3

5
a) *A*
b) C
c) D
d) B
e) D
f) C
g) A
h) B
i) A
j) B

6
1) *introduction*
2) successful
3) attention
4) unreadable
5) failure
6) revision
7) mistaken
8) absences
9) punishments
10) gifted

7
a) *done*
b) taking
c) done
d) made
e) made
f) take
g) made
h) take
i) took/made
j) does

8
a) *knowledge*
b) discipline
c) education
d) dictionary
e) calculator
f) university
g) intelligence
h) comprehension
i) secondary
j) experiments

9
a) *up*
b) to
c) in
d) for
e) at
f) by
g) about/on
h) in
i) by
j) up

10
1) *C*
2) B
3) A
4) D
5) D
6) B
7) A
8) C
9) B
10) D
11) D
12) A
13) B
14) C
15) B

Vocabulary 19

1
a) *disobedient*
b) unlikely
c) misunderstood
d) outstanding
e) co-operate
f) submarine
g) pre-cooked
h) multi-millionaire

2
a) *dissatisfied*
b) unusual
c) transatlantic
d) vice-president
e) non-smoker
f) informal
g) rewritten
h) overcooked

3
a) *freedom*
b) thoughtful
c) musician
d) shortage
e) leading
f) astonishment
g) foolish
h) backwards

4
a) *overnight*
b) careless
c) mispronounce
d) friendship
e) postponement
f) dissatisfied
g) outskirts
h) overcharged
i) employee
j) homeless

5
a) *gunfire*
b) thunderstorm
c) handwriting
d) haircut
e) soap powder
f) crash helmet

g) bookcase
h) rainbow
i) footsteps
j) fireplace

6 1) *secretarial*
2) occupation
3) frozen
4) carpentry
5) explanation
6) solution
7) failure
8) successful
9) construction
10) embarrassment

7 a) *thin*
b) cool
c) nodded
d) worthless
e) high
f) lovely
g) tasty
h) dangerous
i) bored
j) angry

8 a) *making*
b) feel
c) take
d) set
e) gave
f) do
g) getting
h) put
i) fallen
j) draw

9 (*Suggested*)
a) *The forest outside the town caught fire last night.*
b) Suddenly Janet burst into tears.
c) What do you do (for a living)?
d) We'll have to make/take a decision soon.
e) Can you take care of my plants while I'm away?
f) You will keep in touch, won't you?
g) Diane gave birth to a baby boy last week.
h) Peter always keeps his head in an emergency.
i) Let go of the steering wheel!
j) He stands no chance of winning the race.

Vocabulary 20

1 a) *overwork*
b) invisible
c) subway
d) autobiography
e) ex-wife
f) misleading
g) semi-final
h) unable
i) non-stop
j) disappeared

2 a) *neighbourhood*
b) employer
c) widen
d) handful
e) hopeless
f) greenish
g) partnership
h) drinkable
i) equality
j) harmful

3 a) *inedible*
b) youngster
c) semi-circle
d) friendly
e) foreground
f) mountaineer
g) tricycle
h) hopeful
i) international
j) artist

4 1) *politician*
2) shyness
3) sympathised
4) disorganized
5) replacement
6) straighten
7) personal
8) innocence
9) imagination
10) uninterested

5 a) *bus station*
b) part-time
c) well-dressed
d) old-fashioned
e) car park
f) well-known
g) haircut
h) first class
i) homemade

6 a) *kind-hearted*
b) empty-handed
c) fully-clothed
d) long-legged
e) absent-minded
f) good-looking

g) loud-mouthed
h) short-tempered
i) dog-eared

7 a) *defeat*
b) safe
c) decline/refuse
d) pass
e) landing
f) stale
g) buried
h) similar
i) ending

8 a) *make*
b) lose
c) bear
d) drop
e) waste
f) catch
g) think
h) gain
i) take
j) break

9 (*Suggested*)
a) *Nothing you do will make any difference.*
b) I hope it's not too much trouble/I hope I'm not putting you to any trouble.
c) Let's take measurements of the room.
d) Mark's face fell when I told him my name.
e) The old car suddenly burst into flames.
f) Susan had lost her way.
g) I can't stand/bear the sight of that boy!
h) Helen was put in charge of/took charge of the business.
i) How did you pass the time while you were waiting for the train?
j) I have changed my mind about this matter.

10 a) *by*
b) by
c) on
d) in
e) under
f) from
g) by
h) on
i) for
j) in

Vocabulary 21

1
a) *Take*
b) have
c) make
d) give
e) give
f) do
g) make
h) take
i) do
j) have
k) give
l) do
m) have
n) make
o) take

2
a) *race*
b) challenge
c) support
d) damage
e) language
f) opportunity
g) technique
h) recording
i) love
j) trend

3
a) *shake/head*
b) suit/mood
c) lose/patience
d) tackle/problem
e) reach/target
f) withdraw/money
g) enrol/course
h) waste/chance

4
a) *dominantly*
b) evidently
c) severely
d) quickly
e) greatly
f) clearly
g) carefully
h) enormously
i) exactly
j) inevitably

5
a) *sales staff*
b) market leader
c) visitor centre
d) crash landing
e) Rice production
f) rubbish collection
g) skills shortage
h) holiday weekend

6
a) *try to*
b) slow to
c) due to
d) hard to
e) happy to
f) asked to
g) dare to
h) allowed to
i) manage to
j) tend to

7
a) *blue*
b) race
c) cheese
d) red
e) cons
f) first
g) cake
h) cards
i) nerves
j) nutshell

8
a) *largely created*
b) absolutely superb
c) seriously overweight
d) virtually destroyed
e) eternally grateful
f) radically changed
g) ridiculously overpriced
h) blissfully happy